**Making Levantine Cuisine**

# Making Levantine Cuisine

## Modern Foodways of the Eastern Mediterranean

EDITED BY ANNY GAUL, GRAHAM AUMAN PITTS, AND VICKI VALOSIK

University of Texas Press ◆ Austin

First edition, 2021

Requests for permission to reproduce material from this work should be sent to:
Permissions
University of Texas Press
P.O. Box 7819
Austin, TX 78713–7819
utpress.utexas.edu/rp-form

♾ The paper used in this book meets the minimum requirements of ANSI/NISO
Z39.48–1992 (R1997) (Permanence of Paper).

**Library of Congress Cataloging-in-Publication Data**

Names: Gaul, Anny, editor, contributor. | Pitts, Graham Auman, editor, contributor. |
    Valosik, Vicki, editor.
Title: Making Levantine cuisine : modern foodways of the Eastern Mediterranean /
    edited by Anny Gaul, Graham Auman Pitts, and Vicki Valosik.
Description: First edition. | Austin : University of Texas Press, 2021. | Includes
    bibliographical references and index.
Identifiers: LCCN 2021012109 (print) | LCCN 2021012110 (e-book)
    ISBN 978-1-4773-2457-8 (hardcover)
    ISBN 978-1-4773-2458-5 (library e-book)
    ISBN 978-1-4773-2459-2 (non-library e-book)
Subjects: LCSH: Cooking—Middle East. | Cooking, Middle Eastern. | Cooking—
    Middle East—History. | Cooking, Middle Eastern—History. | Cooking—Social
    aspects—Middle East—History. | Food—Social aspects—Middle East—History. |
    Food—Middle East.
Classification: LCC TX725.M628 M335 2021 (print) | LCC TX725.M628 (e-book) |
    DDC 641.5956—dc23
LC record available at https://lccn.loc.gov/2021012109
LC e-book record available at https://lccn.loc.gov/2021012110
doi:10.7560/324578

*For Rochelle, with gratitude and admiration*

# Contents

A Note on Transliteration  ix
Preface  xi

Introduction: Making Levantine Cuisine  1
ANNY GAUL AND GRAHAM AUMAN PITTS

PART I. **Making Levantine Food Cultures**

1.  When Did Kibbe Become Lebanese? The Social Origins
    of National Food Culture  23
    GRAHAM AUMAN PITTS AND MICHEL KABALAN

2.  Adana Kebabs and Antep Pistachios: Place, Displacement,
    and Cuisine of the Turkish South  47
    SAMUEL DOLBEE AND CHRIS GRATIEN

3.  The Transformation of Sugar in Syria: From Luxury to
    Everyday Commodity  69
    SARA PEKOW

4.  Pistachios and Pomegranates: Vignettes from Aleppo
    (Essay and Recipe)  85
    ANTONIO TAHHAN

PART II. **Revisiting Foodways in Israel-Palestine**

5.  Urban Food Venues as Contact Zones between
    Arabs and Jews during the British Mandate Period  93
    DAFNA HIRSCH

6.  The Companion to Every Bite: Palestinian Olive Oil in
the Levant  **115**
ANNE MENELEY

7.  Even in a Small Country Like Palestine, Cuisine Is Regional
(Essay and Recipes)  **133**
REEM KASSIS

PART III. **Levantine Cuisine beyond Borders**

8.  Embodying Levantine Cooking in East Amman, Jordan  **153**
SUSAN MACDOUGALL

9.  *Shakshūka* for All Seasons: Tunisian Jewish Foodways at
the Turn of the Twentieth Century  **170**
NOAM SIENNA

10.  Unmaking Levantine Cuisine: The Levant, the Mediterranean,
and the World  **184**
HARRY ELI KASHDAN

11.  Fine Dining to Street Food: Egypt's Restaurant Culture in Transition
(Essay and Recipes)  **199**
SUZANNE ZEIDY

Conclusion: Writing Levantine Cuisine  **210**
ANNY GAUL WITH POETRY BY ZEINA AZZAM

Further Reading and Cooking  **219**
Contributors  **223**
Index  **229**

# A Note on Transliteration

This volume conforms to the *International Journal of Middle East Studies* (*IJMES*) transliteration system for Arabic and Turkish. Place-names with standard English equivalents (such as Aleppo, Beirut, and Zahle) have been rendered as such. Proper names and titles omit diacritical marks except for ʿayn and hamza. Words from foreign languages that appear in the Merriam-Webster dictionary are reproduced as they appear in it (for example, arak, baba ghanoush, hummus, kibbe, tabbouleh). Arabic and Turkish words and phrases that do not appear in the dictionary are fully transliterated with diacritical marks. They are transliterated to reflect their spelling in the original if referencing a written text but transliterated to reflect Levantine Arabic pronunciation if referencing spoken language or colloquial usage: *knāfeh* rather than *kunāfa*, *frīkeh* rather than *farīka*, and so forth.

# Preface

Food has seldom occupied the attention of scholars working on the modern Middle East, despite the voluminous literature about the region. That neglect has been especially pronounced for the Levant. This primarily Arabic-speaking region in the Eastern Mediterranean is home to some of the world's most storied cuisines, from the refined culinary traditions of the city of Aleppo to the chickpea-based favorites falafel and hummus. While the classical and medieval history of the region's foodways are relatively well documented, the historical record is silent on the transformations wrought by the introduction of New World foods, industrialization, colonization, and other modern phenomena—sweeping changes that created the Levantine foods of today.

We began work on this book with a simple question: what is the history of the Levant's cuisine? The silence we encountered in trying to answer the first question led us to another: why have scholars not paid the topic much attention?

Restaurants serving Lebanese and Palestinian food can be found across the globe, from West Africa to Europe to the Americas—although in North America they are more likely to be advertised under the vague label "Mediterranean." The outflux of Syrian refugees since 2011 has placed even more of the world's population in contact with Levantine culture. Yet, despite its fame, the region's recent culinary history remains unwritten.

*Making Levantine Cuisine* is the first book-length scholarly work devoted to the topic. This is not merely an academic book, however: alongside scholarly chapters, readers will find personal essays and recipes that reflect their authors' firsthand culinary experience. This blend of genres stems from our conviction that, as scholars, we should not only address wider audiences but learn from specialists and authorities beyond the academy as well.

It is worth pausing to address how the three of us came to be the editors of this book and how it came to be published in the United States. Concern over appropriation and ownership—who lays claim to what dishes and how they are labeled, marketed, and understood—looms large in discussions about food in the Levant. So it is important to point out that we did not grow up eating Levantine food in our childhood homes. It is not "our" food.

At the same time, the globalization of Levantine food means that it is very much a part of the culture of the southeastern United States, where the three of us were raised (in Charlotte and Greensboro, North Carolina, and Nashville, Tennessee). In our lifetimes, conversations about "American" food culture have increasingly acknowledged and celebrated Arab American and other immigrant cuisines as a part of our collective public culture. We have also gained much-needed clarity about the contributions of Black and Indigenous food cultures to cuisines historically appropriated and claimed by white settlers, particularly in the South, thanks to the work of writers like Michael Twitty and Toni Tipton-Martin and scholars like Psyche Williams-Forson, alongside many others. Both of these shifts signal food history's potential as a means to counter nativist and nationalist cultural logics in the United States and elsewhere.

And yet it is not enough simply to diversify our understanding of food and its history. As bell hooks warns, the commodification and uncritical enjoyment of "Otherness" can lead to a self-satisfied, reductive form of consumption devoid of context or politics. Embracing intercultural exchanges does not erase the structures of domination that frame them.[1] In our case, those structures range from US foreign policy to the formations of ethnonationalism and capitalism.

Our response is to acknowledge the political conditions that shape our encounters with the foods of others—and to provide an accounting of the histories of inequality and struggle that produced them. For us, this means including chapters that historicize the appropriation and expropriation of Palestinian and Armenian foodways and document the resistance embodied in Palestinian olive cultivation. It also means drawing connections between the trajectories of Levantine dishes and vital contemporary conversations taking place about food politics. The following chapters trace the circulation of falafel and *shakshūka* within what Harry Eli Kashdan calls "a denatured global food culture that lacks reference to the histories and contexts of particular recipes" and describe the chasm between those who claim and profit from various food cultures and those whose labor produces, reproduces, innovates, and preserves them.

In striving to offer an account of modern Levantine food history and culture that is both critical and contextualized, this volume reflects a number of commitments.

First is a commitment to taking Levantine cuisine seriously as a subject of scholarly inquiry. We assembled a group of scholars from a range of fields and career stages, from full professors to graduate students and postdoctoral scholars. We sought scholarship that engages rigorously with a wide range of sources in Levantine languages. As a result, this volume reflects a variety of methods used to interpret materials in formal and vernacular registers of Arabic, including Judeo-Arabic, as well as Turkish and Armenian. References also include English, French, and Hebrew sources, reflecting the colonial legacies that lie at the heart of the region's modern cuisines and continue to drive many of its political conflicts. Although linguistic ability should never be confused with an understanding of complex social realities, it is nevertheless an essential foundation for the study of a culture and its history and is especially important given the industries of US "expertise" about the Arab world that engage with non-English sources superficially or not at all.

Our next commitment was to a diversity of perspectives, including writing by those who grew up cooking and eating Levantine foods at home. Beyond personal experience, we sought to recognize culinary expertise as a significant form of knowledge in its own right. Each of the book's three thematic sections includes a chapter that reflects firsthand culinary knowledge, from running a restaurant to developing recipes for popular audiences and home cooks. This in turn speaks to our final commitment: to make this volume's collective insights accessible to as broad an audience as possible in both its style and its content.

These commitments, and our individual intellectual pursuits, partly explain how we came to coordinate this effort as coeditors. Working on a book about famine in Mount Lebanon, Graham Pitts discovered that his project required more knowledge about Levantine foodways than was available. Anny Gaul offered her background studying the cuisines of the Arabic-speaking world as well as an interest in reframing the study of foodways beyond national categories. Vicki Valosik lent her skills as an editor specialized in translating scholarly writing (particularly on topics related to the Arab world) into accessible prose. Each of us is also invested in collaborative approaches to scholarly work.

There are also structural reasons that explain why this volume came to be. This work was produced from within the North American academy because of the financial resources of institutions like Georgetown University and the historical privileging of Euro-American academic knowledge production about the Arab world. These chapters are attuned to the way that social and political inequalities have contributed to the making of Levantine cuisine, so we would be remiss not to acknowledge that inequalities within systems of higher education and knowledge production on a global scale have also determined the conditions that produced this book. Proceeds from the sale of this book will be donated to fund scholarships at Georgetown University's Center for Contemporary Arab Studies (CCAS).

Fifteen authors share their work here, but the network that made this work possible is much broader. Institutional support from Georgetown's CCAS was essential in bringing this project to fruition. The center hosted a day-long workshop for the volume's contributors, followed by a collaborative cooking demonstration and dinner. CCAS also cosponsored a public event hosted at the Freer and Sackler Galleries, the Smithsonian's National Museum of Asian Art, featuring talks by several of the chapter authors. The CCAS drew on an endowment provided by the American Druze Foundation and funding from a Department of Education Title VI Grant designating CCAS as a National Resource Center on the Middle East and North Africa (NRC-MENA).

Crucially, this support allowed us to create an environment for collectively workshopping these essays in a manner that paralleled our approach to scholarship beyond the academic realm: cooking and eating together enriched our work as much as sitting around the seminar table, papers in hand.

We would like to thank several individuals who made this unique collaborative environment possible. Dana Al Dairani, CCAS associate director, has been tireless in her support of this project since its inception. Maddie Fisher, CCAS events coordinator, was a diligent collaborator helping to ensure that the workshop, dinner, and public talks were successful. We would also like to thank the management of the Leo J. O'Donovan Dining Hall at Georgetown University, particularly Joelle Valbrun-Bailey and her team, for graciously opening their kitchen and beautiful dining space to us and providing staff support for our communal dinner. We thank Antonio Tahhan and Laila El-Haddad for leading interactive cooking demonstrations focused on Aleppan and Gazan cuisines, respectively. The contributions of Annia Ciezadlo and Adel Iskander to our workshop enriched and enlivened the discussions. We are grateful to Grace Murray from the Smithsonian's Freer and Sackler Galleries for hosting a day of public events featuring the book's contributors and to Majd AlGhatrif, Syrian restaurateur and cardiologist, who served attendees a meal catered by his restaurant, Syriana, which is located in Ellicott City, Maryland.

Jim Burr and Sarah McGavick of the University of Texas Press have been patient and encouraging throughout the publication process. Kathy Lewis's editorial acumen greatly improved the manuscript. We were lucky to have partners willing to take a chance on the mix of personal essays, recipes, and academic essays included in this volume. We thank them for sharing our vision and working to make it a reality.

Professor Rochelle Davis, a mentor to each of us, believed in this project from the beginning and gave her time and the center's resources to make it possible. She also came up with the title of the book. During her three years as CCAS director, she established a collaborative atmosphere that served as the context for this project. We dedicate this volume to her.

ANNY GAUL, GRAHAM AUMAN PITTS, AND VICKI VALOSIK

## Note

1. bell hooks, "Eating the Other: Desire and Resistance," in *Black Looks: Race and Representation* (Boston: South End Press, 1992), 21–39.

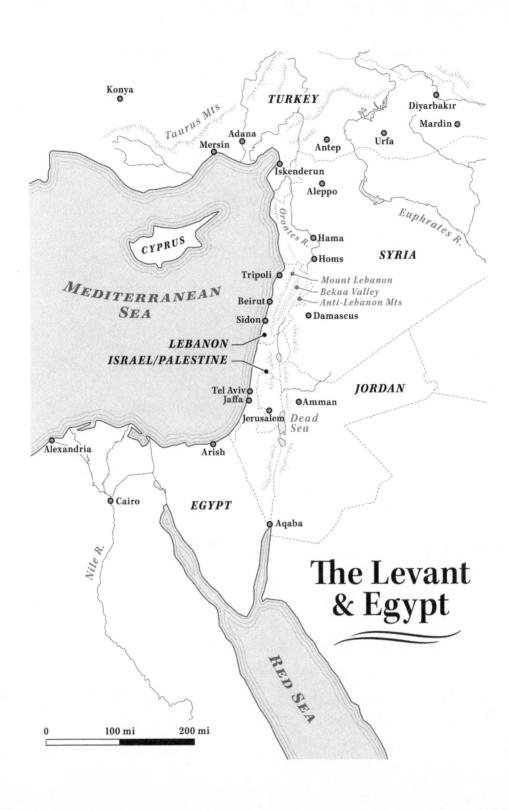

Konya

TURKEY

Diyarbakır

Mardin

Taurus Mts

Adana

Mersin

Antep

Urfa

Iskenderun

Aleppo

Euphrates R.

Orontes R.

Hama

Homs

SYRIA

Tripoli

Mount Lebanon
Bekaa Valley
Anti-Lebanon Mts

CYPRUS

Beirut

MEDITERRANEAN
SEA

Sidon

Damascus

LEBANON

ISRAEL/PALESTINE

Tel Aviv
Jaffa

Amman

JORDAN

Jerusalem

Dead
Sea

Alexandria

Arish

Cairo

EGYPT

Aqaba

Nile R.

# The Levant
# & Egypt

RED SEA

0          100 mi          200 mi

# Introduction: Making Levantine Cuisine

ANNY GAUL AND GRAHAM AUMAN PITTS

In sight of Jerusalem's Damascus Gate, restaurateur and cookbook author Yotam Ottolenghi tells Anthony Bourdain that the Ottoman occupation of Palestine ended "150 years" before their 2013 interview. The cameras for Bourdain's *Parts Unknown* TV series then follow the pair to a falafel stand inside the Old City's Muslim Quarter. In response to Bourdain's query about the origin of the iconic fried chickpea dish, Ottolenghi declares, "There's actually no answer."[1] As the author of several best-selling cookbooks (including *Jerusalem: A Cookbook*), Ottolenghi, along with his collaborator Sami Tamimi, is perhaps the most prominent chronicler of the Levant's cuisine. However, his answers to Bourdain distort the history of Levantine food. The Ottoman occupation ended in late 1917, not even 100 years before the "Jerusalem" episode was recorded. Ottolenghi and Tamimi's cookbook does correctly cite the date for the Ottoman withdrawal but reproduces a tired Orientalist cliché, describing the early twentieth-century city as "miserable, congested, and squalid."[2] The history section glosses over Zionist immigration from Europe, the signal development of modern Palestine's history. The falafel that Zionist settlers eventually came to claim as their national food was made by Palestinians first. It belongs to a family of fritters made with fava beans, or chickpeas in the Palestinian version, that had long been shared throughout the Arab Eastern Mediterranean, from Alexandria and Port Said in Egypt to Beirut in Lebanon.[3]

The cookbook authors also make a "leap of faith . . . that hummus will eventually bring Jerusalemites together," yet such assumptions disregard the history of that dish and the broader progression of cultural encounters in Israel-Palestine.[4] Historically, the appropriation of Levantine foods like hummus by European Jews has corresponded not with improving intercommunal relations but rather with the further entrenchment of Israeli colonialism. Misconceptions about one of the world's most prominent cuisines persist, given the scarcity of scholarship on its origins.[5]

Ottolenghi and Tamimi's commodification of their "Jerusalem" brand is typical of how the forms of dispossession essential to modern Levantine cuisine, in its different guises, have been obscured. Turkey and Israel both assembled their national cuisines from the traditions of populations marginalized in the making of those nations. In adopting Arab and Armenian dishes, Turkey's national food culture attempted to obscure a non-Turkish past. Since Israel's founding in 1948, the uneven and shifting attitudes within mainstream culture toward the foods of marginalized communities masked a history of violent dispossession, in the case of Palestinians, and systemic discrimination, in the case of Jewish populations who immigrated to Israel from the Arab world. Each project for a national cuisine undermines its nationalist aims by tacitly revealing a diverse past and the persistent cultural unity of a politically divided region.

In addition to ethnocentric nationalist agendas, conventional discourse has concealed the inequalities of class and gender essential to making modern Levantine cuisine. Paid and unpaid female laborers have been key to the reproduction of Levantine foodways. This modern food culture began to develop once capitalist social relations took hold in nineteenth-century Beirut. Unlike the traditional mode of production, where the terms of exploitation are obvious, they remain hidden under capitalism. It is the task of critique to reveal them.[6] In centering questions of labor and inequality, this volume peels away the ideological branding that has largely defined this cuisine.[7]

*Making Levantine Cuisine* is the first book-length scholarly work devoted to Levantine food and foodways. The concept "foodways" shifts our focus beyond food itself to a framing that considers the social contexts that make food and make food meaningful—spanning from fields to markets to kitchens, factory spaces, and restaurants. Eight chapters by anthropologists, historians, and critical theorists address this gap in our knowledge of global food history and culture. From a range of disciplinary perspectives, we address several broad questions: What is Levantine cuisine, historically, culturally, and gastronomically? What is the relationship between national and regional cuisines in the Levant? How does cuisine offer a way of conceptualizing the Levant beyond its traditional national borders? How are its national and regional variants known, consumed, and discussed by those inside the region and outside of it? Can studying the region's food and foodways help us better define or understand what constitutes "the Levant" or what counts as "Levantine" and how they came to be?

Supplementing these scholarly perspectives on what "makes" cuisine Levantine are essays and recipes that offer a glimpse into the kitchens where Levantine cuisine is made in a more tangible sense. This combination of scholarly, practical, and personal literature reflects both a feminist commitment to the validity of diverse perspectives and a conviction that as food scholars we have much to learn from matters of practice and lived experience.

The volume begins with the local and granular and gradually expands to encompass the Mediterranean and the world beyond. These accounts reveal an understanding of Levantine cuisine as an entity that has never mapped neatly onto political boundaries. They also look beyond the region to show how culinary styles most commonly known today as "Lebanese," "Israeli," or variants of the vaguer "Mediterranean" coalesced in the twentieth century as the product of global diasporas, modernization, and national tradition-making. Stories centered on food, in turn, recast the histories of these national communities.

This book sets Levantine cuisine in its global context. While firmly rooted in the Eastern Mediterranean, the cuisine of the Levant is now found far beyond its shores. Many outsiders have encountered this region through its food, now ubiquitous around the globe. Often disguised as "Greek" or "Mediterranean," Levantine cuisine appears in restaurants from Hong Kong to Mexico City in innumerable iterations. Just as Ottolenghi and Tamimi's "Jerusalem" took shape in London, the contemporary foodways of the Levantine region more broadly have emerged as part of the encounter between the Eastern Mediterranean region and the rest of the world.[8]

## What Is the Levant?

How do we assert the coherence of the Levant as a region? In the way we use it here, "Levant" is equivalent to historical Syria (as distinct from the modern nation-state, which covers less territory).[9] The Levant rises between the Mediterranean Sea and the Euphrates River in Lebanon, Syria, and Turkey. No clear boundary exists to the north. The region transcends the contemporary border between Syria and Turkey. Israel-Palestine and Jordan occupy the region's southern half, where the desert provides a natural border to the east. The Ottoman Empire ruled the region for four hundred years from the early sixteenth century into the twentieth. In the early Islamic period, the northern portion of the empire became known as Bilad al-Sham, while Damascus, the capital of the Syrian provinces, was referred to as al-Sham. While those toponyms remain in use for Arabic speakers, "Levant" offers the most useful equivalent in contemporary English.[10]

Unified but not uniform, the Levant possesses multilayered diversity in addition to a clear cultural and historical unity.[11] Its Arabic dialects are diverse but mutually intelligible. The sectarian differentiation within its Christian, Jewish, and Muslim populations defies summary. The region's ecology reflects this core unity and broad diversity. The mountains that rise above the Mediterranean, from the coastal region of contemporary Syria to the hills of the West Bank, provide its inhabitants the opportunity to grow an array of crops at different elevations. Subtropical crops, like bananas and citrus, can be grown only a short distance away from pit fruits such as apples, cherries, and peaches. Vegetables grow across all of the Levant's ecosystems along with the trio of grain, olives, and vines typical of the Mediterranean. Inland, the hill country gives way to steppe and then desert. A close juxtaposition of different rainfall zones encouraged specialization and market exchange throughout human history. That fact encouraged specialization in tree crops in areas of higher rainfall, grain in dry-farmed regions, and livestock among nomadic populations.[12]

More than just a cliché, the region's geographical position at the confluence of three continents encouraged biodiversity. Wheat, as is well known, originated in the Eastern Mediterranean area. Figs, grapes, and olives were all also first domesticated in the Levant.[13] A market network integrated the region's foodways from early human history and enriched its cuisine through successive waves of crop and cultural exchanges. Mediterranean seaways exposed the Levant to the food cultures of the rest of the basin and allowed for the exportation of the region's wine centuries before the Common Era. Under the aegis of Islamic rule, a new high cuisine dominated by Persianate influences expanded the Levant's culinary repertoire, infusing it with new ingredients like eggplant, new processing methods for rice and sugar, and new culinary techniques, such as preparing meat in vinegar or pomegranate juice.[14] Beginning in the sixteenth century, the Columbian Exchange brought the final package of crops that came to characterize the region's cuisine as we know it today: tomatoes, beans, and peppers.

While the echoes of some dishes from earlier periods still resonate, something recognizable as contemporary Levantine cuisine began to take shape only in the nineteenth century. The integration of the Levant into the global industrial economy did not cause the regional economy to segment. Instead, it heightened the integration of the Levant both economically and culturally. Coastal cities (especially Beirut, Haifa, and Jaffa) received migrants from the interior and developed a newly extractive relationship with the surrounding countryside. Population growth and the dispossession of an indebted peasant class spurred broad labor migration as capitalism took hold. Rural areas devoted to commercial export agriculture, like Mount Lebanon and Palestine's citrus region around Jaffa, imported staple foodstuffs from the surrounding region. The presence of a mobile and predominantly male labor force spurred the creation of new kinds of food preparations, like the Adana kebab, designed to feed them while they were working. Meanwhile, rising populations and prosperity saw the growth of the middle class in cities like Beirut as villagers migrated to urban centers. The consequent melding of village foodways with the customs of the urban upper class provided the context for the production of a repertoire of dishes that would become "Lebanese" cuisine.[15] Beirut and other coastal cities hosted an increasing number of Europeans and a growing middle class with new consumption habits. It was in the urban Levant of this period that the region developed a self-conscious middle-class food culture predicated on new forms of class formation (see chapter 1).

Global mobility was a key factor in shaping the modern Levant and its foodways. The first destination for Levantines was Egypt—where they brought their food customs and influenced the urban culinary cultures of Alexandria and Cairo. Beginning in the 1880s, emigration to the Americas began. Migrants left their homes in the Eastern Mediterranean for Argentina, Brazil, and the United States. One in three inhabitants of Ottoman Mount Lebanon had migrated to the Americas by 1914, and remittances had become the largest source of income in Mount Lebanon. In the diaspora, food was a key identity marker for Levantine migrants and their descendants. Wealth generated in the settler colonies of the Americas underpinned middle-class prosperity. Levantine cuisine developed in this context of a globalizing and increasingly integrated Levant immersed in an intensive cultural encounter with Europe and the Americas.[16]

The region's imbrication in the global food economy was not without its perils. Networks of grain provisioning extended across the region and as far afield as Australia. In one sense, the coastal population's ability to import wheat and barley was a sign of its prosperity. It also represented a key vulnerability. During World War I, when the British and French navies blockaded the Ottoman Empire, food became scarce. The ensuing famine took the lives of about half a million people. After catalyzing the famine, Britain and France used the population's desperation to impose colonial authority once the Ottomans had been defeated in 1918.[17] Food insecurity persisted after the war, leading to a reliance on imported staple grains that has been a persistent force undermining Levantine autonomy up to the present day.[18]

The integration that characterized the late Ottoman period continued apace under colonialism. Under the auspices of "mandates" established by the League of Nations, France and Britain administered the Levant until after World War II. The territories that would become Lebanon and Syria were subject to French rule, while Palestine and Jordan were British. The conventional wisdom that British and French colonialists simply drew artificial borders on a map, thereby creating the problems from which the Levant has long suffered, is misleading. Under the aegis of colonialism, the principle of dividing the Eastern Mediterranean into discrete states was established, but those borders were ultimately defined in military conflicts. Ironically, during the two decades of mandate rule, the Levant became more integrated culturally and economically than ever before.[19]

The watershed historical moment came after the departure of the British and French, when the creation of modern nation-states in the twentieth century signaled not only the marking of physical boundaries but the conceptual production of national cuisines that belied both the village-level variation and the regional coherence of the Levantine table.[20] As Sami Zubaida argues in an influential meditation on the subject, the "nationalization" of cuisines concealed a deeper history of exchange.[21] Turkish cuisine, for example, took many of its core elements from the Levantine region that became its southwestern provinces: the Adana kebab, with its flaked Aleppo pepper, as well as Syrian pistachios, rebranded as if they originated from the town of Antep (see chapter 2). Efforts to codify national cuisines did not destroy internal diversity and often even celebrated it. When chronicling their national cuisines, Palestinian and Lebanese cookbook authors highlight regionally distinctive versions of popular dishes. Laila El-Haddad and Maggie Schmitt's work has chronicled the particularity of Gazan cuisine, which uses more "spicy heat" than the rest of the Levant.[22] The region's culinary traditions have been and remain diverse. Our intention is not to reify the Levant but rather to suggest that a cultural unity that developed in the nineteenth and twentieth centuries is still evident in the region's shared cuisine.

## Writing Middle Eastern Food Histories

The historiography of Levantine cuisine fittingly reflects both the histories of migration that transported it around the globe and the discursive reconfigurations that produce a slippage among Middle Eastern, Mediterranean, and more specific national or regional categories. Arguably the field's foundational text is not a scholarly volume but a migrant's cookbook: Claudia Roden's *A Book of Middle Eastern Food.*[23] As Harry Eli Kashdan points out, unlike other popular Anglophone cookbooks about the Mediterranean, *A Book of Middle Eastern Food* reflects its author's departure from the region where the recipes originated, not travel to it. Roden's Sephardic Jewish roots meant that her family's culinary traditions included foods from Istanbul, Aleppo, and Cairo, the city where she was born, which her family left in 1956. When she resettled in London, Roden began to assemble recipes from across the wider Middle East, writing to friends and family and other contacts similarly scattered outside the Levant. Kashdan writes that Roden's account of her own methodology "sketches a diasporic network, bringing together the experiences and memories of an emerging community of Middle Eastern expatriates in London."[24] Her collection reflects both centuries of Sephardic migration patterns and the diffuse category of a Western "Middle Eastern" imaginary, with recipes from Fez to Istanbul to Alexandria to Baghdad.

Roden's writing was also shaped by scholarly communities, including the Oxford Food Symposium (formerly the Oxford Symposium on Food and Cookery), of which she is currently president. Regular attendees include Sami Zubaida and Charles Perry, scholars whose published work frequently addresses Middle Eastern food history. As a result, Roden's work includes not only the quasi-ethnographic assemblage of a "diasporic network" (to echo Kashdan) but also emerging scholarship on the region's foodways, which has emphasized the cuisines of the medieval Arabic tradition (discussed in more detail later).

A major uptick in both popular and scholarly works on Middle Eastern cuisines started in the mid-1990s, when Roden published *The Book of Jewish Food: An Odyssey from Samarkand to New York*. A revised edition of her original cookbook soon followed, now updated with full-color images, an expanded biographical introduction, and more prominent text boxes next to the recipes, featuring proverbs, historical episodes, and other supplementary material.[25] We might read Roden's more recent work in the context of the growing popular genre of the food memoir.[26] Although Roden is not a trained academic and her books are not conventional works of scholarship, her work also shares many features with a great deal of the scholarly literature in Middle East food studies—features that arguably make this subfield unique. These include detailed attention to the rich corpus of classical and medieval Arabic texts about food, an emphasis on recipes, and a tendency to favor a broad and diffuse framing of the region. Sami Zubaida and Richard Tapper's landmark edited collection *A Taste of Thyme: Culinary Cultures in the Middle East* (with a foreword by Roden) is a case in point: its chapters address both medieval and modern cookbooks and discuss cases from Morocco to Iran and the Caucasus to Yemen.[27]

Over the subsequent quarter-century, sources from medieval Arabic culinary, historical, and belletristic literature received the most comprehensive scholarly coverage within an emerging subfield of Middle East food studies, including translations of nearly all of the known medieval Arabic cookbooks into English.[28] Scholarship in Middle East food studies that addresses more recent periods has tended to feature more articles, edited volumes, and translations of cookbooks than dedicated monographs.[29] Overwhelmingly, what has been documented about the history of Middle Eastern foods in both popular and scholarly texts still relies heavily on classical and medieval sources. The work of Farouk Mardam-Bey, who was born in Syria and is based in Paris, is one example. His fanciful but thorough gastronomic columns for *Qantara*, now published in book form in French, English, and Arabic, detail an array of key dishes and ingredients from throughout the Middle East and North Africa and their histories. His work (like Claudia Roden's) combines exquisite, precise descriptions of contemporary recipes and techniques with extensively researched background notes that draw almost exclusively on classical and medieval texts.[30]

This straddling of a centuries-wide gap between textual sources and contemporary descriptions of the region's food represents a creative, and arguably necessary, approach to an underdocumented history. Practically speaking, a paucity of primary and secondary sources addressing Levantine food between the medieval era and the mid-nineteenth century, a period roughly coinciding with Ottoman rule in the Levant, presents a formidable challenge. What we do know of Levantine foodways during this period is largely filtered through sources that center on Istanbul, whose court cuisine and charitable institutions, like soup kitchens, have been well documented by historians.[31] And yet this gap presents a number of problems. On the most basic level, the absence of sources from a period during which massive social, political, and economic developments transformed landscapes, markets, and kitchens presents empirical challenges to historicizing today's cuisines. Furthermore, as Edward Said argued, the Orientalist legacy of extrapolating from classical Arabic texts to interpretations of modern Arab or Muslim society has long underpinned perceptions of "an unchanging Orient."[32] That is not to say that medieval sources have nothing to contribute to understandings of contemporary cuisines; the opposite is true. But chronicling the many changes that those cuisines have undergone in more recent centuries is an essential direction for the field of Middle East food studies to take.

*Making Levantine Cuisine* joins a limited but growing number of edited volumes that address, at least in part, more modern and contemporary aspects of Middle Eastern food and foodways.[33] These, in turn, are part of a broader recent trend in food studies that has produced similar edited collections about other regions outside of Europe.[34] At the same time, recent edited volumes in Middle East food studies have tended to adopt broad scopes along the same lines as Roden's culinary universe, using the Western-coined term "Middle East" as a central geographical framing rather than more specific (and locally legible) subregional categories like the Levant.[35] Our chief contribution to the study of the region's food is to extend it beyond the realms of elite cuisine and past the medieval period while narrowing our regional scope to the Levant in order to produce a coherent, albeit not comprehensive, narrative. As Sara Pekow's contribution to the volume demonstrates (chapter 3), this does not mean altogether jettisoning the medieval evidence at our disposal, but rather a commitment to historicizing it in light of the transformations of the past two centuries. In this sense, we consider food scholarship as a means to counter outdated and reductive narratives of an ancient and unchanging Middle Eastern "other."

## Locating the Levant in Middle Eastern Culinary Scholarship

Despite its popularity as a global culinary trend, the cuisine of the modern Levant has played a relatively minor role in Middle Eastern food studies until recently.[36] Several subsets of contemporary food studies literature, however, represent exceptions to this trend, pointing to an increasing interest in modern Levantine cuisine. The first such exception is a noteworthy juxtaposition: a flourishing of scholarly work on the food and foodways of Israel and the concurrent rise of Palestinian cookbooks, both within the past decade. The former includes a flurry of articles in food studies and anthropology journals as well as a number of scholarly monographs.[37] What the style magazine of the *New York Times* recently referred to as "the rise of Palestinian food," by contrast, has largely occurred in the realm of cookbooks like Laila El-Haddad and Maggie Schmitt's *The Gaza Kitchen: A Palestinian Culinary Journey*, volume contributor Reem Kassis's *The Palestinian Table*, and Joudie Kalla's *Palestine on a Plate* and *Baladi*, among others.[38]

Many authors in this emerging cookbook genre incorporate ethnographic and historical accounts, positioning food as a means to focus a lens on the plight of the Palestinian people. This approach has moved beyond the pages of cookbooks into broader conversations within the food world. In a discussion published in *Bon Appétit* involving El-Haddad, Schmitt, and Ottolenghi, El-Haddad and Schmitt pushed back against the lack of material context, questions of appropriation, and use of the "Arab/Jew" binary in Ottolenghi's popular cookbook *Jerusalem*. Ottolenghi responded, "I think now I would have taken the whole aspect of appropriation and ownership more seriously . . . it's very hard to say who is the originator of each dish, but it's also overwhelmingly true that some of these dishes are the symbols of the Palestinian culture, and as such they just cannot become everybody's sign of culture or identity."[39] By comparison with Israeli foodways, there has been far less direct discussion of Palestinian foodways in the academic literature, with the exception of Anne

Meneley's extensive work on Palestinian olive oil (including chapter 6 of this volume).[40]

Given these dynamic and ongoing discussions in both the food world and the field of food studies, *Making Levantine Cuisine* includes a section devoted to revisiting foodways in Israel-Palestine with chapters that speak to many of the issues raised in this recent work, with contributions from the voices at the heart of these conversations: Dafna Hirsch, Anne Meneley, and Reem Kassis.

A second major exception where scholars are engaged in conversations about the history and culture of Levantine cuisine is a rich line of inquiry showing how food mediated the encounter between the Middle East and the rest of the world. Gary Nabhan's work charts connections between the Arab world and the Americas over the *longue durée*, shedding light on the history of Levantine flavors like the Aleppo pepper.[41] Matthew Jaber Stiffler has charted how the practice of self-Orientalism helped Arab-Americans fashion "exotic and unusual, but inviting" restaurants that would entice consumers and secure their place in American culture. For subsequent generations of Arab Americans, food became a key link to their heritage.[42] Beginning in the 1960s, as Jennifer Dueck has shown, cookbooks written by Arab, Armenian, Persian, and Turkish authors projected authentic and timeless Middle Eastern cultural landscapes or "foodsheds" to appeal to the mid-century cosmopolitanism of consumers in the United States.[43] "Lebanese" restaurants were common in the United States and Canada by the 1970s.[44] Recreating the experience of cooking and hospitality is one way that the current wave of Syrian refugees has reconstructed a sense of normalcy in exile.[45] Researchers' careful attention to these moments of cross-cultural interaction invites further inquiry into the globalization of Levantine foodways.

*Making Levantine Cuisine* seeks to build on this emerging body of literature, both scholarly and popular, by presenting a set of essays that cohere around the key themes and questions raised by writers on the issue. Collectively workshopped and discussed over both the conference table and the dinner table in June 2019, they offer a model for the expansion of Middle East food studies scholarship as a field now poised to systematically study the richness of the region's culinary cultures with ethnographic and historical rigor.

### Themes and Chapters

#### Part I. Making Levantine Food Cultures

For many, the concept of "Levantine cuisine" evokes the storied urban food cultures of Aleppo, Damascus, and Beirut. As the chapters in this section demonstrate, however, we cannot understand the traditional foodways of these cities without accounting for the modernizing processes of nationalism and industrialization. Writers working in the service of nationalist agendas have done much to chronicle the region's cuisine. In depicting national culture ahistorically and uncritically, their work tends to conflict with contemporary academic sensibilities. In order to discover how "Lebanese" cuisine became codified as such, Graham Auman Pitts and Michel Kabalan read key texts against the grain by historicizing Lebanon's supposedly authentic, unchanging foodways. They focus on the many incarnations of the dish kibbe, which is a mainstay of the Levant's modern cuisine. Their work shows that the codification of Levantine and later Lebanese cuisine happened at two key moments of flight from the countryside and urbanization in the nineteenth and twentieth centuries. A repertoire that is recognizably Levantine first coalesced as a product of an emergent Beiruti middle-class culture in the late nineteenth century. In the twentieth century, as it became coded as "Lebanese," the cuisine preserved a nostalgic image of an authentic, fading village life.

Samuel Dolbee and Chris Gratien explain how foods emblematic of Turkey's southern borderlands with Syria were incorporated into a Turkish national culinary tradition. Their history of pistachios and kebabs belies the notion that the incorporation of these provincial elements into a national food culture in Turkey was a smooth process. The chapter details state efforts to rebrand pistachios as originating not from Syrian Damascus but from Turkish Antep. They also show how industrialization saw regional foods made by women in the home—such as kebabs from the southern city of Adana—become commodified street foods in major urban centers like Ankara, Istanbul, and Izmir. Dolbee and Gratien suggest that Turkey's national cuisine incorporated Levantine traditions in critical but unacknowledged ways.

Sara Pekow also reveals how industrial foodways made emergent national cuisines available to the masses. Her chapter describes the transformation of sugar from an unattainable luxury to a widely available commodity in urban Syria—the result of a combination of factors, from technological improvements to Syria's integration into a global market economy. By the end of the interwar period, she argues, most Syrians had access to both refined sugar and manufactured sweets, meaning that elite consumption practices could be reinvented as newly national traditions.

Antonio Tahhan's essay and his family recipe offer a personal reflection that echoes many themes raised by the preceding chapters, from Syrian sweets made with refined sugar to the way that Levantine foodstuffs like pistachios and pomegranates are embedded in a dense web of rural landscapes, urban markets, cultural values, and human relationships.

## Part II. Revisiting Foodways in Israel-Palestine

As in Turkey, national tradition-making in the context of Israeli cuisine has been characterized by attempts to appropriate foods from the surrounding region and recast them as national dishes. Starting with the founding of Israel in 1948 and intensifying in recent decades, Israelis of European descent have adopted and at times laid claim to both Palestinian dishes and Jewish dishes from the Maghreb, Iraq, Yemen, and elsewhere in the Levant. Food writers including Rafram Chaddad, Yigal Nizri, and volume contributor Reem Kassis have pointed out that this process is especially glaring when it comes to Palestinian foods in particular.[46] They have explained, for instance, that dishes from Arab countries in North Africa or elsewhere in the Middle East, like Iraq, might be hyphenated as Tunisian-Israeli (as in the case of *shakshūka*, the subject of chapter 9), while the Palestinian origin of foods incorporated into the Israeli culinary repertoire is completely elided. This elision finds direct parallels both in the elision of Palestinian identity within Israel as euphemistically and generically "Arab" and in conflicts over land and resources, most obviously the blockade of Gaza since 2007 and the occupation of the West Bank since 1967. As Kassis put it in a recent essay, "presenting dishes of Palestinian provenance as 'Israeli' not only denies the Palestinian contribution to Israeli cuisine, but it erases our very history and existence."[47]

This section aims to revisit foodways in Israel-Palestine from a number of new perspectives, building on an academic body of literature on Israeli foodways that, while extensive, tends to depend upon binaries like Israeli/Palestinian and Arab/Jewish. These chapters contend that moving beyond those binaries, using the granularity of detail offered by food, can recontextualize and reinvigorate these discussions through focusing on the food of the Mizrahim (Jewish Israelis of Arab origin), the fundamental relationship between people and landscape typified by the Palestinian olive tree, and Palestine's regional and local culinary diversity.

Dafna Hirsch describes urban commercial food venues in Mandate Palestine (1920–1948) as "contact zones" where European Jews, Middle Eastern Jews, and Palestinians encountered one another in a range of ways. She demonstrates how Middle Eastern Jews (later referred to as Mizrahim) were mediators between Ashkenazi and Palestinian populations, especially when it came to cuisine. Perhaps most crucially, she highlights the ambivalence of Ashkenazi Jews about the local cuisine in Palestine during the mandate years, stressing the need to understand culinary appropriation as predicated upon specific historical developments rather than as the inevitable result of power imbalances.

Extending analysis beyond urban foodways to questions of landscape, Anne Meneley discusses the political ecology of Palestine through an extended meditation on the olive tree and its significance in Palestinian culture, from poetry and the visual arts to the substances and textures of everyday life. Olive trees and olive oil provide an especially potent lens for discussing the tension between rootedness and displacement on the one hand and regional particularism within Palestine and the common ecology of the Mediterranean writ large on the other.

Reem Kassis's contribution builds on questions of regionalism raised in earlier chapters with a direct discussion of the different ways we might approach Palestinian cuisine as a set of regional culinary cultures, bringing together factors as disparate as migration, displacement, cultural exchange, and landscape. At the same time, she acknowledges the importance of the idea of national cuisine for Palestinians in particular, echoing a wide consensus about the singular significance of a national cuisine in the absence of a state.[48] Her chapter is accompanied by recipes that demonstrate the regional breadth of Palestinian cuisine.

## Part III: Levantine Cuisine beyond Borders

The book's final section looks outward to the ways that Levantine cuisine travels and evolves as people and recipes migrate within and beyond the region proper. Susan MacDougall describes the way that a number of women in East Amman with Palestinian and Iraqi roots embody the Levantine cuisine as a "sensory, embodied, social, and cultural" entity that has traveled over space and time and has been reproduced over multiple generations, but whose embodied forms of knowledge remain within the evolving realm of feminine norms. Citing rich ethnographic evidence, she describes "Levantine food" as a term that includes both the local and particular and regional variations. Ultimately, she argues that the cuisine's survival and reproduction remain bound up with both its role in community-making and the labor of women.

Noam Sienna's chapter traces a different trajectory altogether: the journey of the North African dish *shakshūka* from the Maghreb to the Levant through the prism of Jewish foodways. Parsing the relationship between Jewish and other culinary cultures throughout the Mediterranean, he describes several early twentieth-century recipes for *shakshūka* that attest to its movement across the Maghreb, Levant, and Europe.

Harry Eli Kashdan carefully traces the globalization of popular Levantine street foods like falafel and shawarma, including the slippage between Levantine and Mediterranean culinary categories as dishes are remixed and represented on menus in the context of "a denatured global food culture."

The section ends with a personal essay and recipes from Suzanne Zeidy, who describes the resurgence of the Levantine culinary practice of eating mezze and associated forms of sociability in the wake of the 2011 uprisings in Egypt. From the perspective of an experienced restaurateur, Levantine cuisine emerges as a means to study cultures of consumption and the tension between regional and national modes of belonging within the Arab world.

## Conclusion

In Jacqueline Kahanoff's formulation, the Levant is less aptly described through the metaphor of a mosaic than as "a prism whose various facets are joined by the sharp edge of differences, each of which . . . reflects or refracts light."[49] We have assembled a dozen essays that together present an account of modern Levantine cuisine as a multifaceted entity that students, scholars, and home cooks can use to view the region from a slightly different vantage. Their authors have collected and mediated materials in Armenian, English, French, Judeo-Arabic, Hebrew, and multiple registers of Arabic and Turkish. Through collected recipes, thick description, archival research, and close readings of understudied cookbooks and restaurant menus, they present an argument for a deterritorialized understanding of Levantine cuisine.

By "deterritorialized," we mean several things that on the surface may appear contradictory. First, this book locates Levantine cuisine beyond the fields that produced its ingredients, the places that its cooking styles first developed, and the geographical borders of a short list of nation-states in the Eastern Mediterranean. In this volume, you will find Levantine cuisine appearing in Aleppo, Beirut, and Jerusalem but also in Palestinian and Syrian kitchens in Jordan as well as farther afield in Venezuela, the Netherlands, and the United States.

Second, by limiting our scope to the region of the Levant, we are also honing in on a specific set of environments and landscapes that produce the food we discuss. In doing so, however, we adopt a critical approach. We join the ranks of food scholars who have criticized, in the words of Kyla Wazana Tompkins, the "romanticized and insufficiently theorized attachments to 'local' or organic foodways, attachments that sometimes echo nativist ideological formations," which underpin much of contemporary (and privileged) "foodie culture."[50] Without losing sight of the importance of attachments to local ecologies and places to the making of Levantine cuisine, we aim to resist taking them at face value. The association of foods or ingredients with specific places is common and more often than not contains at least a kernel of truth; but it often illuminates more about who is making the association than it does about the place.

Presenting an understanding of Levantine cuisine that originates and resides within specific borders *and* travels beyond them produces a tension that runs throughout this book, but it is a tension that we embrace rather than seek to resolve. The culinary culture elucidated in the following chapters took shape both discursively and materially only as the geographical Levant became integrated within a global capitalist system over the course of the nineteenth and twentieth centuries—and its inhabitants left their home shores and villages. The stakes of national identification were heightened by displacement, population transfers, the fragmenting of empires, and decolonization. Industrialization reconfigured foodways and drove internal and external migration that in turn rendered a set of regional and home-cooked recipes into commercial dishes that became known from Istanbul to New York and beyond. Writing the history and present of Levantine cuisine requires placing narratives of movement and migration in conversation with renewed attachments to the local within the region itself.

To write the rhythms and sensory richness of food, past or present, always proves an elusive task. Like making kibbe or stuffing grape leaves, we believe it is a task best done collectively. What follows is our attempt to put down in words the making of Levantine cuisine.

## Notes

1. *Parts Unknown*, season 2, episode 1, "Jerusalem," written by Anthony Bourdain, directed by Sally Freeman, aired 15 September 2013 on CNN.

2. Yotam Ottolenghi and Sami Tamimi, *Jerusalem: A Cookbook* (Berkeley, CA: Ten Speed Press, 2012), 21.

3. Falafel was part of the indigenous Arab cuisine when Zionist settlers arrived. Its traditional Palestinian identity remained "self-evident" until after 1948, when "its transformation into an icon of Israeli culture was rushed and deliberate." Yael Raviv, "Falafel: A National Icon," *Gastronomica* 3, no. 3 (2003): 20. Raviv argues that the origin of the dish may be Egyptian, but Zionist settlers adopted the Palestinian version of falafel with chickpeas instead of fava beans in *Falafel Nation: Cuisine and the Making of National Identity in Israel* (Lincoln: University of Nebraska Press, 2015), 16.

4. Ottolenghi and Tamimi, *Jerusalem*, 13.

5. As we explain below, most of the extant scholarly literature on the food of the modern Levant focuses either on the culture and politics of foodways in Israel after 1948 or on questions of Levantine cuisine outside its region of origin. Despite the ostensible intensity of interest in the topic, the history of Palestinian cuisine remains to be written. One exception that does give significant attention to Palestinian foodways, albeit within the framework of modern Israeli society, is Liora Gvion, *Beyond Hummus*

*and Falafel: Social and Political Aspects of Palestinian Food in Israel* (Berkeley: University of California Press, 2012).

6. Samir Amin, *The Law of Worldwide Value* (1978) (New York: Monthly Review Press, 2010), 32.

7. Food studies have often neglected questions of labor. Sarah Besky and Sandy Brown, "Looking for Work: Placing Labor in Food Studies," *Labor* 12, nos. 1–2 (2015): 19–43.

8. Harry Eli Kashdan, "Jerusalem in London: Yotam Ottolenghi and Sami Tamimi's Diasporic World," *Mashriq & Mahjar* 6, no. 2 (2019): 1–35.

9. A Syrian regional identity dates from the Roman period. Nathanael Andrade, *Syrian Identity in the Greco-Roman World* (Cambridge: Cambridge University Press, 2013).

10. The region's precise borders have been the object of long-standing historical debate. See, for instance, the lengthy discussion on the matter in Muhammad Kurd ʿAli, *Kitab Khitat al-Sham*, vol. 1 (Damascus: al-Matbaʿa al-Haditha, 1925), 47–52.

11. A recent monograph puts this diversity in stark relief based on an analysis of court records. The city of Tripoli was specialized in urban horticulture in the early eighteenth century, especially citrus, silk, and olives. That political ecology corresponded with a large middle stratum and the high involvement of women in commerce. In Nablus, meanwhile, 250 kilometers south and further inland, a population of urban merchants traded in grains, legumes, and olives. In contrast to the situation in Tripoli, women almost never represented themselves in court. Both cities served as capitals for the surrounding villages and had textile and olive-soap manufacturing industries. The contrast and similarities between them encapsulate this unity and diversity of the Levantine region. Beshara Doumani, *Family Life in the Ottoman Mediterranean: A Social History* (Cambridge: Cambridge University Press, 2017).

12. J. R. McNeill, "The Eccentricity of the Middle East and North Africa's Environmental History," in *Water on Sand: Environmental Histories of the Middle East and North Africa*, ed. Alan Mikhail (Oxford: Oxford University Press, 2013), 27–50. Contact with nomadic populations brought fermented milk dishes such as *kishk* into the Levantine repertoire. Despite its nomadic origins, *kishk* is not currently consumed predominantly by bedouin communities. For a detailed comparison of the bedouin diet with that of the settled populations, see Carol Palmer, "Milk and Cereals: Identifying Food and Food Identity among Fallahin and Bedouin in Jordan," *Levant* 34, no. 1 (2002): 173–195.

13. Daniel Zohary, Maria Hopf, and Ehud Weiss, *Domestication of Plants in the Old World: The Origin and Spread of Cultivated Plants in West Asia, Europe, and the Nile Valley*, 4th ed. (Oxford: Oxford University Press, 2012); Dafna Langgut, Rachid Cheddadi, José Sebastián Carrión, Mark Cavanagh, Daniele Colombaroli, Warren John Eastwood, Raphael Greenberg, et al., "The Origin and Spread of Olive Cultivation in the Mediterranean Basin: The Fossil Pollen Evidence," *Holocene* 29, no. 5 (May 2019): 902–922.

14. Rachel Laudan, *Cuisine and Empire: Cooking in World History* (Berkeley: University of California Press, 2013), 139–140.

15. The Lebanese folklorist Anis Frayha argues that "original [*aṣīl*] Lebanese village cooking does not have very much art or skill to it. What is erroneously called Lebanese cuisine is in reality Eastern food (more specifically Perso-Turkish) learned by the

Lebanese from the residents of coastal cities or from the cooks of feudal princes." Anis Frayha, *al-Qariya al-Lubnaniyya: Hadara fi Tariq al-Zawal* (1957) (Beirut: Dar al-Nahar, 1980), 100–102. Salim Tamari has recently questioned how rigid a cultural divide existed between the highlands and lowlands in *Mountain against the Sea: Essays on Palestinian Society and Culture* (Berkeley: University of California Press, 2008).

16. On the diaspora, see Akram Khater, *Inventing Home: Emigration, Gender, and the Middle Class in Lebanon, 1870–1920* (Berkeley: University of California Press, 2001); Andrew Arsan, *Interlopers of Empire: The Lebanese Diaspora in Colonial French West Africa* (Oxford: Oxford University Press, 2014); Stacy Fahrenthold, *Between the Ottomans and the Entente: The First World War in the Syrian and Lebanese Diaspora, 1908–1925* (Oxford: Oxford University Press, 2019); Graham Auman Pitts, "The Ecology of Migration: Remittances in World War I Mount Lebanon," *Arab Studies Journal* 26, no. 2 (Fall 2018): 102–129.

17. Graham Auman Pitts, "'Make Them Hated in All the Arab Countries': France, Famine and the Making of Lebanon," in *Environmental Histories of World War I*, ed. Richard P. Tucker, Tait Keller, J. R. McNeill, and Martin Schmid (Cambridge: Cambridge University Press, 2018), 175–190.

18. Jane Harrigan, *The Political Economy of Arab Food Sovereignty* (New York: Palgrave MacMillan, 2014).

19. Cyrus Schayegh, *The Middle East and the Making of the Modern World* (Cambridge, MA: Harvard University Press, 2017), 9.

20. The unity of the region had already been undermined when the Republic of Turkey subsumed portions of the Levant that it won from France in the armed conflict of the early 1920s and through diplomacy in 1939.

21. Sami Zubaida, "National, Communal, and Global Dimensions in Middle Eastern Food Cultures," in *A Taste of Thyme: Culinary Cultures of the Middle East* (1994), ed. Sami Zubaida and Richard Tapper (London: I. B. Tauris, 2000), 33–45.

22. Laila M. El-Haddad and Maggie Schmitt, *The Gaza Kitchen: A Palestinian Culinary Journey* (Charlottesville, VA: Just World Books, 2012), 16.

23. Claudia Roden, *A Book of Middle Eastern Food* (London: Nelson, 1968).

24. Harry Eli Kashdan, "Anglophone Cookbooks and the Making of the Mediterranean," *Food and Foodways* 25, no. 1 (2017): 4–5.

25. Claudia Roden, *The Book of Jewish Food: An Odyssey from Samarkand to New York* (New York: Knopf, 1996); Claudia Roden, *The New Book of Middle Eastern Food*, rev. ed. (New York: Knopf, 2000).

26. Perhaps the best-known book of this genre is Frances Mayes, *Under the Tuscan Sun: At Home in Italy*, first published in 1996 (San Francisco: Chronicle Books) For a well-researched example from the Eastern Mediterranean, see Sonia Uvezian, *Recipes and Remembrances from an Eastern Mediterranean Kitchen* (Austin: University of Texas Press, 1999).

27. Sami Zubaida and Richard Tapper, eds., *A Taste of Thyme: Culinary Cultures of the Middle East* (1994) (London: I. B. Tauris, 2000).

28. Geert Jan van Gelder, *Of Dishes and Discourse: Classical Arabic Literary Representations of Food* (London: Curzon, 2000); Maxime Rodinson, A. J. Arberry, and Charles Perry, eds., *Medieval Arab Cookery* (Devon, UK: Prospect Books, 2006); Lilia Zaouali, *Medieval Cuisine of the Islamic World: A Concise History with 174 Recipes* (Berkeley: University of California Press, 2007); al-Muzaffar ibn Nasr Ibn Sayyar al-Warraq, *Annals*

*of the Caliphs' Kitchens: Ibn Sayyar al-Warraq's Tenth-Century Baghdadi Cookbook*, trans. Nawal Nasrallah (Leiden: Brill, 2007); David Waines, *Food Culture and Health in Pre-Modern Islamic Societies* (Leiden: Brill, 2011); Paulina B. Lewicka, *Food and Foodways of Medieval Cairenes: Aspects of Life in an Islamic Metropolis of the Eastern Mediterranean* (Leiden: Brill, 2011); Anonymous, *Scents and Flavors: A Syrian Cookbook*, trans. Charles Perry (New York: New York University Press, 2017); Anonymous, *Treasure Trove of Benefits and Variety at the Table: A Fourteenth-Century Egyptian Cookbook*, trans. Nawal Nasrallah (Leiden: Brill, 2018). An example of a monograph that addresses medieval Anatolia, rather than the medieval Arab world, is Nicolas Trépanier, *Foodways and Daily Life in Medieval Anatolia: A New Social History* (Austin: University of Texas Press, 2014).

29. Examples include an edited collection on early modern Ottoman foodways, focused largely on Anatolia, and a recent translation of an early modern Persian cookbook: Amy Singer, ed., *Starting with Food: Culinary Approaches to Ottoman History* (Princeton: Markus Wiener Publishers, 2011); Bavarchi Baqdadi, *A Persian Cookbook: The Manual*, trans. Saman Hassibi and Amir Sayadabdi (London: Prospect Books, 2018). Three contributors to the present volume wrote doctoral dissertations on modern Middle Eastern and North African food history and culture and have book manuscripts in development.

30. Farouk Mardam-Bey, *Ziryab: Authentic Arab Cuisine* (Woodbury, CT: Ici La Press, 2002). One notable exception is Mardam-Bey's discussion of the history of the tomato.

31. Tulay Artan, "Aspects of the Ottoman Elite's Food Consumption: Looking for 'Staples,' 'Luxuries,' and 'Delicacies' in a Changing Century," in *Consumption Studies and the History of the Ottoman Empire, 1550–1922: An Introduction*, ed. Donald Quataert, SUNY Series in the Social and Economic History of the Middle East (Albany: State University of New York Press, 2000), 107–165; Özge Samancı, "The Cuisine of Istanbul between East and West during the 19th Century," in *Earthly Delights: Economies and Cultures of Food in Ottoman and Danubian Europe, c. 1500–1900* (Leiden: Brill, 2018), 77–98; Amy Singer, *Constructing Ottoman Beneficence: An Imperial Soup Kitchen in Jerusalem*, SUNY Series in Near Eastern Studies (Albany: State University of New York Press, 2002); Singer, *Starting with Food*.

32. Edward Said, *Orientalism* (New York: Vintage Books, 1979), 96.

33. Recent edited volumes include Malak Rouchdy and Iman Hamdy, eds., *The Food Question in the Middle East*, Cairo Papers in Social Science, vol. 34, no. 4 (Cairo: American University in Cairo Press, 2017); Kirill Dmitriev, Julia Hauser, and Bilal Orfali, eds., *Insatiable Appetite: Food as a Cultural Signifier in the Middle East and Beyond* (Leiden: Brill, 2019).

34. Katarzyna Joanna Cwiertka and Boudewijn Walraven, *Asian Food: The Global and the Local* (Honolulu: University of Hawai'i Press, 2001); Krishnendu Ray and Tulasi Srinivas, eds., *Curried Cultures: Globalization, Food, and South Asia* (Berkeley: University of California Press, 2012); Michelle Tien King, ed., *Culinary Nationalism in Asia* (London: Bloomsbury Academic, 2019); Steffan Igor Ayora-Diaz, ed., *Taste, Politics, and Identities in Mexican Food* (London: Bloomsbury Academic, 2019).

35. Dmitriev, Hauser, and Orfali's *Insatiable Appetite*, for example, includes chapters on wine in early Arabic love poetry as well as the politics of halal certification in contemporary South Africa. For a discussion of the "Middle East" as a culinary category, see chapter 10 of this volume.

36. Zubaida and Tapper's *A Taste of Thyme* includes no chapter dedicated to Levantine food, for example, and more recent edited volumes such as Rouchdy and Hamdy's *The Food Question in the Middle East* and Dmitriev, Hauser, and Orfali's *Insatiable Appetite* include only a handful: Saker El Nour, "Agri-Food System Dynamics in a South Lebanon Village, 1920–2015," in *The Food Question in the Middle East*; Christian Saßmannshausen, "Eating Up: Food Consumption and Social Status in Late Ottoman Greater Syria"; and Tylor Brand, "Some Eat to Remember, Some to Forget," both in *Insatiable Appetite*. It is worth noting that *Insatiable Appetite* does feature more chapters that focus on the classical, medieval, and Ottoman Levant. See also Sara Pekow, "From Farm to Table: The Foodways Connection between Rural and Urban Women in Syria after World War I," *Mashriq & Mahjar* 6, no. 2 (2019): 75–99.

37. Examples of recent journal articles published on Israeli foodways include Ari Ariel, "The Hummus Wars," *Gastronomica* 12, no. 1 (2012): 34–42; Dafna Hirsch and Ofra Tene, "Hummus: The Making of an Israeli Culinary Cult," *Journal of Consumer Culture* 13, no. 1 (2013): 25–45; Azri Amram, "Digesting the Massacre: Food Tours in Palestinian Towns in Israel," *Gastronomica* 19, no. 4 (2019): 60–73. Monographs include Julia Bernstein, *Food for Thought: Transnational Contested Identities and Food Practices of Russian-Speaking Jewish Migrants in Israel and Germany* (Frankfurt: Campus Verlag, 2010); Gvion, *Beyond Hummus and Falafel*; Raviv, *Falafel Nation*; Nir Avieli, *Food and Power: A Culinary Ethnography of Israel* (Berkeley: University of California Press, 2018).

38. Ligaya Mishan, "The Rise of Palestinian Food," *T: The New York Times Style Magazine*, 12 February 2020, nytimes.com/2020/02/12/t-magazine/palestinian-food.html.

39. Sam Dean, "Yotam Ottolenghi and the Authors of 'The Gaza Kitchen' Discuss Food, Conflict, Culture," *Bon Appétit*, 27 March 2013, bonappetit.com/people/chefs/article/ottolenghi-gaza-kitchen-conversation; see also Yasmin Khan's recent essay "'You Can't Discuss Palestinian Food without Talking about the Occupation,'" *Literary Hub*, 5 February 2019, lithub.com/you-cant-discuss-palestinian-food-without-talking-about-the-occupation.

40. Anne Meneley's publications on the topic include "Time in a Bottle: The Uneasy Circulation of Palestinian Olive Oil," *Middle East Report* 248 (Fall 2008), merip.org/2008/09/time-in-a-bottle; "Blood Sweat and Tears in a Bottle of Palestinian Extra-Virgin Olive Oil," *Food, Culture & Society* 14, no. 2 (2011): 275–292; "Discourses of Distinction in Contemporary Palestinian Extra-Virgin Olive Oil Production," *Food and Foodways* 22, nos. 1–2 (2014): 48–64; and "The Accidental Pilgrims: Olive Pickers in Palestine," *Religion and Society* 5, no. 1 (2014): 186–199.

41. Gary Paul Nabhan, *Cumin, Camels, and Caravans: A Spice Odyssey* (Berkeley: University of California Press, 2014), 246–248; see also Gary Paul Nabhan, *Arab/American: Landscape, Culture, and Cuisine in Two Great Deserts* (Tucson: University of Arizona Press, 2008).

42. Matthew Jaber Stiffler, "Consuming Orientalism: Public Foodways of Arab American Christians," *Mashriq & Mahjar* 2, no. 2 (2014): 111–138 (quotation on 112). In an early example of this strategy, Elias Kirdahy and Joseph Kirdahy renamed their New York restaurant (originally established in 1913) "The Sheik" in the mid-1920s. South Americans of Palestinian descent also connect with their heritage, and a legacy of resistance in particular, through cuisine. Nicholas Bascuñan-Wiley, "Sumud and Food:

Remembering Palestine through Cuisine in Chile," *Mashriq & Mahjar* 6, no. 2 (2019): 100–131.

43. Jennifer Dueck, "Foreign Kitchens, Foreign Lands: Middle Eastern Foodsheds for American Consumers," *Global Food History* 5, no. 3 (2019): 144–161.

44. The disruption of the cross-border traffic after 9/11 between Detroit, Michigan, and Windsor, Ontario, revealed how central restaurant culture is to the Levantine diaspora in North America and how it functions as a contact zone with the rest of the population. Robert Nelson, "Pitas and Passports: Arab Foodways in the Windsor-Detroit Borderlands," *Mashriq & Mahjar* 6, no. 2 (2019): 57–74.

45. Leila Hudson, "'They Gave Us Cheese Sandwiches': Foodways of War and Flight," *Mashriq & Mahjar* 6, no. 2 (2019): 151–168.

46. Rafram Chaddad and Yigal Nizri, "Culinary Collisions," *Haaretz*, 22 November 2019.

47. Reem Kassis, "Here's Why Palestinians Object to the Term 'Israeli Food': It Erases Us from History," *Washington Post*, 18 February 2020.

48. See Ligaya Mishan, "The Rise of Palestinian Food," *T: The New York Times Style Magazine*, 12 February 2020, nytimes.com/2020/02/12/t-magazine/palestinian-food .html.

49. Quoted in Ammiel Alcalay, *After Jews and Arabs: Remaking Levantine Culture* (Minneapolis: University of Minnesota Press, 1993), 72.

50. Kyla Wazana Tompkins, *Racial Indigestion: Eating Bodies in the 19th Century* (New York: New York University Press, 2012), 2.

# PART I

# MAKING LEVANTINE FOOD CULTURES

# When Did Kibbe Become Lebanese?
# The Social Origins of National Food Culture

GRAHAM AUMAN PITTS AND MICHEL KABALAN

*You could call them dumplings, but they are a many-splendoured thing that defies characterization.*
CLAUDIA RODEN

A US-born Methodist minister, William McLure Thomson, visited the Levantine port city of Sidon on a pilgrimage in 1857. His memoir noted the sound of wooden pestles "braying" wheat in stone mortars "to make kibby ... at all hours as you walk the streets of the city." The dish was, in his view, "the national dish of the Arabs, and a very good one." Kibbe (*kubba* in formal Arabic) consists of pounded bulgur wheat and meat, shaped and stuffed, eaten baked, boiled, fried, or raw. Any of its ingredients can be replaced. Salim, Thomson's assistant, prepared him "kibbet samak" (fish kibbe), but the pastor noted that "it is more commonly made of mutton, mixed with fat from the large tail of the sheep. When thoroughly pounded, it is sent to the oven, and baked in a copper dish made for the purpose."[1] This preparation, kibbe *bi-l-ṣīnīyya* (on a tray), remains common today, although aluminum has now replaced copper. Throughout the nineteenth century until today, kibbe has been a staple of the Levantine table. Thomson's account suggests that the consumption of kibbe was not limited to rural and urban communities or to a particular class. It was neither "high" nor "humble" cuisine, to invoke the binary that animates Rachel Laudan's analysis of global food history. Neither was it the "middling" cuisine of the industrializing West.[2]

Although part of the Ottoman Empire since the early sixteenth century, the Levant had its own particular food culture. For instance, kibbe was typical across the nineteenth-century Levant, rather than in the entire Ottoman sphere.[3] Yet there is scant evidence to confirm Thomson's assertion that kibbe represented an Arab nation, or any other, in the eyes of those Levantines who cooked and consumed it in the mid-nineteenth century. Lebanon did not exist in its current borders until 1920. The Ottoman province of Mount Lebanon was a third of the size of the contemporary nation. Beirut, although surrounded by Mount Lebanon, was not included in its administrative boundaries; nor were the ports of Sidon, Tripoli, or Tyre or the rural areas of 'Akkar, the Bekaa Valley, and Jabal 'Amil. Before it was codified in cookbooks, a unified Levantine cuisine transcended these administrative boundaries.

This chapter explores kibbe's modern history and the cuisine of which it forms part, based on a critical interpretation of the most widely read Arabic-language cookbooks published in Beirut. Modern Levantine food coalesced not as the popular adoption of upper-class mores but rather as a bourgeois re-creation of traditional foodways in capitalist Beirut. Subsequently, the class aspect of that project became increasingly more implicit in favor of a diverse but unified national Lebanese cuisine.

A self-conscious modern food culture first emerged in late nineteenth-century Beirut when the city's nascent bourgeoisie melded traditional dishes like kibbe into new social mores.[4] Elsewhere in the Arab world, this broad transformation of domesticity coincided with the production of nationalist identities in the twentieth century.[5] However, in the Levant, it preceded a specific nationalist project. The early appearance of modern cookbooks in the Levantine cultural and economic capital of Beirut stems from the intensity of capitalist social transformation and the region's cultural encounter with Europe and the Americas. This culinary project remained inclusively Levantine until the second half of the twentieth century, when cookbook authors began to posit the existence of a "Lebanese" cuisine distinct from the rest of the Levant.

The production of this culinary authenticity coincided with the alienation of an emergent middle class from traditional food production. Tradition, in this sense, denotes what preceded this modern project of print codification and capitalist commodification. Levantine and later Lebanese cuisine emerged as an attempt to re-create a culture that had been refashioned under capitalism. In each period, these cookbooks captured something that risked being lost.

Kibbe has always been central to modern Levantine cuisine and featured prominently in the first widely read nineteenth-century Arabic cookbook. *Tadhkirat al-Khawatin wa-Ustadh al-Tabbakhin* (A Manual for Ladies and the Master Chef) by Khalil Sarkis was the core text on Levantine cuisine for more than seven decades.[6] Published in 1885 in Beirut, *Ustadh al-Tabbakhin* was reprinted for the sixth and final time in 1931, although Sarkis died in 1915. Its recipes surfaced verbatim in other texts throughout the twentieth century, including a popular cookbook sold by peddlers, *Dalil al-Tabbakhin* (Cook's Guide) as late as 1947.[7] *Ustadh al-Tabbakhin* instructed an emergent Beiruti middle class in how to cook, dress, and perform hospitality according to ostensibly global norms adapted to the local milieu. Sarkis's cookbook reveals not only an idealized domesticity but also the material social relations of his society. In tandem with the landlord class represented by Sarkis, migrants from rural Mount Lebanon moved to Beirut to rent rooms and work for wages. The reproduction of village foodways in modernizing Levantine homes was predicated on their labor time, purchased with profits gleaned from commerce and real estate. This systematic bifurcation between classes, at the material and discursive level, was the necessary condition for Levantine cuisine's emergence as a self-conscious, coherent whole in *Ustadh al-Tabbakhin*.

In the second half of the twentieth century a standardized and simplified version of the regional cuisine came into existence as "Lebanese." Lebanon gained independence from France in 1943 but remained under occupation for three more years. George al-Rayyis first published *Kitab Fann al-Tabkh* (The Art of Cooking) in 1951. He included Lebanese dishes alongside recipes from Dutch, French, German, and Turkish cuisines. His book, in its Arabic and French versions, was the signal work for the postindependence era. His project also represented the demands of capital, but differently than *Ustadh al-Tabbakhin*. In a departure from Sarkis's emphasis on domestic food preparation, Rayyis primarily aims to inform restaurant cooking.[8] Food service and tourism were both the object of investment for capitalists and a source of employment for the working class. Like the context that produced Sarkis, Rayyis's Lebanon experienced a gilded age of unprecedented urban middle-class prosperity and a wave of mass attrition from the countryside to urban areas and abroad. As village life languished, cookbooks more fully embraced rural traditions. The emergence of TV chef and writer Ramzi Choueiri (born 1971) in the 1990s epitomized this celebration of rural Lebanon. His book *Min Turath Lubnan* (From Lebanon's Heritage) cataloged thirty-seven kibbe recipes associated with individual villages.[9]

In what follows, we trace culinary and social history through the codification of this cuisine as it evolved from Levantine to Lebanese. Sarkis and Rayyis were the most widely read Arabic-language cookbook authors while they were in print. Ramzi Choueiri was the Arab world's first TV chef and the most prominent chronicler of Lebanese cuisine in the late 1990s and early 2000s. One constant feature of these cookbooks, written by men, was that women or employed cooks were supposed to shoulder the labor of food preparation. Each successive author assumes less tacit knowledge necessary to prepare Levantine dishes. Fundamental techniques receive more detailed attention over time.[10] That trend suggests that this project aimed to capture traditions as they were progressively being lost to capitalism's creative destruction. Beirut's globally minded bourgeoisie, its dynamic publishing industry, and its urban restaurant culture worked to salvage those traditions in a new social context. The energy that has gone into producing an authentic and timeless Lebanese cuisine has obscured these material processes behind its creation. To unlock that history, we read these texts against their efforts to naturalize a bourgeois food culture.

## Khalil Sarkis and the Bourgeois Origins of the Modern Levantine Kitchen

"The peasant moved to the city and all he missed was molasses and tahini" (*nizil al-fallāḥ ʿal-madineh mā istaḥlā ghayr al-dibs wa-l-ṭaḥīneh*).[11] Recorded in early twentieth-century Beirut, this colloquial proverb captured the experience of rural migration to the city from Mount Lebanon. Molasses, made from grapes or carob seeds, would keep for the winter like tahini, a paste made from sesame seeds and oil. Rural folk would have eaten a mixture of the two with fresh bread. It suggests that workers who moved to the city ate a humble diet, in great contrast with the class who employed them. Crucially, it shows that village life had become unviable, apart from lingering nostalgia for the products of rural foodways.

Peasants left behind an especially diverse ecology of food production in Mount Lebanon. Cultivation on terraces occurred at varying elevations—a practice that amplified the diversity of Levantine cuisine. Relatively abundant springs facilitated intensive agriculture impossible on the rain-fed plains of the Syrian interior. These factors promoted a dense population of peasant farmers whose labor facilitated the establishment of a capitalist silk industry in the mid-nineteenth century.

Capitalism created social mobility and prosperity alongside vulnerability and instability for Mount Lebanon's market-dependent population. When the price of silk collapsed in the 1870s, peasants sought to find their fortunes elsewhere. Opportunity in Beirut enticed many to migrate from the villages of adjacent Mount Lebanon to the city (and abroad). Migration to Egypt began in the 1860s, followed by a substantial outflux of inhabitants to the Americas that started in the 1880s. One in three inhabitants of Mount Lebanon had emigrated by 1914.[12]

Beirut also attracted wealthy migrants from around the Levant. Starting in the first half of the nineteenth century, the city offered merchants freedom from traditional sources of power and the ability to trade directly with Europe. They came first from Damascus and later from Acre, Sidon, and Tripoli.[13] An amalgam of the Levantine region's population, the city's population grew from 7,000 at the turn of the nineteenth century to almost 150,000 by the outbreak of World War I. European and American diplomats, merchants, and missionaries also settled in Beirut by the thousands. Steamer traffic facilitated the export of silk and the import of manufactured goods as Beirut became the Levant's principal commercial capital and port. In 1888, three years after the publication of *Ustadh al-Tabbakhin*, Beirut became the capital of its own province for the first time. That development testified to the city's rising commercial and political power.

Beirut experienced unprecedented integration with the surrounding region, the rest of the Ottoman Empire, Europe, and the Americas. With this dynamic cultural backdrop, the city developed a vigorous book and newspaper publishing industry. Khalil Sarkis, born in the town of Abeih in 1842, moved—like many others from Lebanese villages—to the burgeoning port city of Beirut, where he became a prominent newspaper publisher.[14] He went into the publishing business with his father-in-law, the famous author Butrus al-Bustani, before founding his own press in the mid-1870s. Often appreciated for its contribution to nascent Arab nationalisms, Beirut's publishing industry was also the expression of bourgeois class formation. Sarkis, from the very first lines of *Ustadh al-Tabbakhin*, reveals the geographic, gender, and class dimensions of his worldview in terms that chime with historian Toufoul Abou-Hodeib's analysis. He represented an emergent bourgeoisie that she has shown was "middling" in two regards: according to the terms of its own civilizational hierarchy and its conceptual place between the lower and upper class. This process corresponds to Pierre Bourdieu's distinction framework but with the extra global dimension invisible in the French sociologist's focus on self-contained national cultural units.[15] Although her "cultural history of domesticity" does not consider food in detail, the codification of the indigenous cuisine confirms what Abou-Hodeib describes as the "unsettled" modern project of the Beirut middle class, "laying claim to aspects of modernity while trying to emphasize what it is about that class that makes it specifically local."[16]

At no point in his book does Sarkis identify the recipes as Beiruti or Lebanese. Instead, he chronicles a regional cuisine that is implicitly Levantine. In the 1885 introduction, Sarkis confirms (explicitly) that the recipes in a later section of the book focus "specifically" on dishes found in the Levant (*khuṣūṣan fī aqṭārinā al-Suriyya*), although the section title refers to them generically as "Eastern-style foods" (*al-ṭaʿām ʿalā al-ṭarīqa al-sharqiyya*).[17] Subsequent editions dropped the reference to Syria in favor of an unnamed "nation" (*waṭan*).[18]

We know that this is a reference to the Levant because dishes from elsewhere are labeled as such. For instance, lamb preparations are "Egyptian" or "Persian" or "Indian."[19] "Foreign" food occupied the enormous majority of *Ustadh al-Tabbakhin*'s original recipes and enjoyed place of pride in the text. However, by the time of the 1931 edition, the recipe order had been switched so that the local foods, including kibbe, came first. A plain civilizational hierarchy is implied by the book's recommendation to unite the cuisine of "our Eastern lands" (*aqtāruṇā al-sharqiyya*) with the cuisine of "foreign lands" (*al-aqṭār al-ajnabiyya*) that have excelled in this modern domestic craft (*ṣinā'a*) and ascended "the ladder of progress."[20]

Sarkis's reader learns how to cultivate an authentically local and middle-class identity that advertises education, good taste, and thrift. His kibbe recipes assume the use of the heavy mortar and pestle (*jurn*). Intensive, prolonged pounding labor was required to make kibbe dough using this age-old technology. It found a new home in the separated kitchens that the wealthy built, distinct from the other rooms of the house. Adjacent would be the dining room with a dinner table that had a tight-fitting tablecloth, with cutlery and plates specialized for each course. In Sarkis's ideal home, kibbe was to be served at a dinner party as one course among several, individually plated for each guest.[21] Imported wines were to be paired with each course. He recommends that a dinner party end with the woman of the house serving drinks in the sitting room with fine bottles of liquor displayed to show that she had chosen the finest in the world for her guests.[22] This aspirational ideal home featured a blend of global and local comestibles and customs. As Christian Saßmannshausen has shown, "only a small privileged circle managed to participate in these practices comprehensively."[23] Self-consciously Westernized, Sarkis's recommendations for organizing the home and hosting guests contrast with nonbourgeois traditions. In traditional Mount Lebanon, according to Ma'luf, the hosts did not sit with their guests at a high table as in Sarkis's vision of proper bourgeois customs but instead served them around a low table (*ṭabliyya*) on earthenware plates.[24]

Although Sarkis's household employs servants, the woman of the house engages in domestic work. In that regard, this authentic local modernity distinguishes itself from an upper class that eschews domestic labor altogether.[25] The laborious task of preparing a multicourse dinner for several invited guests could be accomplished only with hired servants. Sarkis recommended inspecting the fingers of a potential cook to gauge his cleanliness. The task of preparing meals could not be left to an "ignorant female servant" and must be performed by an educated person. Yet the woman of the house (*rabbat al-manzil*) must be involved, because relying solely on hired help for food preparation risks

**Table 1.1. Kibbe Dishes in Sarkis, *Tadhkirat al-Khawatin* (1885)**

| Name in Formal Arabic | Preparation Method and Translation |
|---|---|
| *al-kubayba bi-l-ṣīnīyya mamdūda* | Kibbe on a cooking tray with a stuffing of onion, pine nuts, and cooked meat between the two layers |
| *al-kubayba bi-l-ṣīnīyya aqrāsān* | Stuffed kibbe balls on a cooking tray |
| *al-kubayba mashwiyya* | Grilled kibbe balls |
| *al-kubayba al-Ḥalabiyya* | "Aleppan kibbe" balls in tomato sauce |
| *al-kubayba ʿalā yakhnā al-banādūrā* [sic] | Kibbe balls in a tomato stew |
| *al-kubayba ʿalā yakhnā* [sic] *al-bādhinjān* | Kibbe balls in an eggplant stew |
| *al-kubayba bi-labaniyya* | Kibbe balls in yogurt sauce served with rice |
| *al-kubayba al-arnabiyya* | Kibbe balls in a tahini, lemon, and meat sauce |
| *kubbat al-aruzz* | Meat and rice dough kibbe layered with stuffing |
| *al-tabkha al-fākhtiyya* (or *kubaybat al-arnabīṭ* [1931]) | Meat, cauliflower, and bulgur with tahini and yoghurt sauce |
| *al-kubayba bi-l-kishk* | Fermented milk and bulgur, meat, and chickpeas |
| *kubaybat al-samak* | Fish-based dish with bulgur cooked in the oven |
| *kubaybat al-ḥīla* | Vegetarian "trick" kibbe with rice and bulgur |
| *kubbat al-yaqṭīn* | Pumpkin kibbe with bulgur (vegetarian) |
| *kubaybat al-baṭāṭā* | Potato kibbe with bulgur |

"disaster."[26] The book leaves ambiguous exactly how much of the kitchen labor should be taken up by a hired cook versus the *rabbat al-manzil*. Servants "quiet and calm like a soldier on the battlefield" would serve the food.[27] Beirut's new domesticity required both sides of the coin: a growing bourgeoisie to supervise a class of workers willing to sell their labor as household servants.[28] The book's full title reveals this class dynamic: *Tadhkirat al-Khawatin*, "a manual for [elite] ladies," and *Ustadh al-Tabbakhin*, "the master chef."

Demand for foodstuffs among Beirut's growing consumer class in the late nineteenth century reoriented agricultural production in the surrounding areas toward production for the city's market. Proximate to the diverse agricultural ecologies of Mount Lebanon, the Bekaa, and the Syrian interior, Beiruti consumers had access to a wealth of foodstuffs. Fruits and vegetables came from close by, grain and livestock from elsewhere in the Levant. The best grains, which were boiled and cracked to make bulgur—the base ingredient of kibbe—came from a variety produced on Syria's Hawran plain.[29] Sarkis provides instructions for preparing fifteen different types of kibbe (see table 1.1), revealing the diversity of the surrounding agricultural ecology with its variable microclimates, elevation, and rainfall. As bulgur and meat were available year-round, kibbe provided a vehicle to cook different combinations of seasonally available ingredients as part of these preparations. Eggplant and tomato kibbe would have been enjoyed in the summer, pumpkin in the fall. As an ensemble, these recipes are a celebration of the agricultural and culinary diversity that surrounded Beirut.

While Sarkis defines kibbe as "good minced meat and bulgur in various forms," that description does not fit all of his recipes.[30] There are a variety of vegetarian kibbes, such as *kubaybat al-ḥila* ("trick" kibbe made with rice and bulgur), *kubbat al-yaqṭīn* (pumpkin kibbe with bulgur), and *kubaybat al-baṭāṭā* (potato kibbe). The extensive array of nonmeat options throughout the cookbook derives in large part from the Christian abstention from meat on fast days. Two seafood kibbe recipes, fish and octopus, would have also been appropriate for fasting. While Sarkis does not explicitly imbue his local subject with any specific religion, the references to pork and wine and the extended recipes devoted to dishes for Christian fasting suggest the prominent role that Christians played in the codification of this cuisine.[31]

The nature of the ingredients in some of the preparations suggests that they are of mid-nineteenth-century vintage. *Al-kubayba al-Ḥalabiyya* (Aleppan kibbe) was made of small balls "the size of a large walnut" served in a tomato sauce (*ṣālṣa*) with pine nuts. Notably, tomatoes were only introduced in the city of Aleppo in the early 1850s.[32] So the tomato must have been incorporated into the making of a sauce for kibbe balls sometime after mid-century and subsequently become understood in 1880s Beirut as a dish typical of Aleppo. Of the kibbe recipes offered by Sarkis in *Tadhkirat al-Khawatin*, it is the only one tied to a specific place. The reference to Aleppo is a testament to that city's particular culinary heritage (see chapter 2 of this book), also a telling acknowledgment that his kibbe recipes reflect variations on a theme found across the Levant.

First in Sarkis's list is the well-known kibbe *bi-l-ṣīnīyya*, which he refers to in formal Arabic: *al-kubayba bi-l-ṣīnīyya mamdūda* (kibbe spread on a cooking tray). He notes that it was also called *kubayba bi-l-furn* (kibbe in the oven).

[Use a ratio] of one *aqa* [1.28 kilograms] of meat for an *aqa* and a half of bulgur. Cut and debone the meat, reserving an *ūqiyya* [213 grams] and a half. Mince finely. Take the two onions, mince them finely, and fry in ghee [*samn*] until they mellow. Add the minced meat on top and half an *ūqiyya* of pine nuts, salt, spices. Fry well. Then mortar-mince the [rest of the] meat well, take it out of the *jurn*, and reserve it in a bowl. Take the onions and grind them well with salt and spices. Then add the [reserved] ground meat and put the rinsed bulgur on top of the meat and knead with both hands well until the kibbe becomes like a dough. Butter a cooking tray [ṣīnīyya] with ghee and take a piece of the kibbe, remove any veins [naqha min al-'urūq], and pound it; spread it as one layer on the tray, taking the stuffing and spreading it over the kibbe. Take a piece of the kibbe and flatten it in a thicker layer than the first, spreading it over the stuffing and smoothing it well. Cut it like baklava [in rectangular shapes] and put about an ūqiyya and a half of ghee on top. Bake it in the oven.[33]

Some details stand out as distinct from the contemporary preparations. This recipe is heavier in fat than the current versions, for instance. The overall technique, however, remains similar except for the obvious difference entailed by the transition from the *jurn* to food processors in the late twentieth century (as discussed later). Only two of the recipes disappeared from the "Lebanese" cookbooks we discuss.[34] Kibbe's prominence is one key point of continuity between today and the late Ottoman cuisine of Beirut, Mount Lebanon, and the broader Levantine region.

Sarkis never mentions that the food he describes is particularly Beiruti or Lebanese. That distinction would likely not have been meaningful to his audience. Writing on the cusp of the transition between Ottoman and French rule, notable and author 'Isa Iskandar al-Ma'luf attempted to characterize the cuisine of Mount Lebanon. After mentioning *kishk* and kibbe, dishes found throughout the region, he had to opt for something rather obscure to distinguish it from the rest of the Levant region. The Lebanese "specialize in snails, just like the Damascenes do in frogs and crabs."[35] His reliance on these obscure details indicates that there was little to distinguish Lebanese cuisine from Levantine. His description contains some dishes well known globally now, such as *mujaddara* (rice, lentils, and onions) and stuffed grape leaves, along with some that are less well known but still prepared, such as *makhlūṭa* (a stew of bulgur, chickpeas, and lentils), *harīsa* (bone-in meat with wheat hearts cooked into a porridge), and *rishta* (a stew of pasta and lentils). Dishes that form the core of today's stereotypical Lebanese cuisine were absent, especially hummus, baba ghanoush, and tabbouleh.[36]

The differences between the first and final editions of *Ustadh al-Tabbakhin* are negligible. If the cookbook's longevity is any measure, there was a great continuity in approach from the last three decades of Ottoman rule through almost three decades of French rule. One change is the foregrounding of local recipes in the 1931 edition and the more locally appropriate lists of fruits and vegetables in the monthly lists of common foods.[37] That development suggests that the project became increasingly comfortable asserting an authentically local alternative modernity as time went on. That trend would continue in the second half of the twentieth century as Lebanese national cuisine came into existence.

## The Birth of the Authentic Lebanese Kitchen, 1951–2002

Following Sarkis's tome, which was reprinted and reproduced throughout the period of French colonization of Lebanon and Syria (1918–1946), no new cookbooks devoted to the Levant or any of its subregions were published until the second half of the twentieth century. A new generation of Arabic-language cookbooks after World War II would assert the coherence of an authentic Lebanese national cuisine during another period of punctuated social change like the one that produced *Ustadh al-Tabbakhin*. Read against the grain of their attempt to dehistoricize and reify tradition, these texts reveal the contradictions entailed by an effort to codify national Lebanese food culture.

Folklorist Anis Frayha, writing in the late 1950s, aimed to capture the essence of Lebanese village life before it was "invaded" by Western influence.[38] Born in 1903, he idealizes the village of his childhood. The contradiction entailed in his periodization, however, is plain. Mount Lebanon had always been linked to the outside world, but its encounters with the West intensified in the nineteenth century with the region's integration into the global industrial economy and the arrival of Christian missionaries. Emigration to the Americas had reached full tilt in Frayha's first years of life. Returning migrants had brought back "Western" influence to their villages since the 1880s. Frayha's nostalgic version of the village never existed, but his attempt to reconstruct it is emblematic of how writing about traditional foodways reflects an inclination to posit them as an authentic local alternative to their Western industrial counterpart. Frayha sublimated the class agenda that had been so explicit in Sarkis's writing. His village, and by extension the nation, had no social tension.[39] Lebanon's projected image of prosperity belied simmering inequality and political instability. Frayha wrote at a moment when many Lebanese households were buying cars, canned food, and televisions. His version of the pure Lebanese village remained influential, despite the fact that it excluded the country's Muslim inhabitants.[40]

As in the historical canon more broadly, cooking and cuisine are an afterthought in Frayha's work. At the end of his discussion of women in traditional village culture, he mentions the "Lebanese kitchen" (*al-maṭbakh al-Lubnāni*). However, the term itself does not apply to his purported object of study: Frayha's traditional Lebanese house did not have a space exclusively dedicated to food preparation, which was done in the upper room (al-'ulliya) or outside. "Authentic" Lebanese village cuisine, according to him, was "simple and primitive," lacking "art or innovation." Complex preparations had been learned from the people of the coast or the upper class. These represented a "Turco-Persian [kitchen] erroneously called Lebanese."[41] Where in this dichotomy did kibbe fit? If Lebanese cuisine included meat only sparingly, did the mixing of grain and lamb in kibbe represent a method of making precious meat go as far as possible? Or was it a dish of the Ottoman elite not generally prepared by Lebanese peasants? For Frayha, it was authentic Lebanese food, but he defers to other texts (unnamed but most likely Sarkis) that he says have described its history and preparation. Kibbe disrupts the binary that he constructed between "Oriental" and traditional Lebanese cuisine. His attempt to project a culinary distinction between Mount Lebanon and the rest of the region back in time falters when he broaches a dish that has a clear heritage throughout the region.

Frayha's literary production of an authentic Lebanese village coincided with the Lebanese state's investment in the production of a national cuisine. George al-Rayyis was Lebanon's minister of tourism when he published the first book devoted to "Lebanese" foods, *Fann al-Tabkh*, in 1951. Rather than being the explicit domestic project of a particular class, the new national cuisine was purportedly in the interest of the national economy and aimed at reforming practices of the public sphere. Rayyis adapted the book's "Lebanese" recipes from a book already published by his ministry under the supervision of two chefs: Najib Elias Abi 'Ad and Thabet Iskandar Abi 'Ad. The government of newly independent Lebanon hoped to build an infrastructure to attract tourists and in doing so wanted to equip the staff of hotels and restaurants to prepare foreign cuisine that visitors would recognize and enjoy. Rayyis suggests that foreign recipes would make tourists feel at home in the hotels and restaurants that receive them. Equally, his project aimed to codify the Lebanese repertoire and to recognize and project the nation's food in a positive and systematic fashion.

During the mid-twentieth century, convincing tourists to eat Lebanese food was not necessarily an easy task. A United States Information Service guide to Beirut described kibbe as a "glorified hamburger" and counseled those visitors who were not "gastronomically adventurous" to stick to the conventional "French cooking" widely available in the city's hotels and restaurants. The writer added, however, that "one does not know Lebanon" without tasting kibbe and stuffed zucchini (kūsā maḥshī). A 1953 guide recommended places in Beirut to stock up for a road trip—"Western style." Small cafés in rural villages would "not be up to preparing such meals" suited to foreigners. Only "adventuresome travelers will want to try local foods."[42] The same book

**Table 1.2. Kibbe Dishes in *Fann al-Tabkh* (1951)**

| Name of the Kibbe Dish | Preparation Method and Translation |
| --- | --- |
| kubba nī'a | Raw kibbe of meat, bulgur, and onion |
| kubba nī'a ma'a al-muhammaṣa | Raw meat, bulgur, and onion served with a butter sauce of onions, ground meat, and pine nuts |
| kubba bi-l-ṣīnīyya | Kibbe on a cooking tray with a stuffing of onion, pine nuts, and cooked meat between the two layers |
| kubba mashwiyya | Kibbe shaped into small balls, stuffed and grilled |
| kubba mashwiyya bi-l-furn (aqrās kabīra) | Large kibbe balls "grilled" in the oven |
| kubba maqliyya bi-l-zayt | Kibbe balls fried in oil |
| kubba ma'a yakhnī al-bādhinjān | Kibbe balls served in eggplant stew |
| kubba ma'a al-kūsā aw ghayrihi min al-khuḍār | Kibbe balls served in zucchini (or other vegetable) stew |
| kubba labaniyya | Kibbe balls in yogurt sauce |
| kubba ma'a shīshbarak | Kibbe balls with dumplings in yogurt sauce |
| kubba ma'a al-kishk | Kibbe balls with *kishk* (fermented milk and bulgur) served with cooked cabbage |
| kubba arnabiyya | Kibbe balls in lemony meat stock with tahini and chickpeas |
| kubba rummāniyya (Ṭarābulusiyya) | Kibbe balls in pomegranate sauce (from Tripoli, Lebanon) |
| kubbat al-samak | Fish kibbe baked on a cooking tray or in balls |

divides restaurants between "oriental and Western" categories, recommending that the best bet (paradoxically) was to eat "favorite Lebanese dishes" at Western-style hotels and not in "oriental cafes catering to the local trade."[43] Local outdoor cafes, according to the guide, would be a nice place to enjoy beer or anise-flavored grape liquor, arak, with an array of mezze including both familiar dishes such as kibbe, introduced as "the national dish of Lebanon," and bread, hummus, baba ghanoush, and the now less common roasted *'aṣāfīr* (quail or similar small birds), raw or fried liver, spleen, or brains.[44] Beirut's vibrant restaurant culture was reflected in Rayyis's concern with restaurant cooking.

Compared with Sarkis, Rayyis and Frayha are more comfortable accentuating all aspects of the village tradition. The first kibbe listed among George al-Rayyis's thirteen recipes (see table 1.2) was notably absent in *Ustadh al-Tabbakhin*: raw (*nī'a*) kibbe, spiced and mixed with onions. Rayyis recommended a higher percentage of lean mutton to bulgur than in his cooked preparation of kibbe. *Ustadh al-Tabbakhin*'s sanitary sensibility likely proscribed serving uncooked meat, although raw kibbe was consumed in the nineteenth-century rural Levant.[45] It became the headliner of Lebanon's national kibbe recipes in the mid-twentieth century. What changed? As the twentieth century progressed and the trappings of modernity became ever more ubiquitous, the food culture increasingly embraced its origins. That trend continued with Rayyis and accounts for his inclusion of raw kibbe. Refrigeration, of course, also made it safer to store and transport raw meat.

The proliferation of industrial technologies made the reproduction of labor-intensive traditional cuisine feasible in restaurants and homes. Rayyis offered the traditional option of the *jurn* alongside the alternative of the food processor. The preparation of kibbe became a task that could be accomplished quickly, without hours of labor beating the mixture into a dough. Kibbe only took twenty minutes in the food processor: ten minutes for the spiced meat alone and another ten mixed with bulgur. Ice—not as readily available in late-nineteenth century Beirut—was used to help the meat adhere. It, too, was a time-saving shortcut to making the kibbe into a dough that could be shaped and cooked.[46] Frozen and canned vegetables made some key ingredients available year-round so that tabbouleh and hummus and other spreads could become ubiquitous on the "Lebanese" table. During this period, Lebanese cuisine took shape with the core repertoire for which it is known globally today.[47]

This embrace of village culture came as Lebanon's countryside confronted a crisis. While Beirut of the 1950s and 1960s was noted for its prosperity, the country's open economy offered no protection for small agricultural producers amid the massive commercialization of global food production. The growing irrelevance of the agricultural sector and the production of new inequalities again spurred emigration from the countryside. Much like the late nineteenth-century period that produced *Ustadh al-Tabbakhin*, independent Lebanon experienced economic and social transformations and the rapid adoption of new customs and technologies. That context once again produced a need to codify and commodify an authentic version of the local cuisine, this time in the form of a Lebanese national project. Once again, the cookbook aimed to capture something as it was fading away, a process that would repeat toward the end of the century in the era of television chefs.

## Chef Ramzi and the Neoliberal Embrace of Lebanon's Rural Kibbe

As we have seen, the apparent prosperity of the decades that followed World War II masked a profound instability in Lebanon. As in the late nineteenth century, market forces displaced a significant portion of the rural population.

This trend, global in scope, was particularly intense in Lebanon because of the proximity of a major center of finance capital to a dense rural population engaged in traditional agriculture. This contradiction was the context for Frayha's ethnography and the state's investment in a Lebanese national cuisine. Such projects aimed to suture over Lebanon's growing divides, which exploded in the Lebanese Civil War (1975–1990).[48]

Rayyis was not displaced as the premier chronicler of Lebanese food until after the war, during another era of massive but deeply unequal economic growth in the 1990s. Ramzi Choueiri was born in 1971. His grandfather had accumulated wealth as a merchant in Louisiana in the early twentieth century before returning to Lebanon after World War I. In 1957 Ramzi's father, Nadim, abandoned a career in finance and real estate to establish al-Kafa'at, a technical school for underprivileged and disabled youth. During the Lebanese Civil War, when his wife and children were in exile in France, he added a catering school. Nadim visited his family in Lyon, France, and encouraged his children to prepare themselves to contribute to the school once they returned. Ramzi studied culinary arts and hospitality in England and France before returning to Lebanon to work at the catering school in 1993.[49]

Ramzi then began his career as a Lebanese television celebrity chef. Between 1994 and 2011 he hosted a daily show on the Lebanese channel Future TV. Choueiri's work reflected the ethos of a post–civil war national healing predicated on neoliberal economic prosperity. The reconstruction of downtown Beirut under the aegis of the holding company Solidere was to be the cornerstone of a new Lebanon. Rafiq al-Hariri was the majority shareholder in the company and owner of Future TV while he served as Lebanon's prime minister. Chef Ramzi's show was sometimes broadcast from downtown Beirut, intimately linking Choueiri to the Hariri reconstruction project predicated on private capital.[50]

Choueiri's kibbe recipes numbered thirty-seven, compared to Rayyis's fifteen and Sarkis's sixteen. Choueiri's books describe in great detail the mechanical processes that facilitated making such an array of kibbe preparations.[51] The labor regime had evolved in other ways too. After Lebanon's civil war, households with the means to do so stopped hiring Arabic-speaking household servants, instead drawing on global labor markets. Women from Ethiopia, the Philippines, and Sri Lanka provided much of the intensive kitchen labor for the reproduction of the indigenous cuisine in bourgeois households.[52] This new domestic labor regime underpinned a reassertion of local Lebanese identity through food culture.

Like Sarkis, Choueiri initially focused on foreign foods but became a famous best-selling author by turning toward an exploration of Lebanon's varied interpretations of classic dishes. Choueiri's show had a run of more than 3,000 episodes, leading one critic to acknowledge that "every housewife" had the name of "Chef Ramzi for so long on her lips."[53] In his cookbook *Min Turath Lubnan*, Ramzi Choueiri explicitly links each kibbe variation to a specific Lebanese village (see table 1.3). For instance, he manages to identify at least four recipes for pumpkin kibbe, each from a different location: Saghbine in the West Bekaa, Kherbit Selm and Deir Kontar near Bint Jbeil, 'Akkar, and Ehden or Hasroun in the north of Lebanon. He details the use of rice, bulgur, white flour, and chickpeas in kibbe. He notices, for example, more chickpeas in the south of Lebanon and more bulgur and rice in the north. Not just the kibbe but every recipe is attributed to a specific Lebanese town. The technique of *jarm al-kharūf*, which is a traditional method of butchering and deboning lamb or mutton, comes from Dhour Shweir, while *faṭā'ir bi-baqla* (herb samosas) are exclusively prepared with sumac in Beirut.[54] Moreover, most of the recipes in Choueiri's work are "quintessentially" Lebanese, distinguished from their equivalents in the Syrian hinterland or Palestinian south by the small omnipresent Lebanese flag.[55] Choueiri asserts the place of Lebanese cuisine amid its global counterparts with unprecedented confidence, mining each village for its *typicités* (typical items) in a mode akin to the same process of cataloging regional diversity in France.

Choueiri's cookbooks preserve a village lifestyle increasingly imperiled by the difficulties posed by social reproduction in the Lebanese countryside before, during, and after the civil war. Farmers could count on little protection from the government in terms of tariffs and extension services. Pollution of groundwater resources was a constant menace. Uncontrolled development of agricultural land, already substantially unplanned, accelerated during the civil war. Once again, as Lebanese village life faced unprecedented challenges, the rural sector was profoundly unsettled. Chef Ramzi Choueiri celebrated village foodways at the moment when the economic importance of Lebanese agriculture had reached its nadir.[56]

This analysis, it should be noted, does not seek to implicate Chef Ramzi or those who preceded him in chronicling Lebanon's foodways in the dispossession of Lebanon's rural population. They performed the service of detailing culinary customs for posterity. Sarkis's project was quite different from the project of those who followed him, predicated as it was on explicit class distinction in an urban milieu. Rayyis's massive cookbook celebrated the nation and shed all of the additional class-conscious advice that accompanied the recipes in Sarkis. Choueiri expanded his perspective to include and celebrate Lebanon's villages. Despite their differences, and the lack of explicit dialogue between the texts, they each perform a parallel function of salvaging a culinary tradition during

**Table 1.3. Kibbe Dishes in _Min Turath Lubnan_ (2002)**

| Name of the Kibbe Dish | Place of Origin | Preparation Method |
|---|---|---|
| _kubba arnabiyya_ | Baabda, Mount Lebanon | Meat-based, served in a tahini and citrus sauce |
| _kubba aqrāṣ_ | ʿAkkar, northern Lebanon | Meat-based kibbe balls, fried or grilled |
| _kubbat al-aruzz_ | Kesrewan, Mount Lebanon | Prepared with rice, meat-based |
| _kubbat al-baṭāṭā_ | Hermel, Bekaa | Potato dough, meat-based |
| _kubbat al-baṭāṭā_ | Bint Jbeil, southern Lebanon | Potato bulgur dough, with cumin |
| _kubbat al-baṭāṭā bi-l-jawz_ | Bsharri, northern Lebanon | Potato bulgur dough, stuffed with walnuts |
| _kubbat al-banadūra_ | West Bekaa | Tomato bulgur dough |
| _kubbat al-banadūra_ | Aleyh, Mount Lebanon | Tomato-based dough |
| _kubbat al-ḥazīna_ | Jbeil, Mount Lebanon | Bulgur and potato based |
| _kubbat al-ḥīla al-nīʾa_ | Al-Chouf, Mount Lebanon | Potato-based dough |
| _kubbat al-ḥīla bi-l-hummus_ [1] | Bint Jbeil, southern Lebanon | White flour–based with a chickpea stew |
| _kubbat al-ḥīla bi-l-hummus_ [2] | Bint Jbeil, southern Lebanon | Vegetarian with a chickpea stew |
| _kubbat al-ḥīla bi-l-laban_ | Bint Jbeil, southern Lebanon | Vegetarian with yogurt |
| _kubbat al-ḥīla maʿa al-baṣal_ | Batrun, Mount Lebanon | Vegetarian with an onion stew |
| _kubbat al-dajāj_ | ʿAkkar, northern Lebanon | Chicken-based dough |
| _kubbat al-dajāj_ | Kesrewen, Mount Lebanon | Chicken-based dough |
| _kubbat al-rāḥib_ | ʿAkkar | Vegetarian with beans |
| _kubbat al-rāḥib_ | Tripoli | Vegetarian with beans |
| _kubbat al-samak_ | Tyre | Fish-based dough |

| Dish | Location | Description |
| --- | --- | --- |
| *kubbat al-ʿadas* | Bint Jbeil, southern Lebanon | Lentil-based |
| *kubbat al-ʿadas maʿa al-filayfila al-ḥamra* | Bint Jbeil, southern Lebanon | Lentils and red pepper paste |
| *kubbat al-qāṭiʿa aw Kūrāniyya* | Koura, northern Lebanon | Bulgur and white flour–based |
| *kubbat al-qawurma bi-l-kishk* | Batroun, Mount Lebanon | *Qawurma* and *kishk* |
| *kubbat al-yaqṭīn* | Zahle, Bekaa | Pumpkin-based |
| *kubbat al-yaqṭīn* | ʿAkkar, northern Lebanon | Pumpkin-based |
| *kubbat al-yaqṭīn* | West Bekaa | Pumpkin-based |
| *kubba bi-l-ḥāmiḍ* | West Bekaa | Bulgur-potato-based with a lemon sauce |
| *kubbat rummān* | Tripoli | Meat-based, with pomegranate molasses |
| *kubba Zghartawiyya* | Zgharta, northern Lebanon | Meat-based oven pie |
| *kubbat shīsh barak* | Batroun, northern Lebanon | Meat-based with dumplings and yogurt sauce |
| *kubbat ʿadas kadhābiyya* | Bint Jbeil | Lentil-based vegetarian "lying" kibbe |
| *kubba qāṭiʿa mashshwa maslūqa bi-l-ʿadas* | Koura, northern Lebanon | Lentil-based |
| *kubba mūṭabbaqa* | Zgharta, northern Lebanon | Spread and baked in a pan |
| *kubba mukabkaba* | Zgharta, northern Lebanon | Meat-based, large balls |
| *kubba mamdūda maʿa al-ṣanawbar wa-l-baṣal* | Zgharta, northern Lebanon | Baked kibbe with pine nuts and onions |
| *kubba niʾa* | Zgharta, northern Lebanon | Raw kibbe |
| *kubayba ʿalā yakhnit al-bādhinjān* | Tyre | Kibbe balls in eggplant stew |

a moment of capitalist expansion: the first in the late nineteenth century, the second in the mid-twentieth century, and the third in the 1990s. The cuisine—Levantine and then Lebanese—was a product of that creative destruction: both a remnant of the old and the expression of a new kind of class formation.

## Conclusion

"I have often wondered if the reputation of Lebanese cuisine might not be slightly overrated. After much thinking on the subject, I must say that it is totally justified."[57] Syrian author Farouk Mardam-Bey, a key literary voice on Arab cuisine and scholar of its history, gives grudging praise while taking it for granted that Lebanese cuisine represents a coherent category of analysis. This history has shown that a cuisine understood to be distinctively "Lebanese" does not have roots that extend back farther than the mid-twentieth century. The different Lebanese cuisines share so much with Syrian food that the utility of distinguishing them for anything but nationalist purposes remains unclear. The energy surrounding the production of ostensibly distinct Lebanese, Palestinian, and Syrian food or that of individual cities obscures their commonality.

Kibbe is a case in point. It was a key part of the Levantine foodways before and after this modern move for codification. Sometimes kibbe is associated with national units and sometimes with subregions or cities. Although now consistently recognized as "Lebanese," kibbe is nonetheless equally associated with the city of Aleppo's particular food culture. Some food writers claim that Aleppo is not only the epicenter of kibbe culture but indeed of Arab cuisine. For Claudia Roden, "kibbeh are the hallmark of Syrian cooking—the standard by which once upon a time women were judged—even if it was the cook who made them."[58] The commonality between Aleppo and Sarkis's Beirut is the refinement of the local food tradition by the urban middle class. Women and servants undertook the complex labor of making kibbe in an urban house. Men wrote the cookbooks to construct this new authentically local modern identity. This study has focused on how the expropriation of the peasant majority was necessary for the production of a new urban bourgeois domesticity first codified in Beirut. This food culture did not represent an emulation of upper-class mores by a growing middle class but rather the reproduction of a regional craft in a new capitalist social context.

Social history also illuminates the circumstances in which cookbook authors constructed a purportedly authentic Lebanese national cuisine. The project to codify Lebanese food coincided with three rounds of capital expansion that unsettled life in the surrounding countryside and reshaped social relations in urban Beirut. The class dimension of this project became more implicit over time, while the local cuisine gained prominence versus global alternatives. Choueiri devotes more attention to the details of culinary diversity than any author who preceded him. The explicit class agenda in Sarkis's work grew fainter and finally disappeared by the end of the twentieth century. Choueiri's oeuvre contained an implicit message of class and sectarian unity. Despite these important differences in presentation, each of these cookbook authors sought to capture the essence of village foodways as they threatened to disappear amid the long decline of rural life that began in the late nineteenth century.

This chapter has so far left the origin of kibbe unexamined. Mardam-Bey believes that the adoption of bulgur dates from the early Ottoman era.[59] If that is the case, then kibbe must too. The technique of pounding grain in a mortar, however, is very old. Further study will have to trace the dish's history before the period considered in this study. The paucity of studies on the core aspects of one of the world's most prominent food cultures remains a puzzle. Why, despite all of the global energy devoted to the cuisine of Lebanon, has this story not been told? The purported distinction between Levantine and Lebanese is thin: perhaps the obvious threat to the nationalist understanding posed by historical inquiry has discouraged researchers.

A common perception maintains that the repertoire of dishes in Lebanon has become much more simplified. As it became enshrined in cookbooks, however, it expanded. This inverse correlation confirms that modern food culture, as manifested in Arabic-language cookbooks, aimed at preserving a purportedly traditional way of life. As a sense of loss intensified, so did the effort to chronicle the diversity of village cuisine in increasing detail. New sources will have to show precisely how this trend reflected changing patterns of consumption. This study concludes that the construction of this ideal cuisine masked the class dynamics that shaped it.

## Acknowledgments

The labor that produced this chapter is far from ours alone. Sarah Mink edited an early draft. She and Maria Joana Gomes supported us throughout the process. Idun Hauge generously shared her research from the American University of Beirut. Pascale Graham sent us the 1931 edition of Sarkis's cookbook, without which we would have been unable to pursue this line of research. When we were separated from our source material during the COVID-19 pandemic, two people saved the project. Therese Elkhoury Kabalan in Zahle photographed cookbooks in her personal collection. Maia Tabet kindly sent us a rare copy of *Kitab Fann al-Tabkh*. Robert and Laura Pitts helped cook some of the historical kibbe recipes. The Agrarian Question workshop gave trenchant comments on a late version of this chapter. We thank Kellan Anfison, Gabi Kirk, Paul Kohlbry, and China Sajadian for their insights. Paul ended up editing the manuscript more than once. China was especially generous with her insight into questions of labor in rural Lebanon. Sam Dolbee also provided a valuable critique of an earlier incarnation of the manuscript. Antonio Tahhan and Reem Bailony were kind to read the piece and consult their kin in Aleppo and the Aleppan diaspora about the particularities of the city's kibbe. Sylvie Durmelat wrote us detailed feedback that was invaluable in clarifying our core argument. Finally, Anny Gaul's astute commentary and Vicki Valosik's keen editorial eye made this chapter much more rigorous. Any errors are our responsibility alone.

## Notes

1. William McClure Thomson, *The Land and the Book* (London: T. Nelson, 1861), 94–95.

2. Rachel Laudan, *Cuisine and Empire: Cooking in World History* (Berkeley: University of California Press, 2015).

3. Monks served a British traveler kibbe as a second course on a visit to Saydanaya and Malula in 1829. Those towns are on the eastern slope of the Anti-Lebanon Mountains in what is now Syria. John Fuller, *Narrative of a Tour through Some Parts of the Turkish Empire* (London: Richard Taylor, 1829). Lady Hester Stanhope found that kibbe was a common dish as far east as Palmyra among the settled inhabitants. "They made kubby by pounding together husked wheat and minced mutton, or goats' flesh, in a mortar: this they mould into hollow spheres, and boil or fry." Charles Lewis Meryon, *Travels of Lady Hester Stanhope: Forming the Completion of Her Memoirs*, vol. 2 (London: Henry Colburn, 1846), 145. Kibbe does not appear in an otherwise comprehensive mid–nineteenth-century cookbook published in Istanbul: Mehmet Kamil Bey, *Melceü't Tabbahin* (Istanbul: n.p., 1844).

4. A recent study has defined Beirut's rise to its status as the cultural and economic "gravitational point" in the patchwork of the urban Levant: Cyrus Schayegh, *The Middle East and the Making of the Modern World* (Cambridge, MA: Harvard University Press, 2017), 54–65. Schayegh asserts Beirut's particular importance as the region's key interface with the rest of the world and the importance of its merchants, but he does not characterize social relations in the city as predominantly capitalist. The most prominent monograph on the role of local capital and class formation in Beirut's late Ottoman history is Jens Hanssen, *Fin de Siècle Beirut: The Making of an Ottoman Provincial Capital* (Oxford: Oxford University Press, 2005). Toufoul Abou-Hodeib has shown how the middle-class "attempt to forge a cultural hegemony through domesticity" was a sa-

lient aspect of Beiruti social relations under capitalism in *A Taste for Home: The Modern Middle Class in Ottoman Beirut* (Stanford: Stanford University Press, 2017), 47. A recent study argues that Levantine capitalism, centered in Beirut, deserves to be seen as a full-fledged historical formation in its own right: Kristen Alff, "Levantine Joint-Stock Companies, Trans-Mediterranean Partnerships, and Nineteenth-Century Capitalist Development," *Comparative Studies in Society and History* 60, no. 1 (2018): 150–177.

5. The production of this modern "kitchen" coincided with the formation of national identities in Egypt and later Morocco. Ann Marie (Anny) Gaul, "Kitchen Histories in Modern North Africa" (PhD diss., Georgetown University, 2019). See also Anny Gaul, "Food, Happiness, and the Egyptian Kitchen (1900–1952)," in *Insatiable Appetite: Food as a Cultural Signifier in the Middle East and Beyond*, ed. Kirill Dmitriev, Julia Hauser, and Bilal Orfali (Leiden: Brill, 2019), 121–141. In the 1930s and 1940s in Palestine, as well, the production of the "national economy" was predicated on a modern bourgeois domesticity. Sherene Seikaly, *Men of Capital: Scarcity and Economy in Mandate Palestine* (Stanford: Stanford University Press, 2015), 40–41. Beirut's experience predated these cases, and the class element eclipsed the national project.

6. Khalil Sarkis, *Tadhkirat al-Khawatin wa-Ustadh al-Tabbakhin* (Beirut: al-Matba'a al-Adabiyya, 1885). The title was later modified: Khalil Sarkis, *Kitab Ustadh al-Tabbakhin* (Beirut: al-Matba'a al-Adabiyya, 1931). In this chapter we refer to the 1885 edition as *Tadhkirat al-Khawatin* and the 1931 edition as *Ustadh al-Tabbakhin*. Another Beiruti cookbook preceded Sarkis, which unfortunately we could neither locate nor consult: Shahin Hanna 'Eid, *Kitab al-Tabkh* (Beirut: al-Matba'a al-Adabiya, 1878).

7. An early twentieth-century almanac on Mount Lebanon included a substantial number of recipes from Sarkis: Ibrahim al-Aswad, *Dalil Lubnan* (Ba'abda, Lebanon: al-Matba'a al-'Uthmaniya, 1906), 422–472. Maxime Rodinson offered these details on *Dalil al-Tabbakhin wa-l-Tabbakh al-Manzili al-Hadith* (Kafr Shima, Lebanon: al-Matba'a al-Rashidiyya, n.d.). Published anonymously and without a date, the previous edition had been "decorated with a cover adorned with an illustration borrowed from some old European cookbook"; in a new printing in 1947 it was replaced with a "more modern presentation." Maxime Rodinson, "Recherches sur les documents arabes relatifs à la cuisine," *Revue des études islamiques* 17 (1949): 108.

8. We have consulted the final Arabic-language edition: George al-Rayyis, *Kitab Fann al-Tabkh* (1951), 3rd ed. (Beirut: Maktabat Antwan, 1969).

9. Ramzi Choueiri, *al-Shif Ramzi: Min Turath Lubnan* (Beirut: Akadimiyya, 2002).

10. For example, Sarkis uses a colloquialism to refer to a preparation *munazzala* (colloquial: *mnazzaleh*), in which an eggplant is cooked separately from the rest of the stew's ingredients. He assumes that his reader knows the word already. Sarkis, *Ustadh al-Tabbakhin*, 67. Folklorist Anis Frayha felt obligated to define the technique in the 1950s in *al-Qariya al-Lubnaniyya: Hadara fi Tariq al-Zawal* (1957) (Beirut: Dar al-Nahar, 1980), 103. In the same period, Rayyis gave detailed attention to basic techniques and provided detailed instructions in recipes designed for use in commercial kitchens. Rayyis, *Fann al-Tabkh*, 24–31. Similarly, Choueiri has opened his books with even more basic information in recent decades. He defined the roles and ranks in a commercial kitchen and explained techniques as basic as boiling. Ramzi Choueiri, *al-Shif Ramzi fi 'Alam al-Sabah: Mawsu'a Shamila fi al-Tabkh wa-l-Halwiyat* (Beirut: Akadimiyya, 1998).

11. This proverb appeared in a chapter authored by a notable from Zahle, 'Isa

Iskandar al-Maʿluf, in a collection of essays produced about Ottoman Mount Lebanon during World War I: "al-Akhlaq wa-l-ʿAdat al-Lubnaniyya," in Haqqi Bey, *Lubnan*, vol. 1 (Beirut: al-Matbaʿa al-Adabiyya, 1334 [1918]), 170. All translations by authors unless otherwise noted.

12. Akram Khater, *Inventing Home: Emigration, Gender, and the Middle Class in Lebanon, 1870–1920* (Berkeley: University of California Press, 2001).

13. Hanssen, *Fin de Siècle Beirut*, 35–36.

14. For Sarkis's career as a publisher, see Ami Ayalon, "Private Publishing in the Nahda," *International Journal of Middle East Studies* 40, no. 4 (2008): 561–577.

15. Abou-Hodeib, *A Taste for Home*, 39–40.

16. Abou-Hodeib, *A Taste for Home*, 32–33.

17. Sarkis, *Tadhkirat al-Khawatin*, 404.

18. Sarkis, *Ustadh al-Tabbakhin*, 23.

19. Sarkis, *Ustadh al-Tabbakhin*, 108–110.

20. Sarkis, *Tadhkirat al-Khawatin*, n.p. (introduction).

21. Sarkis, *Tadhkirat al-Khawatin*, 416.

22. Sarkis, *Tadhkirat al-Khawatin*, 39.

23. Christian Saßmannshausen, "Eating Up: Food Consumption and Social Status in Late Ottoman Greater Syria," in *Insatiable Appetite: Food as a Cultural Signifier in the Middle East and Beyond* (Leiden: Brill, 2019), 33.

24. [Maʿluf], "al-Akhlaq wa-l-ʿAdat al-Lubnaniyya," 157.

25. This process matches a global trend visible elsewhere in the Arab world. Gaul, "Kitchen Histories in Modern North Africa," 22.

26. Sarkis, *Tadhkirat al-Khawatin*, n.p. (introduction).

27. Sarkis, *Tadhkirat al-Khawatin*, 37–38.

28. Sarkis, *Ustadh al-Tabbakhin*, 45.

29. Frayha, *al-Qariya al-Lubnaniyya*, 73–74. On the preparation of bulgur, see Aïda Kanafani-Zahar, "Le burghul, un emblème de la table villageoise libanaise," in *Couscous, boulgour et polenta: Transformer et consommer les céréales dans le monde*, ed. Monique Chastanet and François Sigaut (Paris: Karthala, 2010), 93–103.

30. Sarkis, *Tadhkirat al-Khawatin*, 414; Sarkis, *Ustadh al-Tabbakhin*, 65.

31. Europeans took inspiration from the vegetarian practices of Arab Christians, even if they misunderstood them. Julia Hauser, "A Frugal Crescent: Perceptions of Foodways in the Ottoman Empire and Egypt in Nineteenth-Century Vegetarian Discourse," in *Insatiable Appetite*, 292–318.

32. Sarkis, *Ustadh al-Tabbakhin*, 67. The 1885 version offers a different transliteration ("salsa") in an otherwise nearly identical recipe. Sarkis, *Tadhkirat al-Khawatin*, 415. This fact about tomatoes comes from Kamil al-Ghazzi, *Nahr al-Dhahab fi Tarikh Halab*, vol. 3, cited in Charles Issawi, *The Fertile Crescent, 1800–1914: A Documentary Economic History* (Oxford: Oxford University Press, 1988), 87. We thank Daniel Neep for this citation.

33. Sarkis, *Ustadh al-Tabbakhin*, 65–66.

34. Octopus kibbe was one (although it appears to have survived in the diaspora). Another was called *al-tabkha al-fākhtiyya* in the 1885 edition of *Ustadh al-Tabbakhin*: cauliflower kibbe made with yogurt and tahini sauce. A mid–twentieth century cookbook suggests that this is a version of kibbe *arnabiyya*, which retained the name *al-fākhtiyya* in Damascus. The sauce contains pomegranate juice, lemon, and tahini.

Muhammad bin al-Hasan and Fakhri al-Barudi, *Kitab al-Tabikh wa Ma'akil al-Dimashqiyya* (1964) (Windsor, UK: Hindawi, 2018), 81.

35. [Ma'luf], "al-Akhlaq wa-l-'Adat al-Lubnaniyya," 170.

36. Absent from Ma'luf's description, hummus does appear in Sarkis, although as an evident afterthought. Sarkis, *Tadhkirat al-Khawatin*, 471; Sarkis, *Ustadh al-Tabbakhin*, 133.

37. Sarkis, *Tadhkirat al-Khawatin*, 19; Sarkis, *Ustadh al-Tabbakhin*, 133.

38. Frayha, *al-Qariya al-Lubnaniyya*, n.p. (introduction).

39. While not acknowledging any systemic class tension, the book does contain reference to differentiation along class lines. The "rich" or "middling" peasant is the class depicted. Frayha, *al-Qariya al-Lubnaniyya*, 37, 91.

40. Christopher Stone, *Popular Culture and Nationalism in Lebanon: The Fairouz and Rahbani Nation* (London: Routledge, 2007), 27, 74.

41. Frayha, *al-Qariya al-Lubnaniyya*, 100–102.

42. United States Information Service, *Visitor's Guide to Lebanon* (Beirut: American Press, 1948), 14; Margaret Clark Keatinge, *Beirut: Guidebook* (Beirut: Catholic Press, 1953), 16–17. I thank Idun Hauge for sharing her notes on these materials, accessed in Jafet Library at the American University of Beirut.

43. Keatinge, *Beirut*, 35.

44. Keatinge, *Beirut*, 46.

45. Meryon, *Travels of Lady Hester Stanhope*, 348. For the early twentieth century, see [Ma'luf], "al-Akhlaq wa-l-'Adat al-Lubnaniyya," 170.

46. Rayyis, *Fann al-Tabkh*, 28.

47. In this regard, it is notable that tabbouleh and hummus did not appear in English-language published texts until 1955, while travel guides referenced kibbe as early as 1816. See "Kibbeh," "Tabbouleh," and "Hummus," in the *OED Online* (March 2021), Oxford University Press.

48. Although conventionally understood as a sectarian conflict, the Lebanese Civil War began in large part because of instability that stemmed from the unsettling of the countryside. Salim Nasr, "Backdrop to Civil War: The Crisis of Lebanese Capitalism," *Merip Reports* 73 (1978): 3–13. For a broader consideration of Lebanon's agrarian question, see Ahmad Ba'albaki, *al-Zira'a al-Lubnaniyya wa Tadakhulat al-Dawla fi al-Ariyaf min al-Istiqlal ila al-Harb al-Ahliya* (Beirut: Manshurat Bahar al-Mutawassit, 1985).

49. These details appear in a book of family history penned by Ramzi's brother: Raif Shwayri, *Beirut on the Bayou: Alfred Nicola, Louisiana, and the Making of Modern Lebanon* (Albany: SUNY Press, 2015).

50. Choueiri, *Fi 'Alam al-Sabah*. On neoliberalism in Lebanon, see Hannes Baumann, *Citizen Hariri: Lebanon's Neoliberal Reconstruction* (Oxford: Oxford University Press, 2016).

51. Choueiri, *Min Turath Lubnan*, 640.

52. Ray Jureidini, "In the Shadows of Family Life: Toward a History of Domestic Service in Lebanon," *Journal of Middle East Women's Studies* 5, no. 3 (2009): 74–101.

53. Zaynab Hawi, "al-Shif Ramzi . . . Kan Ya Ma Kan!," *al-Akhbar* (Beirut), 31 August 2017.

54. Choueiri, *Min Turath Lubnan*.

55. Choueiri, *Fi 'Alam al-Sabah*.

56. For an overview of environmental challenges facing Lebanon, see Eric Verdeil,

Ghaleb Faour, and Mouin Hamzé, eds., *Atlas du Liban: Les nouveaux défis* (Beirut: Presses de l'Ifpo/CNRS Liban, 2016).

57. Farouk Mardam-Bey, *Ziryab: Authentic Arab Cuisine* (Woodbury, CT: Ici La Press, 2002), 188.

58. Claudia Roden, *The Book of Jewish Food: An Odyssey from Samarkand to New York* (New York: Knopf, 1996), 354.

59. Mardam-Bey, *Ziryab*, 123–124.

CHAPTER 2

# Adana Kebabs and Antep Pistachios: Place, Displacement, and Cuisine of the Turkish South

SAMUEL DOLBEE AND CHRIS GRATIEN

In the summer of 2018 the Turkish food writer and television host Vedat Milor reviewed a Syrian restaurant in Istanbul, named Saruja in honor of the neighborhood in Damascus (the hometown of its owner, Bilal Khalaf).[1] Saruja impressed Milor, but notions of difference still underpinned much of his positive review. He warned his predominantly Turkish audience that much of the food was different from "our version."[2] The kebabs were good, but "the spices" made them distinct from Adana kebabs, a more familiar variety named for the southern Turkish city close to the border with Syria. For dessert, the restaurant served *şamfıstıklı* baklava, with pistachios named for Şam (Arabic al-Shām), which refers to Damascus in both Turkish and Arabic but also can mean greater Syria. Many welcomed Milor's review, but it also incited an internet backlash among those who objected to giving a Syrian restaurant so much attention. Some Twitter users complained that Turkey would soon become an Arab country. Others suggested that Syrians should go home. What is striking about both Milor's review and the xenophobic response from a historical perspective is that the ingredients and dishes of Turkey's south that Milor categorized as distinctly "ours" were themselves newly a product of a Turkish national culture.

In fact, food of the flavor termed "ours" by Milor had for many years been perceived as exotic or alien, in no small part because of its connections to southern Turkey and northern Syria (see map in frontmatter).[3] The kebabs of Adana that Milor mentioned in his review had long been viewed like the migrants from the Turkish south who brought them to Turkey's cities from the mid-twentieth century onward: low-class and of potentially alien origin. Moreover, Milor's reference to Şam pistachios to describe the distinctive Syrian baklava concealed the protracted struggle over the nut's identity. The Şam pistachio had long been associated with Syria but rebranded as the "Antep pistachio" in Turkey thanks to considerable effort on the part of state officials over the course of the twentieth century. Yet during that period the nuts became an intimate part of daily life all across Turkey as migrants from the south asserted their presence beyond their home regions. Whether in the form of late-night kebabs, pistachio-flavored ice cream bars, or new restaurants that elevated these flavors to the forefront of the national cuisine, the food of southern Turkey has entered the mainstream and even become a culinary export.

Food exposes connections between Syria and Turkey that are typically obscured by nationalism. Turkey and its neighboring countries of the Arabic-speaking Levant are not always imagined as part of a shared space today, though these regions were part of the same polity before the fall of the Ottoman Empire. In Turkey, the Arab countries of the south are sometimes imagined as "the others," who betrayed the Ottoman cause.[4] Across the border to the south, Turkey is sometimes presented as little more than the successor of a former foreign occupier, remembered primarily for its role in the famine years of World War I.[5] Neither view is entirely accurate. But the division between Turkey and the places connected to it has nevertheless been reinforced by academic scholarship that approaches the Arab world and Turkey as separate objects of study, an approach that risks giving the arbitrary post-Ottoman borders more power than they deserve.[6] With these legacies, as well as ongoing controversy connected to the status of the millions of Syrian refugees in Turkey, it can be difficult to see the long-standing continuities between these places.

Food offers one path forward. A look at the history of two items that Milor mentioned in his review—pistachios and kebabs—reveals these dynamics quite profoundly. Nuts and grilled meat serve different purposes in terms of culinary culture. Pistachios act as ingredients in both sweet and savory dishes or as snacks on their own. Kebabs represent a prepared dish. Also different are the ways in which the foods spread from the border with Syria across Turkey. Pistachios represent a food commodity built on the expropriation of Armenian property in the wake of the Armenian genocide and the end of the Ottoman Empire. They were subsequently rebranded as a Turkish national product through heavy state involvement. Kebabs, in contrast, journeyed to Turkey's cities with migrants from the Turkish south. One variety became known as Adana kebab, not through heavy state involvement—as in the case of Antep pistachios—but rather through humble grill-masters who, much like many of their patrons, established new lives far from home.

Together, Antep pistachios and Adana kebabs highlight two dynamics. First, they are both expressions of a Turkish national culture born of dispossession and migrant labor. The foods from the Turkish south took time and work to spread to the cosmopolitan confines of Istanbul. But now, thanks to migration, as well as the emergence of a national taste, they can be found all over the country. Moreover, Antep pistachios and Adana kebabs reveal a considerable overlap with the cuisine of northern Syria, where nuts grown in much the same soil are called Aleppo pistachios and meats spiced in similar ways also take different names. The product of these two dynamics—the expansion of these foods across Turkey and their connections to the cuisines of Syria—perhaps has a provocative implication. Istanbul might not typically be thought of as part of the Levant—a term usually applied to the Arabic-speaking Eastern Mediterranean. But migration from the south has made the city and much of the country part of that space, at least in culinary terms.

To explain these transformations, we chart how the distinctive flavors of Turkey's Eastern Mediterranean, defined by legendary street foods, large helpings of meat, and a bold embrace of red pepper (most readily symbolized by Adana kebab) came to be seen as part and parcel of Turkey's mainstream cuisine, as opposed to alien and low-class. We argue that this process began with the commercialization of the countryside in the late Ottoman Levant, giving rise to a new class of migrant workers in growing cities like Adana and Mersin, and ended with a second wave of migration from this region to cities like Istanbul and Ankara during the 1960s and 1970s that profoundly shaped mainstream Turkish cuisine. We also explore the attempt to rebrand the pistachio—a longtime product of the Antep region that nevertheless remained associated with Syria—as a Turkish national product during roughly the same period. In doing so, we study how the food culture of the Republic of Turkey incorporated and rendered domestic a region of the Eastern Mediterranean that we refer to here as the "Turkish south," the swath of territory extending from Adana to Antep and farther east along the Syrian border, inhabited today by large populations of Syrian refugees but also the longtime home of Kurdish- and Arabic-speaking citizens of the Republic of Turkey. In closing, we examine how these culinary influences have spread around the world.

## Foodways of Southeastern Anatolia during the Late Ottoman Period

From high cuisine to back-alley barbeque, the kebab is ubiquitous in modern-day Turkey, although it cannot be claimed to be an exclusively Turkish national dish. Various parts of the "Balkans to Bengal" region share terminologies, methods, and ingredients with regard to meat-based recipes. The term "kebab," used in many variants throughout the former Ottoman, Safavid, and Mughal Empires, is old and has been applied to a wide variety of dishes. The famous seventeenth-century Ottoman traveler and sometime fabulist Evliya

Çelebi mentioned encounters with kebabs of dazzling variety from the Balkans and Crimea to Egypt and Anatolia during the seventeenth century.[7] In addition to kebab cooked on a skewer (*şiş*), he also mentioned grilling and tandoor ovens being used in the preparation of dishes containing every sort of animal flesh: lamb, of course, but also beef, various fowl, fish, pork, and even crocodile in the case of Egypt. Kebab was common in the Ottoman capital of Istanbul, primarily as a form of street food. Evliya mentions roughly 1,500 people who roamed the city cooking and selling kebab and other ground meats like *köfte* (meatballs) from decorated *tahtırevan*s: roughly 400 small structures used as the mobile base for shops that could be carried from place to place by hand, akin to modern food trucks.

Thus, traditions of grilled meat consumption had been in place across the Ottoman Empire for centuries. But these traditions would come to change considerably thanks to economic transformations of the nineteenth century that began to shape the cuisine of what would become the Turkish south. One center of economic growth was a region known today as Çukurova, centered on the cities of Adana and Mersin. Before the mid-nineteenth century, the main products of the region came from sheep and goats tended by villagers and seminomadic pastoralists. The region's economy and population expanded in the late nineteenth century with the spread of commercial agriculture. This growth earned it the nickname "the Second Egypt."[8] Çukurova's main export was cotton. Tens of thousands of seasonal laborers came to the region each year for planting and harvesting. These workers were a diverse group, including Nusayri Arabs from northern Syria as well as Kurdish, Turkish, Armenian, and Assyrian migrants from as far east as the Iranian side of the Ottoman-Qajar borderlands.[9] These transformations also shifted the region's geographic gravity toward Çukurova. During Ottoman provincial reorganization, Adana had briefly been part of the province of Aleppo, a much more important political and economic center. But Adana had attained a great deal of economic power in its own right by the early twentieth century. For this reason, in 1913 merchants from Aleppo's main port city of Iskenderun petitioned to be attached to Adana province.[10]

The mobile labor force and the region's rich tradition of animal husbandry created a culinary laboratory of sorts. The journalist and politician Abdülkadir Kemali (the father of the novelist Orhan Kemal) recalled the region's street food fondly. While still a primary-school student, Abdülkadir was waiting alone in his father's office, where he found a handkerchief full of money in the pocket of a jacket. He took the money and headed straight for the market. "In the center of Ceyhan's market, itinerant cooks would make *mumbar* (stuffed sheep intestines with rice and meat), *işkembe dolması* (stuffed tripe), and liver to sell to the workers who came from the various regions of the East," he recalled. "Every time I would pass by, I wanted to have some of what those workers were eating, but I could never find the chance. . . . Those were the days when you could get five or six skewers of liver kebab with a piece of bread for a penny. The ones in those days were enough to fill a large man, let alone a child like me." He went to the little shop of a kebab chef known as Ali Banda and ordered liver kebab and bread. Moments later, "the kebab was ready, he set it in front of me, and I began to eat with gusto. I ordered *mumbar* and *işkembe dolması* on top of that." Young Abdülkadir blissfully double-fisted kebab and dolma until he was located and reprimanded by a colleague of his father.[11]

Among the workers of Çukurova, regional specialties coalesced into a rich corpus of street food: skewers of liver cubes, *mumbar*, *şırdan* (sheep stomach stuffed with rice and meat), and Mersin's iconic *tantuni* (a sandwich of strips of beef or lamb boiled and stir-fried in cottonseed oil: perhaps the clearest example of how cotton both created the need for cheap workers' fare and shaped food preparation techniques). And of course alongside all of these dishes was Adana's *kıyma kebabı* (grilled ground mutton spiced with lots of red pepper), which would later come to be called Adana kebab. While grilled meat was not exclusive to the Adana region, the cuisine's cavalier use of red pepper was distinctive and continues to characterize the borderlands of Turkey and Syria today, as historian Sami Zubaida notes.[12] This regional proclivity for a spicy flavor profile is also expressed in the use of pickled hot peppers as garnish on kebab and *tantuni* as well as a key ingredient of *şalgam suyu*, a fermented beverage made from red carrots and bulgur wheat once produced only in the Adana region. Though it comes in different forms, the spicy *acılı* variety is considered an essential companion to Adana kebab.

To the east of the emerging economic region of Çukurova was Aleppo and its hinterland, where the provincial city of Antep was also growing in the late Ottoman period. If the ascendant commercial class of Adana made fortunes from cotton, pistachios were one of the principal sources of wealth for Antep families who owned land in the agriculturally productive countryside as far as Kilis and Nizip. There were even stories that an Armenian named Jurjy Chamichian—known as "king of the pistachios"—had brought saplings with him when his family moved to Antep from Persia.[13] The provenance of this story is unclear, but many notable Armenian families in Antep owned large tracts of pistachio trees.[14] Because the trees took decades to bear fruit, pistachios did not offer a fast track to riches the way cotton did in Adana. Significantly, however, the trees required little precipitation and could produce tons of nuts on a biannual basis, even in agriculturally marginal environments.

Pistachio growers from Antep expanded their area of cultivation into the arid countryside by grafting new pistachio trees onto the preexisting roots of *menengiç* or "wild pistachios" that clung to the dry soil.[15] The province of Aleppo—of which Antep was a part—produced a whopping 960,000 *kiyye* (a little more than a kilogram) of pistachios by 1914, which amounted to about 95 percent of total Ottoman pistachio production.[16] All of these pistachios came from the Rumkale district, located east of Antep on the banks of the Euphrates, home of the vaunted pistachio fields of Nizip.[17] Though pistachios defined late Ottoman Antep's countryside, the nuts were by no means new in the region; as far back as the seventeenth century, Evliya Çelebi wrote that Antep was distinctive in exporting the nuts by the camel load to the rest of the Arab world, Iran, and even India.[18] Wherever these pistachios went, they served as sophisticated embellishments of dishes both sweet and savory, whether as a crucial ingredient for baklava or a subtle addition to kebab and *köfte* dishes.[19]

Although Antep was the pistachio heartland of the Ottoman Empire, Damascus got most of the credit, as the nuts were commonly referred to in Turkish as Şam *fıstığı*: Damascus or Syrian pistachio. That was how they were listed in a register of gifts from Damascus to the Ottoman palace in 1765, when a number of top officials received foodstuffs like Şam apricots and Hama herbs, but only the sultan received "shelled Şam pistachios."[20] The name stuck through much of the nineteenth century, appearing among the flavors of ice cream listed in Ayşe Fahriye's cookbook *Ev Kadını* (1883) and in one of the first English-language cookbooks of Ottoman cuisine: Ardeshes Hagop Keoleian's *The Oriental Cookbook* (1913). Pistachios, Keoleian reassured any potentially nervous readers, were "easily digested."[21] Yet by the time many of these works were written, most pistachios decidedly did not come from Damascus. Indeed, when Ottoman officials sought to promote pistachio cultivation in regions like the Aegean coast, they contacted not Damascus but rather Aleppo for saplings.[22]

To be sure, the expansive nature of Şam—referring to both Damascus and greater Syria more generally—could often include Aleppo and in some cases even extend to places like Antep.[23] Nonetheless, it is noteworthy that many people at the time were confused that the commodity associated with Şam largely did not grow in Şam's most prominent city but rather in Aleppo and to its north in Antep and Rumkale.[24] Moreover, the preferred term in Arabic, "Aleppo pistachio" (*fustuq Ḥalabi*), contained no reference to Şam or Damascus.[25] As an explanation, a number of people have claimed that Antep's pistachios were exported via or marketed in Damascus and thus took on the better-known city's name.[26] Short-story writer and Antep native Lütfiye Aydın (whose own father was a pistachio farmer) has suggested a different explanation: Antep's products may well have taken on the name of Damascus "because in the Ottoman period Antep was connected to the province of Aleppo," which fell within the confines of greater Syria.[27] In any case, the name "Şam pistachios" emerged from historical economic linkages of Damascus, greater Syria, and Antep. Over the coming years, the transformation of the Şam pistachio to the Antep pistachio would serve as a potent symbol for how post-Ottoman national boundaries would not only separate Turkey from Syria but also delimit the region's pistachios.

## Food in the Making of the Turkish South

In the wake of World War I, the political world of the Ottoman Empire became dismantled. Damascus and Aleppo would form part of a Syrian state administered by the French as part of the League of Nations mandate system. Meanwhile, the region to the north—Antep and Adana included—was occupied in 1918 by French troops, who sought to establish a mandate in this region as well. Invoking the Roman and Armenian term for the region, they called it Cilicia. The logic of the occupation was threefold: (1) the region's cotton would feed French factories; (2) Armenian survivors of the genocide could be repatriated there; and (3) the region itself was an integral part of Syria.[28] However, armed resistance to the French occupation emerged within a year. When the French left at the end of 1921 and the dream of a mandate of Cilicia died, they evacuated the Armenians of the region, many of whom went to Syria and Lebanon.[29] To mark the break with the past and commemorate resistance to the French, the Republic of Turkey—established in 1923—renamed some of the region's cities and towns. Antep became Gaziantep (Antep the Victorious), to commemorate its contribution to the national resistance.

The food of the workers in Adana in the late Ottoman Empire endured as the city emerged as one of the economic powerhouses of Turkey. As the successor state to the Ottoman Empire, Turkey had lost millions of people from its imperial predecessor through territorial losses, ethnic cleansing, and migration—far more than the number of refugees and "exchanged people" who arrived from the Balkans. Non-Muslims had played a large role in Adana's economy as merchants, landowners, and laborers, as in many commercial centers of Ottoman Anatolia. Çukurova's cotton became all the more important in this context, functioning as an engine of Turkish national development. Muslim cultivators and merchants who had established themselves during the late Ottoman period were poised to profit, and new figures like Hacı Ömer Sabancı, who would create one of Turkey's wealthiest business dynasties, moved to the region to capitalize on its economic opportunities.[30] Laborers—whose work made people like Sabancı rich—were not always as warmly welcomed in the new republic as was Çukurova's agricultural output. Many were Arabic or Kurdish speakers, languages that were to be left behind, according to the mantra "citizen, speak Turkish."[31] Workers in Çukurova—particularly the Arabic-speaking Nusayris—came to be referred to pejoratively with the label of *fellah*, deriving from the Arabic word for peasant.[32] Such racial coding took on added importance when Turkey annexed a portion of northern Syria in the late 1930s.[33] Nationalist thinkers and activists insisted that members of the region's largely Arabic-speaking population were genetic descendants of the ancient Hittites of Anatolia and thus Hittite Turks.[34]

Groups such as the Nusayris and others could be imagined as Turks, but it was more difficult to reimagine the region's food as distinctly Turkish. Even as Adana's kebabs gained fame locally, the majority of the city's most talented kebab makers hailed from Turkish cities farther east, including Adıyaman, Diyarbekir, and Mardin.[35] Moreover, most of them were Arab. Their origin was commonly known, as revealed in a piece by the Turkish intellectual Burhan Belge, himself born in Damascus to an Ottoman bureaucratic family (and briefly married to Zsa Zsa Gabor). Belge noted that the types of kebabs referred to as "Aleppo-style" (*Halep işi*) in Ankara or Istanbul were widespread across the southern cities of Turkey.[36] Notions of cultural difference mapped onto these descriptions. Belge called Turkey's relationship to this region "the disease of the south," akin to regional distinctions around the world that overlapped with economic inequality, such as northern Europe versus southern Europe or Russia's relationship with Crimea and the Caucasus.[37] Thus Adana's kebab culture derived its distinctiveness from the region's multiethnic mix. But for the same reason kebabs became an object of exoticized derision, evocative of difference in a nation-state intent on consolidating a homogeneous national identity.

Pistachios also became embroiled in these processes of differentiation. This occurred on a discursive level, as many wondered what the proper name for the nut should be. For example, the New York import group Zaloom Brothers wrote to the American consul in Aleppo in 1925 with a question on this topic.[38] The group imported pistachios through connections in Aleppo and marketed them as "Syria pistachios." Its logo featured an anthropomorphized pistachio walking jauntily, clad in a fez with a crescent and star and brandishing a sword. But Zaloom Brothers noticed that a competitor in the United States was also selling pistachios under the name "Cilician nuts." The label referred to the Cilicia region associated with the French (including Antep) but also, the Zalooms charged, served to take advantage of American consumers who might confuse "Cilician" with "Sicilian," a more familiar association.

To settle the question of whether the pistachio was Syrian or Cilician, the Zalooms asked the American consul whether Antep—the source of the pistachios no matter how they were described—was "a part of Syria." The consul replied categorically that Antep was no longer part of Syria.[39] Though it is unclear what message Zaloom Brothers took from the information, the exchange attests to the blurry boundaries of the post-Ottoman world and the way food products of the emerging borderlands of Syria and Turkey threw this dynamic into relief. Meanwhile, Turkish officials took a more active role in making it clear that Antep was outside of Syria. As they initiated a novel program of language reform, which entailed a purge of many words with Arabic and Persian roots, the implementation of the Latin alphabet in 1928, and changing place-names of Armenian, Greek, or Kurdish origin, one writer even declared that "Şam pistachio" ought to be considered among the many insufficiently Turkish words that were to be rejected and replaced in the post-Ottoman era.[40]

The transformation also occurred on a material level. Turkey's Agriculture Ministry became involved in research to catalyze pistachio production by the 1930s, if not earlier.[41] New trees were planted, though others had been around for many years. This was clear in 1949, when a "white-bearded seventy-three-year-old" told a newspaper reporter outside of Antep that "pistachio trees do not die. Who knows when the trees that you see here are left over from?"[42] His words seemed to allude to the fact that Antep's pistachio trees had survived World War I, while many of Antep's Armenians—including those connected with the pistachio industry—had not.[43] As in Adana, the Turkish state endeavored to rejuvenate this region and its economy in national terms, including ambitious schemes aimed at marketing Antep pistachios toward export markets rather than domestic consumption. As one person connected to the business explained to a reporter, "We export the good product. The bad ones go to Istanbul."[44] Some nuts still remained in Antep, of course, where they played a role in many dishes, particularly on special occasions. At one point during a typically pistachio-swollen banquet in Antep in the 1940s, Turkish prime minister İsmet İnönü is said to have asked for a glass of water, jokingly adding, "Please make it without pistachios!"[45]

In the coming decades, the key ingredient of so many of Antep's delicacies would find its way across the borders of the post-Ottoman world in dizzying ways. With pistachios hailed by Turkey's leading novelists and state officials alike as Antep's national treasure, other provinces began efforts to cultivate the tree.[46] Meanwhile, smugglers began taking the commodity south to Syria.[47] The phenomenon was so widespread that it not only appeared in Aleppo writer Khalid Khalifa's prize-winning novel *No Knives in the Kitchens of*

*This City* but also became an object of discussion in the Turkish parliament.[48] During a 1962 speech, Kadri Eroğan of Urfa—the Turkish province directly east of Antep—spoke of how smuggling ravaged the borderlands of Syria and Turkey to the tune of some 1.5 billion liras annually. No small part of this traffic consisted of pistachios, which Eroğan referred to by their erstwhile name "Şam pistachios." When he corrected his miscue, he called them not "Antep pistachios" but rather "Urfa pistachios." He excused himself: "Forgive me, esteemed residents of Antep."[49] The ambiguity of place cloaked both of these episodes. Pistachios were being smuggled into the place from which they formerly derived their name. In discussions of smuggling, it was unclear what pistachios should be called even within the Republic of Turkey. The Antep pistachio had been invented by the mid-twentieth century, but it was not the unambiguous propellant of the Turkish national economy that state officials had hoped, in terms of both where the pistachios went and what they were called.

### The South Comes to Istanbul

People of the Turkish south increasingly made their way to the burgeoning cities of the Republic of Turkey in the mid-twentieth century. With a major baby boom, agricultural mechanization, and urban industrialization, villagers looked to the city as a source of economic opportunity and social mobility. As they moved, the stature of Adana kebab and Antep pistachios continued to grow. Some have dated the birth of Adana kebab in its present form to 1946, when Mesut Silindir, a kebab maker in Adana, began to cook minced meat on a spit (*şiş*) rather than a grill (*ızgara*).[50] But others claim that the name came into being when the style of kebab left Adana.[51] Whatever the true origin, men who had learned to make kebabs from their mothers in Adana gradually came to open kebab stands as a way of making money. The stands became known as "Adana Kebab Makers," and their distinctively spiced kebabs made from meat minced by hand came to be known as Adana kebab. The kebabs produced by cooks from Urfa came to be called Urfa kebab, known for being less spicy than Adana's.[52]

Migration fueled the spread of Adana kebab, which at the same time came to symbolize some of the complex emotions of displacement as some people left Adana for cities like Istanbul, Izmir, and Ankara, while others left their villages farther east to set off for places like Adana. Some 20,000 natives of the Çukurova region were living in Istanbul in 1965, and some 10,000 in Ankara. Meanwhile another 100,000 from villages farther east headed for the cities of Çukurova. Adana produced cotton and kebabs, but it also produced

Turkey's urban working class in many ways. The large-scale internal migration catalyzed stereotypes that echoed the 1930s discussions of the "disease of the south." When Adana native and sociologist Can Kozanoğlu moved to Istanbul as a child, he quickly realized that "everyone has a certain idea about someone from Adana," ranging from nouveau riche stereotypes of 1960s films to the continued association of borderland cities with smuggling.[53]

Music was one realm where the spicy kebab and the longing for love and home came together. Many of the foremost performers of the genre of Arabesk, for example, who emerged in the 1960s, hailed from places like Adana and Urfa. The songs, like kebabs, played on the fact that *acı* in Turkish referred both to the spiciness of food and to the emotional pain of longing that defined much of the Arabesk aesthetic. Reveling in that longing produced a certain kind of pleasure mixed with the pain involved in migration, not unlike the experience of eating a spicy kebab.[54] Kebabs sometimes even came to be part of iconic Arabesk lyrics. On one record, Urfa native and Arabesk pioneer Seyfettin Sucu sang a free-form ode in Arabic (*ghazal*) before launching back into the song's refrain in Turkish: "Look at that brow, look at that eye, / my liver became kebab on those coals."[55] This bilingual track sizzled with the local flavor of the south. Much like Adana kebab, however, the Arabesk genre was often looked down upon as low-class by Istanbulites, even as they secretly took pleasure in its consumption. Like the cuisine of the south that it accompanied, Arabesk offers evidence of how the region's inhabitants had pushed their way into the mainstream.[56]

Adana kebab and Antep pistachios had both spread from their humble origins in the borderlands of southeastern Turkey by the 1970s. But they did so in distinct ways. Adana kebab had moved with the people who had journeyed to places like Istanbul in search of economic opportunity. The distinctive meat dish may have been on the menu in 1971 at the wedding of one of the scions of the Sabancı family, who had turned their roots in cotton and textiles in Adana into a global business empire that made them part of the Istanbul elite.[57] But in Istanbul the food still carried the connotations of the people with whom it moved, migrants who had worked formerly in the cotton fields and later in the textile workshops of Turkey's burgeoning cities.

Motion was connected to the story of pistachios in a different way, as they continued to be smuggled across borders. In a 1975 parliamentary debate on the topic, Abdi Özkök lamented the practice but further complained that, after being smuggled to places like Lebanon, the "world's best pistachio" was still being called "Şam pistachio." In his view, Turkey received no credit for its delicious nut.[58] Moreover, the economic effects of the smuggling, according to Özkök, left Turkish farmers in a state of "peonage" (*ırgatlık*), while other countries could enjoy "lordship" (*ağalık*). In other words, the smuggling of Antep pistachios moved the region's nuts out of Turkey while migrant workers ensured that Adana kebabs had begun to conquer Turkey's great cities.

## The Global Goes South and the Turkish South Goes Global

Demarcations of difference are still visible among regional cuisines in Turkish cities, but the class signification of kebab has changed with time. One of the foremost figures in this transformation was and is Musa Dağdeviren. His own story intersects in prominent ways with the history of the Turkish south. Hailing from a family that grew olives and pistachios east of Antep in Nizip, he would go to Adana annually to pick cotton during harvest season.[59] After a stint working in a bakery in Nizip and organizing workers there in the early 1980s, he left for Istanbul, where he opened his first Çiya Kebab restaurant. At that time, grilled meat of the southeast was still, as he said in a 2018 episode of the documentary series *Chef's Table*, "something that was made fun of" (*alay konusu*).[60] Through his restaurant, however, Dağdeviren was able to realize his vision of making the food of the Turkish south a gourmet experience: Istanbulites could eat Aleppo-style kebabs while listening to classical music. In a similar way, bottles of *şalgam suyu* found their way to grocery shelves throughout Turkey and onto menus in Istanbul restaurants. Though its alien taste remained unpalatable to many and transplants from the Adana region accounted for much of its consumption, the fact that a spicy and savory beverage made from fermented carrots and pickles had become almost as widely available as soft drinks and the yogurt drink known as *ayran* was further testament to the ascendance and mainstream status attained by cuisines of the Turkish south.

As kebabs rose to a higher status, it seems that in some ways pistachios decreased in value. The Iranian Revolution played a key role. The US embargo on Iranian goods—including significant pistachio imports—provided California growers with the opening they needed to build their industry. Until that time, pistachios consumed in the United States were primarily imports, with domestic production of pistachios limited to an experimental farm in Chico in northern California and, farther south, a few trees dotting the city of Glendale (which has subsequently become home to no shortage of Armenians of Anatolia and their food; one of its revered eateries is even called Adana Restaurant, offering quite a selection of kebabs).[61] But US growers capitalized on their chance and used an Islamophobic marketing campaign to consolidate their place in the pistachio market. A massive ad on Santa Monica Boulevard in Los Angeles depicted a man and a camel in the desert with the caption "Would you rather buy pistachios from this?" beside an image of luxuriant California vegetation with the words "or this?"[62] With the US market closed off, Iranian pistachios that would previously have gone to the United States flooded the world market, driving down prices. Coupled with ongoing violence in southeast Turkey as a result of the state's conflict with the Kurdistan Workers' Party (better known by its Kurdish acronym PKK), the place of pistachios in Turkey was precarious. Amid headlines describing a "pistachio war," one pistachio exporter warned in 1991 that "if it goes on like this, the Gaziantep pistachio will be a thing of the past."[63]

This would not come to be, in part because of continued state support for pistachio cultivation. This support took a number of forms, including an annual Pistachio Festival beginning in 1990.[64] Meanwhile, commercial publications such as *Yöre* (Region) and *Güneydoğubirlik Dergisi* (Southeast Union Journal) emerged, touting the economic prospects of the southeast in general and pistachios in particular. Such initiatives were part of a broader effort on the part of the Turkish state to stimulate economic development in the country's southeast in the form of the Southeast Anatolia Project (Güneydoğu Anadolu Projesi: GAP). The state-directed initiative of hydropower and scientific agriculture aimed to address not only the region's poverty but also its status as the main site of Kurdish political challenge.[65] Pistachio cultivation intersected with this geography of insurrection, with 92.3 percent of the production taking place in the GAP region as of 1993.[66] In this context, state officials hoped to use science to transform the region's possibilities and association with poverty and violence. Organizations like the Antep Pistachio Research Institute hoped to make obsolete the conventional wisdom about the decades necessary for pistachio trees to bear fruit. Sayings like "a pistachio from the grandfather and an olive from the father" attested to this dynamic, but the new scientific agriculture hoped to transform these limitations on production.[67]

Though Adana kebab was never viewed as a national economic product in the same way that pistachios in Antep have been, the city's distinctive kebab culture has increasingly become recognized by state authorities as an opportunity and a kind of heritage that requires protection. The Adana Chamber of Commerce patented the name Adana kebab in 2004, and those who used the term without certification faced at least two and a half years in jail.[68] Among the criteria registered with the Turkish Patent Institute was a specification that the meat had to be taken from animals raised in the Adana region. Many agree that the *terroir* of Adana continues to shape the kebab's distinctive flavor. As Can Kozanoğlu has remarked, kebabs in Istanbul never seemed as good as those in Adana, lending credence to the belief that "if animals do not graze in the Taurus mountains, they do not make good kebabs."[69] An attempt at a festival occurred in 2005 with the "Official Adana Kebab Festival" in Taşköprü, but it did not continue in the following years.[70]

By the time the patent was in place, the fame of Adana's grilled meats had spread even beyond Turkey's borders. A restaurant-owner named Erol Yılkıran decided to attempt to prepare the world's longest Adana kebab in 2010.[71] Yılkıran's Sultan Palace Restaurant in Hanover, Germany, was far from Adana, where the previous record-length kebab of 35 meters had been set at the 2005 festival. But like the vaunted Adana kebabs that traveled throughout Turkey with migrants from the south, kebab more generally—including Adana's spicy variety—had traveled to Germany with the Turkish diaspora. Millions of people—many of whom hailed from the Turkish south—went there beginning with West Germany's Gastarbeiter program.

Antep pistachios did not travel in quite the same way, but the ambiguity about their name remained omnipresent. After the onset of the "Zero Problems with Neighbors" policy in the early 2000s under Turkey's Justice and Development Party, Syria no longer represented what it had in the past: the smuggler's paradise spiriting away Turkey's national wealth of the 1960s and 1970s or the safe haven for the PKK of the 1980s and 1990s. A 2009 trilingual cookbook on the region of Antep and Aleppo trumpeted how southeastern Turkey and northern Syria shared the "same geography, same climate, and similar cultures."[72] What, then, of the pistachios planted on either side of the border? The book offered an answer with its pistachio-heavy recipe for "Antep-style kadayıf," a popular dessert. The Turkish-language version of the recipe called for "Antep pistachio" (*Antepfıstığı*) and the Arabic-language version of the recipe called for "Antep (Aleppo) pistachio" (*fustuq ʿAyntabī [Ḥalabī]*). The English version called simply for "pistachio."[73] Adding another layer of ambiguity, by 2014 the majority of Antep pistachios did not even come from Antep but instead hailed from the neighboring province of Urfa.[74] Numbers be damned: Antep anointed "the world's first and only Pistachio Museum" in honor of it being "the homeland of the pistachio" in 2018.[75] In yet another example of the consolidation of the Antep pistachio, the nut even became involved in the Turkish military's invasion of northern Syria in February 2018. In solidarity with Operation Olive Branch, as it was called, officials in Nizip arranged to have 1 million tons of Antep pistachios sent to the border for the enjoyment of Turkish soldiers.[76] Nearly a century after Ottoman rule ended in what would become Syria, pistachios that had once been seen as evocative of greater Syria thanks to their label of Şam pistachios had entered Syria once again, this time with an army under the Turkish flag.

Meanwhile, the cuisine of the Turkish south has spread beyond Turkey in more peaceful ways too. Musa Dağdeviren has been profiled not only in the aforementioned documentary series *Chef's Table* but also by the *New Yorker*.[77]

Dağdeviren recently published a cookbook that is a compilation of local food traditions, many of them from the Turkish south.[78] It is titled *The Turkish Cookbook*, showing how foods like Adana kebabs and Antep pistachios have entered mainstream Turkish cuisine. But Dağdeviren's work is also a stark rejoinder to those nationalist elites who might have looked down on the flavors of the south and its people. *The Turkish Cookbook* reveals a Turkish cuisine of remarkable diversity, with recipes drawing on Armenian, Assyrian, Arab, Greek, Jewish, Kurdish, and Turkish food traditions among others, though Dağdeviren insists that "food has no ethnicity, only geography."[79] His work thus makes apparent complicated realities that many would prefer to forget, such as the polyglot worlds of migrant workers and nomads that eventually gave birth to Adana kebab or the Şam pistachios grown by Armenians that became Antep pistachios amid post-Ottoman efforts to forge a national economy.

Thanks in no small part to people like Dağdeviren and Gaziantep native and food writer Ayfer Ünsal, a number of chefs have brought the kebabs and pistachios of Turkey's south around the world in a regional fusion billed as both upscale and authentic.[80] A few examples include Rawia Bishara (of Brooklyn's Tanoreen), Yotam Ottolenghi and Sami Tamimi (of London's Ottolenghi suite of restaurants), and Ana Sortun and Maura Kilpatrick (of greater Boston's Sarma and Sofra).[81] In one example of this oeuvre, London-based writer Sabrina Ghayour offers a recipe for "Turkish Adana Köfte Kebabs" that demonstrates the blurriness both of this genre and of the foods of the Turkish south more broadly.[82] To create the dish's distinctive spice mixture, Ghayour calls for Aleppo pepper. In invoking a spice named for a northern Syrian city to make the distinctive meat of a southern Turkish city, Ghayour gestures toward the overlapping food cultures of these regions (although it should be noted that the red peppers of Aleppo, Antep, Maraş, and Urfa are distinct, though related). But the question of Aleppo pepper and its provenance has become more mottled still in recent years. Because of the conflict in Syria, much of the distinctive spice of Aleppo sold around the world today actually comes from southern Turkey.[83] People fleeing northern Syria carried their pepper seeds with them and planted them in southern Turkey, meaning that Adana kebab could very well be made with pepper seeds native to Syria but grown in Turkey.

## Conclusion

In sum, Antep pistachios and Adana kebabs took trajectories at times overlapping and at other times divergent. They both came to colonize Turkish cuisine over the course of the twentieth century as the borderlands of southern

Turkey, its people, and its products became integral to the national economy. Both emerged from the economic transformations and regional connections of the late Ottoman Empire. Grilled meat dishes transformed the Adana region's rich animal husbandry traditions into filling fare for migrants working in the region's cotton fields. Pistachios functioned as an embellishment to sweet or savory dishes, including the famous baklava of places like Antep and Aleppo. While there were kebabs in Adana and pistachios in Antep during the Ottoman period, there was, in a way, no such thing as the "Adana kebab" and "Antep pistachio." These distinctive names found today across Turkey and beyond would come later.

The Antep pistachio emerged thanks to a concerted state effort to present the previous name of the commodity—Şam pistachio—as a relic of an older time. The invention of the Antep pistachio not only represented a severing of Turkey from its Ottoman entanglements with the areas that would become part of Syria. The development of pistachios—some of them expropriated from Ottoman Armenians expelled and killed during and after World War I— was also a crucial part of the creation of a Turkish national economy, complete with an emphasis on scientific improvement of the crops and an orientation toward export.

Cotton in Adana was also envisioned as a way to rejuvenate the post-Ottoman economy of Anatolia. White gold and textiles made some fabulously wealthy, but they also required a mobile labor force. It was with these populations moving from the countryside to places like Adana and subsequently to the growing cities of Ankara, Istanbul, and Izmir that Adana kebab came into its own as a recognizable dish. Unlike Antep pistachios, Adana kebab was coded in the Turkish national imaginary much like the people who brought it to the city, as low-class and of suspect origins, whether Kurdish or Arab, even as Istanbulites indulged in the guilty pleasures of Arabesk tearjerkers that provided the same pleasure mixed with pain as Adana kebab's signature red pepper spices did. By the late twentieth century, the negative associations had begun to change, thanks in part to interventions of people like Musa Dağdeviren, aimed at recuperating the forgotten foodways of Anatolia and elevating them to high cuisine. Meanwhile, local officials scrambled during the 1990s and early 2000s to harness the power of kebabs and pistachios as an indelible part of local culture and an asset to the tourism industry. Museums, statues, and festivals in honor of these foods of the Turkish south and indeed portions of the Levant more broadly are still being created in a time when Syrian refugees shed unprecedented light on the connections and divisions between Syria and Turkey.

The histories of pistachios and kebabs offer cause for hope and despair.

They both point to the long-standing culinary connections between Syria and Turkey. But the histories of Adana kebabs and Antep pistachios also reveal how the connections of these foods with Syria and the Levant more broadly have been erased. As the foods became entrenched in the Turkish nationalist imaginary and economy, Şam pistachios became Antep pistachios. Meanwhile, the spicy meat of the south came to be viewed—much like those migrants who brought them to the city—as part and parcel of Turkey's regional diversity rather than a demonstration of Turkey and Syria's overlapping geography. It is in part because of these long-term processes of disconnecting Syria and Turkey that Vedat Milor could speak of the difference between "our food" and Syrian food in his review of Saruja with which this chapter began. But the history of Antep pistachios and Adana kebabs also undermines the differentiation that Milor was making. The "our food" Milor invoked when referring to Adana kebabs had not long ago been itself associated with places like Aleppo. And the "şamfıstıklı" baklava he delighted in tasting likely took its pistachios from Şam or greater Syria only by a most expansive definition of the region, including places in Turkey like Antep. In the end, this formulation might be accurate. Many have worried in Turkey about how Syrians have changed their country. Unquestioned in many of these arguments, however, is how the traditions of Syria have been a part of Turkey for many years already. The story of Adana kebabs and Antep pistachios reveals the culinary legacy of the late Ottoman Levant in Turkey that is simultaneously hidden and deliciously obvious.

## Notes

1. Vedat Milor, "Saruja: Suriye Mutfağı," *Hürriyet*, 30 June 2018, hurriyet.com.tr /yazarlar/vedat-milor/saruja-suriye-mutfagi-40881555; Dalia Mortada, "Saruja: Return to Mom's Kitchen," *Savoring Syria*, 15 January 2020, culinarybackstreets.com/cities -category/istanbul/2020/saruja-fatih.

2. Milor, "Saruja."

3. Milor is of course aware of the connections between the cuisine of northern Syria and the cuisine of southern Turkey. In his review of Saruja, he even notes that he had tried to visit Aleppo for his television program several years before, but the director refused, saying that Aleppo's food was "more or less the same as that of Antakya." Milor, "Saruja." All translations are by the authors unless otherwise noted.

4. Selim Deringil calls this approach in the early years of the Republic of Turkey the "good riddance syndrome" in *The Ottoman Twilight in Arab Lands: Turkish Memoirs and Testimonies of the Great War* (Boston: Academic Studies Press, 2019), xiii.

5. Salim Tamari, *The Year of the Locust: A Soldier's Diary and the Erasure of Palestine's Ottoman Past* (Berkeley: University of California Press, 2011), 5.

6. Keith Watenpaugh, *Being Modern in the Middle East: Revolution, Nationalism, Colonialism, and the Arab Middle Class* (Princeton: Princeton University Press, 2006),

182. For a growing body of work that has examined the border explicitly, see Seda Altuğ, "Sectarianism in the Syrian Jazira: Community, Land, and Violence in the Memories of World War I and the French Mandate (1915–1939)" (PhD diss., University of Utrecht, 2011); Seda Altuğ and Benjamin White, "Frontière et pouvoir d'état: La frontière turco-syrienne dans les années 1920 et 1930," *Vingtième siècle: Revue d'histoire* 103 (2009): 91–104; Ramazan Hakkı Öztan, "The Great Depression and the Making of Turkish-Syrian Border, 1921–1939," *International Journal of Middle East Studies* 52, no. 2 (2020): 311–326; Vahe Tachjian, *La France en Cilicie et en Haute-Mésopotamie: Aux confins de la Turquie, de la Syrie et de l'Irak (1919–1933)* (Paris: Karthala, 2004); Jordi Tejel, "Des femmes contre des moutons: Franchissements féminins de la frontière turco-syrienne (1929–1944)," *Revue d'histoire* 20/21, no. 145: 35–48; Benjamin White, "Chapter 4: The Border and the Kurds," in *Emergence of Minorities in the Middle East: Politics and Community in French Mandate Syria* (Edinburgh: Edinburgh University Press, 2011), 101–120.

7. Evliya Çelebi, *Evliya Çelebi seyahatnamesi: Topkapi Sarayı Bağdat 305 yazmasinin transkripsiyonu*, ed. Orhan Şaik Gökyay et al., 10 vols. (Istanbul: Yapı Kredi Yayınları, 1999), 1:270.

8. For an overview, see Meltem Toksöz, *Nomads, Migrants and Cotton in the Eastern Mediterranean: The Making of the Adana-Mersin Region 1850–1908* (Leiden: Brill, 2010).

9. On Iranian workers, see Başbakanlık Osmanlı Arşivi (BOA: Ottoman Prime Ministry Archive), İ-DA 8/194 14, Cemazeyilahir 1287 (11 September 1870); DH-MKT 330/45, 12 Receb 1312 (27 December 1895); ŞD 633/18, No. 4 (7 September 1893).

10. BOA, DH-İD 183–2/7, No. 2, 4 Teşrinisani 1329 (17 November 1913).

11. Abdülkadir Kemali and Işık Öğütçü, *Orhan Kemal'in Babası Abdülkadir Kemali Bey'in Anıları* (Istanbul: Everest Yayınları, 2009), 2–4.

12. Sami Zubaida, "National, Communal, and Global Dimensions in Middle Eastern Food Cultures," in *A Taste of Thyme: Culinary Cultures of the Middle East*, ed. Sami Zubaida and Richard Tapper (London: Tauris, 1994), 34.

13. Arthur Hagopian, "The Chamichian Saga: Gold and Pistachios," *Armenian Mirror-Spectator*, 15 December 2016, mirrorspectator.com/2016/12/15/the-chamichian -saga-gold-and-pistachios.

14. G. A. Sarafean, *A Briefer History of Aintab: A Concise History of the Cultural, Religious, Educational, Political, Industrial and Commercial Life of the Armenians of Aintab* (Boston: Union of the Armenians of Aintab, 1957), 289–293.

15. Sarafean, *A Briefer History of Aintab*, 10.

16. *Memalik-i Osmaniyenin 1329 Senesine Ziraat Istatistiki* (Dersaadet: Matbaa-yi Osmaniye, 1332 [1916–1917]), 360, 421.

17. *Memalik-i Osmaniyenin 1329 Senesine Ziraat Istatistiki*, 415.

18. *Evliya Çelebi Seyahatnamesi: Anadolu, Suriye, Hicaz (1671–1672)* (Istanbul: Devlet Matbaası, 1935), 9:358–359.

19. Rose Baboian, *Armenian-American Cook Book: Simplified Armenian Near East Recipes* (Boston: Haig H. Toumanyan, 1964), 99; Cemşid Bender, *Kürt Mutfak Kültürü ve Kürt Yemekleri* (Istanbul: Melsa Yayınları, 1992), 217; Ana Sortun, *Spice: Flavors of the Eastern Mediterranean* (New York: Harper Collins, 2006), 236; Aylın Öney Tan, *A Taste of Sun & Fire: Gaziantep Cookery* (Istanbul: Yapı Kredi Yayınları, 2015), 231; Paula Wolfert, *The Cooking of the Eastern Mediterranean: 215 Healthy, Vibrant, and Inspired Recipes* (New York: HarperCollins Publishers, 1994), 271. For a historical example of these usages, see Boğos Piranyan's 1914 work published in *Merzifon*, which includes a recipe for

"Aleppo köfte" that includes pistachios. Boğos Piranyan, *Aşçının Kitabı*, trans. Takuhi Tovmasyan (Istanbul: Aras Yayıncılık, 2008), 49.

20. BOA, C.SM. 150/7528, 11 Ramazan 1178 (4 March 1765).

21. Özge Samancı, "Kar, Serbet, ve Dondurma," *Yemek ve Kültür*, no. 9 (2007): 150; Özge Samancı, "19 Yüzyılda Osmanlı Saray Mutfağı," *Yemek ve Kültür*, no. 4 (2006): 51; Ardashes Hagop Keoleian, *The Oriental Cook Book: Wholesome, Dainty and Economical Dishes of the Orient, Especially Adapted to American Tastes and Methods of Preparation* (New York: Sully and Kleinteich, 1913), 346.

22. BOA, A.MKT.MHM 436/39, Aydın Governor to Grand Vizier, 3 Şubat 1284 (15 February 1869). On where pistachios did grow, see Vital Cuinet, *La Turquie d'Asie, géographie administrative: Statistique, descriptive et raisonnée de chaque province de l'Asie Mineure,* vol. 2 (Paris: Ernest Leroux, 1891), 143, 157, 166, 256, 265; *Memalik-i Osmaniyenin 1329 Senesine Ziraat Istatistiki* (Dersaadet: Matbaa-yi Osmaniye, 1332 [1916–1917]), 360, 421; *Salname-yi Vilayet-i Haleb 1310,* 112; *Haleb Vilayeti Salnamesi 1326,* 429; *Salname-yi Vilayet-i Haleb 1302,* 191–192.

23. Muhammad Kurd 'Ali, *Khitat al-Sham,* vol. 1, 2nd ed. (Beirut: Dar al-Qalam, 1969), 9.

24. Şerefeddin Mağmumi, *Seyahat Hatıraları* (Cairo: n.p., 1909), 273; Edward Ledwich Mitford, *A Land March from England to Ceylon Forty Years Ago,* vol. 1 (London: W. H. Allen, 1884), 153; G. W. Prothero, ed. *Syria and Palestine* (London: H.M. Stationery Office, 1920), 83; W. J. Childs, *Across Asia Minor on Foot* (London: Blackwood and Sons, 1917), 408.

25. More research is necessary to determine whether or how this term has changed over time. Here are two examples of the use of "Aleppo pistachio" in the latter part of the twentieth century as part of afforestation campaigns in Syria: "Kayfa ahtafalat al-Hassaka bi-l-'id 37 lil-shajara?," *al-Ba'th,* 2 January 1989; 'Imad Fadil, "Al-tashjir silah fa'al didd al-tasahhur: Hizam akhdar min al-zaytun wa-l-fustuq al-halabi," *al-Ba'th,* 19 December 1989.

26. Hıfzı Topuk, "Cenuptan röportajlar 3: Antep fıstığı," *Akşam,* 8 August 1949, 4; "Antepfıstğı," *Güneydoğubirlik Dergisi* 1, no. 1 (April 1993): 17; Osman Yalçın, *Gaziantep* (Istanbul: Ozyürek Yayınları, 1959), 18.

27. Lütfiye Aydın, *Anka Kentim Antep'im* (Istanbul: Heyamola Yayınlarī, 2008), 159.

28. For an overview, see Vahé Tachjian, *La France en Cilicie et en Haute-Mésopotamie.*

29. Vahram L. Shemmassian, "Repatriation of Armenian Refugees," in *Armenian Cilicia,* ed. Richard G. Hovannisian and Simon Payaslian (Costa Mesa, CA: Mazda Publishers, 2008); Benjamin Thomas White, "A Grudging Rescue: France, the Armenians of Cilicia, and the History of Humanitarian Evacuations," *Humanity: An International Journal of Human Rights, Humanitarianism, and Development* 10, no. 1 (2019): 1–27. If it was migrant laborers who brought the cuisine of the Turkish south to places like Istanbul, it was the expelled Armenians of southern Anatolia who brought the same cuisine to places like Beirut and Damascus. For their influence on Aleppo cuisine, see, for example, Marlene Matar, *The Aleppo Cookbook: Celebrating the Legendary Cuisine of Syria* (Northampton, MA: Interlink Books, 2016).

30. For a biography, see Sadun Tanju, *Hacı Ömer* (Istanbul: Apa Ofset Basimevi, 1983).

31. Senem Aslan, "'Citizen, Speak Turkish!': A Nation in the Making," *Nationalism and Ethnic Politics* 13, no. 2 (2007): 245–272.

32. Gisela Procházka-Eisl and Stephan Procházka, *The Plain of Saints and Prophets: The Nusayri-Alawi Community of Cilicia (Southern Turkey) and Its Sacred Places* (Wiesbaden: Harrassowitz Verlag, 2010), 22–23. In class terms, the designation *fellah* was already operative during the Ottoman period. Accounts of the Adana massacres contain disparaging references to *fellah*: Hagop Terzian, *Atanayi keank'ĕ* (Istanbul: Z. N. Perperean, 1909), 7; Arshakuhi Teodik, *Amis mĕ i Kilikia: Kts'ktur nŏt'er* (Istanbul: Ter-Nersesean, 1910), 69.

33. For an overview, see Sarah D. Shields, *Fezzes in the River: Identity Politics and European Diplomacy in the Middle East on the Eve of World War II* (Oxford: Oxford University Press, 2011).

34. Elise K. Burton, "Red Crescents: Race, Genetics, and Sickle Cell Disease in the Middle East," *Isis* 110, no. 2 (2019): 250–269.

35. Musa Dağdeviren, "Adana Mutfağı," in *Adana'ya Kar Yağmış: Adana Üzerine Yazılar*, ed. Behçet Çelik (Istanbul: İletişim Yayınları, 2006), 327; İzzet Öztoprak, Cafer Güler, Murat Karataş, and Güneş Şahin, eds., *Cumhuriyet'in XV. Yılında Türkiye*, vol. 1 (Ankara: Atatürk Araştırma Merkezi, 2014), 36.

36. Burhan Belge, "Adana Hudut Bölgesi," in *Cumhuriyet'in XV. Yılında Türkiye*, vol. 1, 89.

37. Burhan Belge, "Adana Bizim Cenubumuz," in *Cumhuriyet'in XV. Yılında Türkiye*, vol. 1, 85.

38. National Archives and Records Administration (NARA): Record Group 84, Consular Aleppo, Syria, vol. 116: "Zaloom Brothers Company to American Consulate, Aleppo," 21 March 1925. We thank Ramazan Hakkı Öztan for calling our attention to this exchange. For more, see Ramazan Hakkı Öztan, "The Last Ottoman Merchants: Regional Trade and Politics of Tariffs in Aleppo's Hinterland, 1921–29," in *Regimes of Mobility: Borders and State Formation in the Middle East, 1918–1946*, ed. Jordi Tejel and Ramazan Hakkı Öztan (Edinburgh: Edinburgh University Press, forthcoming).

39. NARA: Record Group 84, Consular Aleppo, Syria, vol. 116: "American Consulate, Aleppo, to Joseph A. Zaloom," 16 April 1925.

40. Galip Ataç, *Ulus*, 7 January 1938, in *Gaziantep İçin Söylenenler*, ed. Hulusi Yetkin (Gaziantep: Yeni Matbaası, 1969), 100. As if to substantiate Ataç's argument about Şam pistachios being associated with the past, around the same time Nestlé began marketing a chocolate bar with "Damascus pistachios" (*pistaches de Damas*) called Damak and ads featuring a woman with only her eyes visible behind a veil. Saadet Özen, *Çukulata: A Turkish History of Chocolate*, trans. Stephanie Ateş (Istanbul: Yapı Kredi Yayınları, 2014), 180.

41. İzzet Öztoprak, Cafer Güler, Murat Karataş, and Güneş Şahin, eds., *Cumhuriyet'in XV. Yılında Türkiye*, vol. 4 (Ankara: Atatürk Araştırma Merkezi, 2014), 1846.

42. Topuk, "Cenuptan röportajlar 3: Antep.

43. Ümit Kurt, "Theatres of Violence on the Ottoman Periphery: Exploring the Local Roots of Genocidal Policies in Antep," *Journal of Genocide Research* 20, no. 3 (2018): 369.

44. Topuk, "Cenuptan röportajlar 3: Antep fıstığı."

45. Ayfer T. Ünsal, *Ayıntab'tan Gaziantep'e Yeme İçme* (Istanbul: İletişim, 2002), 238.

46. Yaşar Kemal, "Gaziantep güneyin endüstri merkezi," *Cumhuriyet*, 26 July 1955; Orhan Kemal, *Şahin Gazetesi* (1957), in *Gaziantep İçin Söylenenler*, ed. Hulusi Yetkin

(Gaziantep: Yeni Matbaası, 1969), 95; Sabahattin Ozbek, *Antep Fıstığı Yetiştirilmesi* (Ankara: Yüksek Ziraat Enstitüsü Basımevi, 1945), 11; Osman Yalçın, *Urfa* (Istanbul: Özyürek Yayınları, 1959), 21; Osman Yalçın, *Gaziantep* (Istanbul: Özyürek Yayınları, 1959), 18.

47. "Cenup Bölgesinde Kaçakçılık," *Akşam*, 13 September 1954, 3.

48. Khalid Khalifa, *La Sakakin fi Matabikh hadhihi al-Madina* (Cairo: Dar al-'Ayn lil-Nashr, 2013), 192.

49. *Millet Meclisi Tutanak Dergisi*, C: 2, B: 48, O: 1, 17 February 1962, 470.

50. Mustafa Kurt, "Çek bir Adana, acılı olsun . . . ," *Cumhuriyet*, 29 November 1998, 18.

51. Musa Dağdeviren, "Adana Mutfağı," 327.

52. Musa Dağdeviren, "Kebapçı," *Yemek ve Kültür* 2 (Spring 2005): 153.

53. Can Kozanoğlu, "Adana Dışında Adanalı Olmak," in *Adana'ya Kar Yağmış: Adana Üzerine Yazılar* (Istanbul: İletişim, 2006), 171.

54. İlhan Selçuk, "Pencere: Acının Tadı," *Cumhuriyet*, 22 February 1989, 2. Selçuk frequently discussed this dynamic in his columns. İlhan Selçuk, "Pencere: Acı ve Keder," *Cumhuriyet*, 15 June 1999, 2; İlhan Selçuk, "Pencere: Ağlamasını Bileceksin," *Cumhuriyet*, 31 January 1988, 2.

55. Seyfettin Sucu and Bedir Çağlayan, "Dağlar Ağardı Kardan/Bak Şu Kaşa," Urfa'nın Sesi, 45 rpm vinyl.

56. See Martin Stokes, *The Arabesk Debate: Music and Musicians in Modern Turkey* (Oxford: Oxford University Press, 1992); Nazife Güngör, *Arabesk: Sosyokültürel açidan arabesk müzik* (Ankara: Bilgi Yayinevi, 1993).

57. "Sapancıların Oğlu Evlendi," *Milliyet*, 21 June 1971, 3.

58. *Millet Meclisi Tutanak Dergisi*, C: 10, B: 46, O: 1, 23 February 1975, 77.

59. Musa Dağdeviren, "Adana Mutfağı," 321.

60. *Chef's Table*, season 5, episode 2, "Musa Dağdeviren," directed by Clay Jeter, Netflix, 28 September 2018.

61. Louis S. Badour, "The Pistachio Tree as an Ornamental," *Los Angeles Times*, 1 November 1925; Mark Bittman, "This Armenian Life," *New York Times*, 28 July 2013, nytimes.com/2013/07/28/magazine/this-armenian-life.html.

62. Scott Peterson, "Iran's Prized, and Political, Nuts," *Christian Science Monitor*, 2 December 1999, csmonitor.com/1999/1202/p8s1.html.

63. Ercüment İşleyen, "Fıstık Savaşı," *Milliyet*, 26 February 1991, 9.

64. H. Ziya Biçer, "Fıstık Fıstık Dedikleri," *Yöre* 1, no. 3 (August 1990): 3.

65. Ali Çarkoğlu and Mine Eder, "Development alla Turca: The Southeastern Anatolia Development Project," in *Environmentalism in Turkey: Between Democracy and Development?*, ed. Fikret Adaman and Murat Arsel (Burlington, VT: Ashgate Publishing, 2005), 170.

66. Azmi Ulusaraç, "GAP'ta Antepfıstığının Yeri ve Önemi," *Güneydoğubirlik Dergisi* 1, no. 8 (November 1993): 13.

67. "'Fıstık Dededen Zeytin Babdan' Deyimi Tarihe Karışıyor," *Güneydoğubirlik Dergisi* 1, no. 4 (July 1993): 8.

68. "İzinsiz 'Adana kebabı' yapana 2.5 yıl hapis," *Hürriyet: Kelebek*, 18 June 2004.

69. Can Kozanoğlu, "Adana Dışında Adanalı Olmak," in *Adana'ya Kar Yağmış: Adana Üzerine Yazılar*, 179.

70. İsmail Güneş, *Adana Kent Yazıları* (Adana: Karahan Kitabevi, 2017), 96.

71. Mehmet Uzun, "Dünyanın en uzun Adana kebabını yapacak," *Milliyet*, 27 May 2010, milliyet.com.tr/dunya/dunyanin-en-uzun-adana-kebabini-yapacak-1243383.

72. İsmail Özsabuncuoğlu and İlkay Pınarlı Gök, *Gaziantep-Halep Mutfak Kültürü ve Yemekleri: Benzerlikler ve Farklılıklar* (Gaziantep: Gaziantep University, 2009), 3.

73. Özsabuncuoğlu and Gök, *Gaziantep-Halep Mutfak Kültürü ve Yemekleri*, 219–220.

74. Musa Dağdeviren, "Dalından tadına fıstığın öyküsü," *Yemek ve Kültür* 45 (Fall 2016): 71, 72. The dynamic has prompted some in Urfa to promote a "Şanlıurfa pistachio," a campaign complete with the hashtag "#fıstıkurfanındır" (the pistachio is all Urfa's), and a related Facebook page called "The Pistachio Rebellion" (Fıstığın Isyanı). One of the key figures behind these campaigns is actually the mayor of Birecik, a town located right across the Euphrates from Antep province and the pistachio groves of Rumkale. In the Ottoman period Birecik and Rumkale had both been part of Urfa, until Rumkale was lopped off in 1919, raising the possibility that the simple act of Ottoman redistricting has given Antep a level of fame that Urfa yearns for (albeit perhaps not enough for a proper rebellion). BOA, DH-UMVM 61/69, Mutsarrıf Celal to Dahiliye Nezareti, 9 Şubat 1335 (9 February 1919); DH-MKT 1268/75, Haleb Vilayeti Idare Meclisi to Dahiliye Nezareti, 4 Ağustos 1324 (17 August 1908), in Aylın Çetin, *Nizip Tarihine ait Belgeler* (Izmit: Sesim Ofset, 2014), 97–98, 126–127.

75. "Müzeler Şehri Gaziantep Bir Müzeye Daha Kavuşuyor," *Milliyet*, 11 July 2018, milliyet.com.tr/muzeler-sehri-gaziantep-bir-muzeye-daha-gaziantep-yerelhaber -2914713.

76. Metin İliksoy, "Nizip'ten Mehmetçik'e 1 ton fıstık," *Hürriyet*, 3 February 2018, hurriyet.com.tr/nizipten-mehmetcike-1-ton-fistik-40730439.

77. Elif Batuman, "The Memory Kitchen," *New Yorker*, 19 April 2010, newyorker .com/magazine/2010/04/19/the-memory-kitchen.

78. Musa Dağdeviren, *The Turkish Cookbook* (London: Phaidon Press, 2019).

79. Batuman, "The Memory Kitchen."

80. See Ünsal, *Ayintab'tan Gaziantep'e Yeme İçme*.

81. Rawia Bishara, *Levant: New Middle Eastern Cooking from Tanoreen* (London: Kyle Books, 2018); Rawia Bishara, *Olives, Lemons & Za'atar: The Best Middle Eastern Home Cooking* (London: Kyle Books, 2014); Sabrina Ghayour, *Persiana: Recipes from the Middle East & Beyond* (Northampton, MA: Interlink Books, 2015); Sabrina Ghayour and Haarala Hamilton, *Sirocco: Fabulous Flavors from the Middle East*; Yotam Ottolenghi and Sami Tamimi, *Jerusalem: A Cookbook* (Berkeley: Ten Speed Press, 2012); Ana Sortun and Maura Kilpatrick, *Soframiz: Vibrant Middle Eastern Recipes from Sofra Bakery and Cafe* (Berkeley: Ten Speed Press, 2016).

82. Ghayour, *Persiana*, 122.

83. Tom Verde, "The Long Journey of the Aleppo Pepper," *New York Times*, 9 October 2018, nytimes.com/2018/10/09/dining/aleppo-pepper-syria.html.

CHAPTER 3

# The Transformation of Sugar in Syria: From Luxury to Everyday Commodity

SARA PEKOW

Tamar hindī, sulṭān al-sharāb! *(Tamarind, sultan of drinks!)*
NAJAT QASSAB HASSAN, *HADITH DIMASHQI*

Long before the widespread availability of refrigeration in the Levant, Damascenes enjoyed sweetened cold drinks, ice cream, and sorbet during the hottest months of summer.[1] In the nineteenth and early twentieth centuries, beverage peddlers called out creative phrases—like the one in the epigraph—to advertise their wares as they strolled through the city's alleys and suqs, carrying an animal-skin bag containing a crystal pitcher filled with *tamar hindī* (a juice made of tamarind fruit), along with a few reusable cups. Sometimes they carried other drinks, such as *al-ʿarqsūs* (made from licorice); *al-julāb* (made from raisins); *qamar al-dīn* (made from dried apricots); or lemonade.[2] Beginning each year in early May, enterprising merchants known as *thulāj* would lead donkeys laden with large slabs of ice that had been stored in caves down the steep slopes of the Qalamun Mountains.[3] Hundreds of loads were sold every summer day to drink sellers and restaurants as well as to households, which sometimes would simply add *dibs* (usually produced from grapes boiled down to the consistency of molasses) to the ice for a treat known locally as *suwayqān*.[4]

Wadea Kassab, who spent his childhood in his native Syria during the late nineteenth century before emigrating to the United States, recounts being sent to the market in Damascus to buy a two-pound, foot-long chunk of ice to bring home to make cool drinks when the family had visitors.[5] Nazik Ali Jawdat, who was born in 1903 and raised in an upper-class home in Aleppo, was routinely served *hayṭaliyya*, a local delicacy of iced milk sherbet made from mountain ice, flavored with rose water and served with special china bowls and spoons, after soaking in the neighborhood hammam (bathhouse).[6] The renowned Bakdash ice-cream shop, established in 1895 in Suq al-Hamidiyya in Damascus, also purchased ice brought down from Qalamun to make pistachio *būza* (ice cream). Siham Tergeman recalls groomsmen enjoying it at a wedding she attended as a child in the 1930s.[7]

The production of ice cream in Aleppo dates back to at least the 1630s, when an established guild for makers of ice cream already existed.[8] Jamal al-Din al-Qasimi classifies ice-cream merchants in Damascus by the Turkish term *ḍarḍaramjī* in his famous *Qamus al-Sina'at al-Shamiyya*, a dictionary of trades in Damascus written in the late nineteenth and early twentieth centuries. Ice cream could be purchased by the serving in local suqs as well as from peddlers who adopted a smaller version of the ice-cooling technique used in ice-cream shops.[9] The consumption of ice cream and *hayṭaliyya* was limited to wealthy Syrians due to the cost of materials and the capacity to store an ice delivery, but Syrians of all classes probably could buy an occasional lemonade or other cold drink from a peddler with some spare change. Three ice factories were in operation in Damascus in 1927. Damascus had five ice factories, Aleppo had four, and Hama and Homs had three each by 1945.[10] Ice merchants who delivered ice from the Qalamun Mountains had to find new ways to earn their income.

Just as the production of ice and ice cream underwent a transformation with the technological shifts of the twentieth century, so, too, did the production and consumption of sugar and sweets. Prior to World War I, the price of sugar was too high for it to be used a staple in the kitchens of poor Syrians. This is notable, particularly in contrast with its earlier rise in popularity in England and elsewhere in Western Europe, as documented in Sidney Mintz's influential work, which shows how the taste for sugar grew alongside Britain's emergence as an imperial power.[11] The production of empire was reliant on colonial slave labor for natural resources to fuel industries in the metropole, as workers came to depend on sugar for the physical energy to work in the factory. The rise in sugar consumption in Syria was not tied to the same processes of extraction and industry as seen in Europe, but the expansion of technology and mechanization in Syria did lead to a shift in how products using sugar were produced and distributed. Examining the role of sugar in Syria during the modern period offers a microcosm through which to explore shifts in material, economic, and social history. This chapter demonstrates the importance of sugar as a commodity in Syria during the late nineteenth century and early to mid-twentieth century within the context of the growth of the international production of sugar, how it spurred the expansion of new industries, and the many ways in which Syrians used sugar.

## Sugar in Syria before World War I

Centuries before the start of the transatlantic sugar trade, sugar was cultivated, bought, sold, and consumed in the Eastern Mediterranean, and is thought to have spread from Iran to Iraq beginning in the eighth century. Sugarcane was grown in Homs and Hama, among other areas of the Levant, by the tenth century and expanded to Egypt then North Africa and al-Andalus.[12] Sugar was an essential component of medieval Syrian court cuisine, only available to the wealthy and powerful. The thirteenth-century Syrian cookery book *Scents and Flavors* calls for sugar not only in the majority of sweets and beverage recipes but also in more than half of the seventy-five recipes for chicken dishes as well as a number of meat and pickle recipes.[13] Most Syrians sweetened their food with *dibs*, though this was an ingredient disparaged by wealthy sugar eaters.[14]

After a thousand years of industry dominance, the Mediterranean sugar trade was contracting by the seventeenth century. The Atlantic sugar trade was expanding, fueled by colonial conquest and slave labor. Demographic and climactic shifts added to the demise of the Mediterranean sugar trade. Eighteenth-century sugar consumption in Syria is estimated to have been even lower than during the medieval period. The cost of shipping from Europe or the Americas was especially prohibitive prior to the opening of the Suez Canal and the growth in steamships and train transport.[15] However, sugar had become a staple among the working class in Europe and the Americas by the nineteenth century, particularly in Great Britain, where per-capita annual consumption increased from eighteen pounds in 1800 to ninety pounds a century later.[16] One of the reasons for the massive increase in sugar production in the nineteenth and early twentieth century was the improvement in technology in refining sugar from sugar beets, which favored cooler climates. Only about 50,000 tons of beet sugar were produced globally in 1841, along with 829,000 tons of cane sugar. Production of beet sugar had grown to 8,667,980 tons by 1910, which was slightly higher than the amount of cane sugar produced that year. Germany produced about a third of the total beet sugar on the market, followed by Austria, France, and Russia.

While the market for sugar in Syria did grow with the international sugar boom, it did so primarily later in the nineteenth century, as the Ottoman Empire was incorporated into the global economy. New transnational contacts expanded alongside a burgeoning middle class in the Levant that was now able to buy products such as sewing machines and phonographs that previously had been either unavailable or unaffordable.[17] Sugar imports to Syria and Lebanon grew from £S14,000 (Syrian pounds) in 1837 to £S607,000 in 1913, much of it consumed in Lebanon.[18] As Akram Khater has shown, over a period of twenty years following the opening of the Suez Canal in 1869, the amount of sugar imported to Beirut more than tripled. Consumption expanded not only among middle-class urbanites but also in peasant villages in Mount Lebanon, thanks to the growth of the local silk industry, remittances from abroad, and salaries from young women working as servants in cities.[19] As shown in the following sections, sugar and sweets consumption in Lebanon remained considerably higher than in Syria between the end of World War I and the start of World War II, but the use of sugar throughout Syria exploded: it became a pantry staple for nearly everyone.

### After World War I

The Central and Western European beet-sugar industry, which made up around half of total global sugar yields in the early twentieth century, was devastated during World War I.[20] Just over 4 million tons of beet sugar were produced on the global market in 1920, less than half of the output a decade earlier. Germany's sugar industry did not regain its footing until the late 1920s due to several factors: the continued difficulty of obtaining artificial fertilizer, growing labor unrest, and the loss of 10 percent of the country's sugar factories to Poland in the Treaty of Versailles.[21] Other European beet-sugar producers recovered more quickly: Czechoslovakia was one of the principal suppliers of sugar to Syria by 1924, along with Java, France, and Belgium.[22] Worldwide beet-sugar production doubled between 1920 and 1925 and surpassed its pre-war peak by 1935. Cane-sugar cultivation surged even more dramatically: it was nearly double beet-sugar production by 1940.[23]

The Levant states imported 8,000 tons of sugar and 164 tons of sweets in 1913. During the war, the Allies imposed a blockade on the Ottoman Empire, which was one of the causes of the devastating famine in Syria and Lebanon from approximately 1915 to 1918. Before the direst part of the famine set in, diminishing sugar imports led to a greater reliance on *dibs*.[24] In 1919, immediately after the war, fewer than 4.5 tons of sugar and 48 tons of sweets were imported due to both the contraction in worldwide production and the recovery of local economies.[25]

Paul Huvelin, a French supporter of the mandate who conducted a study of the economic potential of the Levant after World War I, thought that encouraging sugarcane cultivation in the region would allow Lebanon and Syria greater self-sufficiency and an additional cash crop for export.[26] Mohammed Sarrage, a Syrian student at a French university during that period, also recommended cultivating sugarcane and sugar beets in the area of Homs and the Bekaa in Lebanon in his 1935 critique of mandate agricultural policy.[27] France did invest in other cash crops (cotton and tobacco) to the benefit of French businesses while neglecting investment and support of other areas of agriculture, but the cultivation of sugarcane never caught on. A group of Syrian investors seriously began to explore the possibility of growing sugar beets in 1934, however, even sending samples of experimental plants to Italy and planning a refinery in Der-ez-Zor in the east or al-Qamishli in the northeast.[28] A beet-sugar refinery had also been in the works prior to World War I. Though beets have a lower yield than sugarcane, they require less irrigation, fertilization, or mechanized cultivation and add nutrients to the soil, while sugarcane reduces the soil's fertility. Some people claim that they are indistinguishable in taste, though a recent nonscientific blind taste test declared cane sugar a clear winner. Professional chefs assert that there is a difference in cooking properties.[29] The Syrian sugar plan never came to fruition, though small amounts of sugarcane were cultivated during World War II and sent to Egypt to be refined.[30] The first sugar refinery in Syria was built in Homs following the country's independence in 1946.

As the economy gradually began to improve following the war, sugar became more affordable for regular consumers. Sugar cost about 10.54 Syrian piastres (cents) per kilogram in June 1921.[31] The average daily wage of a male industry worker in Aleppo that year was 75 piastres, while a male agricultural worker earned an average of 35 piastres per day.[32] Sugar prices on the Damascus market continued to drop as sugar imports continued to rise; granulated sugar from Java cost 6.7 piastres and sugar cubes cost 7.75 piastres a kilo in March 1935. The amount of crystallized (granulated) sugar imports alone was around 32,000 tons in 1937, rising to nearly 36,000 tons the following year, more than four times the prewar imports. The average daily wage for a worker in Damascus in 1937 was 52 piastres.[33] Due to the instability of the French franc, to which the Syrian pound was tied, it is difficult to compare prices from different periods of the mandate with total accuracy. The clear increase in sugar imports, however, alongside its decreasing price and a rise in wages, indicates an expanding market, in spite of fluctuations that occurred during turbulent periods, such as the Great Revolt in Syria from 1925 to 1927, the Great Depression, and the general strike in 1936. The latter was a two-month boycott successfully led by the political opposition, merchants, and consumers that closed down markets, bringing the country's economy to a halt.[34]

Despite the increase in sugar consumption during the interwar period, some areas of Syria remained outside of the trend. In the remote village of Dayr 'Atiyya in the Qalamun Mountains outside of Damascus, sugar did not become a staple until the 1950s. The village had four commercial producers of *dibs* in the 1930s. Cash was not widely used in the area until the 1940s, but *dibs* was often used as barter. Even though it is less than 60 miles from Damascus, Dayr 'Atiyya's remote location and the lack of motorized vehicle traffic and accessible roads kept it from being fully incorporated into the region's trade.[35]

## Sweets, Past and Present

Syrians have consumed the same types of pastries since at least the eighteenth century, whether made with sugar or *dibs*.[36] In his dictionary of trades in Damascus, Jamal al-Din al-Qasimi describes one of the many sweets specialists: *qaṭīfātī*, the makers of *kunāfa* (a pastry made with dough that resembles shredded noodles layered over cheese) and *qaṭā'if* (a cheese-stuffed sweet pancake).[37] There are numerous variations of *kunāfa*, including *al-biṣāma*, made with pistachios or almonds and layered with a sweet filling made with cheese or cream held between two layers. *Kunāfa al-madlūqa* is uncooked and brushed with sugar and the cooking fat *samn* (ghee), covered with a layer of cream and then sprinkled with toasted pistachios. Najat Qassab Hassan, who was born in Damascus in 1921, devotes a section of his memoir to Damascene sweets, describing a version of *qaṭā'if*, the small round pancakes lightly grilled and then covered in cream and drizzled with sugared syrup. These *qaṭā'if al-aṣāfīr* were so delicious that Hassan describes a friend eating one after the other until he reached a limit, with five of the sweets in his mouth. He could not close his mouth or swallow and had to spit them all out.[38] Hassan, who came from a wealthy family, saw this gluttony as humorous as opposed to wasteful: he had plenty of sugar and sweets to eat.

In his semiautobiographical novel set during the 1930s in northern Syria, Hanna Mina describes a meal prepared by the narrator's aunt and uncle and their neighborhood friends for the Christian Feast of Epiphany, which included *'awāmāt* (fried sweet dough balls) and *zankal* (a similar sweet made with fried dough).[39] For Mina, whose family was mired in poverty during the interwar years and faced starvation during particularly dire moments, the consumption of sweets was limited to holidays.[40] Poor Damascenes could purchase pieces from trays of leftover *kunāfa* for a fraction of the cost of fresh portions of regular size, according to Hassan.[41] Siham Tergeman, whose memoir chronicles her childhood during the mandate in Damascus, was raised in a relatively well-to-do Sunni household, where sweets (which included *'awāmāt, zankal,* and different types of *kunāfa* and *qaṭā'if*) were consumed on a regular basis. Tergeman's mother, who cooked for the family, used both sugar and *dibs*, depending on the dish (*dibs* was sometimes used even when sugar was available because of its specific flavor and consistency).[42]

Even as Syrians became more and more dependent on sugar in their daily lives, the sale of sugar and sweets would rise during holiday seasons. Certain desserts were reserved for special occasions. Tergeman describes eating *karāwiyya*, a sweet pudding prepared with caraway seeds and different types of nuts, at a celebration welcoming a new baby hosted at a neighbor's home. *Aṭbāq al-jirādiq*, a pastry made exclusively during Ramadan, consists of dough cooked over a copper *sāj* and topped with *dibs*—a process that has remained relatively constant from the late nineteenth century to the present.[43] Hassan fondly remembers sweets consumed during Ramadan during his childhood in the 1920s and 1930s, such as *al-kul wa-l-shakūr*, a small pastry similar in appearance to baklava. Among the most famous holiday sweets was *maʿmūl*, a cookie that Hassan notes was usually prepared in the home and enjoyed at Eid al-Fitr. He describes his childhood memory of watching *maʿmūl* bake in the oven as it hardened into its mold.[44]

## Sweets Industry

Except for sugar, almost all of the ingredients in Syrian-made sweets—various nuts, apricots, flour, *samn*, and cream—were produced locally. European-made sweets also found a niche market in the Levant. Syria and Lebanon imported nearly fifty tons of sweets in 1919, mostly from France and Great Britain, including candies, sugared fruits, and jams, amounting to about half of the level of prewar imports. As the economy slowly began to bounce back after the war and the Great Revolt of 1925–1927, the market for sweets rebounded, with 347 tons of sweets imported in 1927, a high for the 1920s and early 1930s.[45] The amount of sweets imports declined between 1928 and 1931, perhaps in part because of the growth in production of local sweets.

The local sweets industry consisted of relatively small operations with or without some form of mechanized production manufacturing candy, sugared fruit, jam, pastries, and chocolates. In Aleppo, 350 men and 400 children were officially employed in candy or pastry production in 1926.[46] A 1926 French study found that the local candy industry produced twenty to thirty tons a year of sugar candies, barley candy, and caramels, prepared in hundreds of small shops (the exact number was impossible to ascertain). These candies, said to be popular among both urban and rural Syrians, could be purchased for twelve piastres per kilo in bulk.[47]

Damascus had two factories making halva (a confection made with sugar and tahini paste), one producer of fruit conserves, and seven manufacturers of candy, nougat, and chocolate by 1934. A 1945 directory of Syrian businesses lists twelve sweets makers in Damascus and six in Aleppo.[48] Syria and Lebanon had far fewer alimentary industries than industries such as textiles and tobacco.[49] It is not clear from labor statistics how many people worked at each establishment. Even after it became easier to import machinery, however, even sweets producers of means were slow to mechanize their production process.[50]

During the early part of the French Mandate, the expansion of industry in Syria and Lebanon stalled due to repressive French tariffs, among other obstacles. French tariff policy was initially based on Ottoman policy, which was an 11 percent tariff on all articles. This was raised to 15 percent in 1924 and then again to 25 percent for League of Nations members in 1926, which included Syria and Lebanon as French Mandates. The tariff was finally readjusted in 1928, at which point industrial machinery and certain raw materials could be imported at a lower rate. The tariffs for items required for candy and sweets production, such as tinfoil and glass containers, were lowered. The sugar duty, however, remained quite high. Tariffs on prepared sweets were also high, which gave prospective native industries incentive to produce lower-cost items for the local market.[51]

Fruit and vegetable conserve factories were among the industries in Syria and Lebanon that benefited from the reduced tariff schedule. The Syrian Conserves Company, founded in 1932 by Shukri al-Quwwatli, a leading member of the National Bloc opposition party, was buoyed by his financial and political connections as well as access to the fruit of the family's orchards in the Ghouta region outside of Damascus. The company employed around 200 workers during canning season by the late 1930s and produced around twenty-five tons of canned fruits and vegetables, which were consumed locally and sold for export.[52] Quwwatli's company produced about 150 tons of fruit conserves in 1942, along with a variety of processed vegetable products, employing around 1,500 workers during the high season.[53] Emile Cortas registered a trademark in Beirut in 1928 for Cortas Brothers jam. It was made from "the best selected fruit and the finest white sugar" according to its label, which was printed in English.[54] Cortas produced 12,000 kilograms of jam in the first trimester of 1934.[55] By World War II, the company had the capacity to employ 400–500 workers during the canning season and 50 workers in the off-season, producing 300 tons of jam a month.[56]

Worldwide chocolate production quadrupled between 1890 and the start of World War I. Chocolate in Syria had been a luxury item before the war due to its short shelf life in warm weather, but its popularity grew locally during the mandate as prices decreased and global production more than doubled between the wars. In his 1919 study of the economic potential of Syria, Paul Huvelin noted that chocolate was popular only among the European community in the Levant, which consumed an average of 100 tons a year before the war, the majority imported from Switzerland.[57] Whether or not his assertion was correct, chocolate makers courted local consumers after the war. The daily Damascus newspaper *Alif Ba'* printed an advertisement for milk chocolate bars from the Swiss company Chocolat Tobler (also known as Toblerone) in 1923. These chocolate bars, which were available for purchase at Suq al-Bazuriyya in Damascus, were said to be low in price and healthy.[58] During the interwar period, Arabic-language Syrian newspapers contained many fewer advertisements than European and American newspapers and generally promoted big-ticket consumer products like cars, electric fans, and radios.[59] The spots purchased by Toblerone or the local distributer of the chocolates indicate that Syria (at least the population of newspaper readers) was seen as a budding market. Another French study in 1926 asserted that chocolate was no longer considered a luxury in the Levant but an everyday item.[60]

Chocolate imports were divided into several categories, the most popular of them being *boules à la crème*. These chocolates from Belgium cost fifty to fifty-five piastres a kilo in 1926, whereas the less popular French version cost between seventy piastres and £S1.15 per kilo. Beirut purchased about 60 percent of the imported *boules à la crème*, Damascus 17 percent, and Aleppo 17 percent. Another type of imported chocolate treat, called "chocolats assortiment riche" by the French, included chocolates made with nougat, pistachios, or praline (an almond-based sweet filling). France provided the Levant with 60 percent of this import, which ranged in price from eighty piastres per kilo for chocolate with nougat, the most popular and least expensive type, to £S2.00 per kilo for chocolate made with almonds. The most important chocolate product in the 1920s on the local market was called *dragées* in French and *malabas* in Arabic. About 200 tons of these small candies with a hard outer shell and a nut or chocolate center were consumed in Syria and Lebanon, most produced locally.[61]

The first establishment specializing in the production of chocolate in the Levant opened in 1925 in Beirut. The factory, which was considered rudimentary by the French, produced *boules à la crème*, *malabas*, and hard candy. Beirut-made *malabas* cost thirty-five to forty piastres per kilo for chocolate filling or seventy-five piastres per kilo for high-quality almond-filled *malabas*, whereas the French product sold for up to £S1.50. Two years later, Beirut, Damascus, and Aleppo each had five similar shops, producing made-to-order chocolates for local clientele.[62] It is not clear whether these chocolate manufacturers were already established as candy makers and then expanded their production to include chocolate, but one Syrian confection maker, Sadek Ghraoui, whose company was founded in Damascus in 1805, began to work with chocolate after visiting a trade fair in Paris in 1931.[63] Though Syrian-manufactured chocolate was considered inferior by the Frenchman who conducted the market study because of the use of lower-quality materials, the local chocolates did well on the market because of their affordability. They were sold in bulk in large, light wooden boxes without special brand markings. This local chocolate sold for about thirty-five Syrian piastres per kilo in 1926.

Nearly 260 tons of chocolate were imported to Syria and Lebanon in 1929, far surpassing the 100 tons imported annually before the war. An article from a 1931 French trade publication claimed that some of the Levantine chocolate establishments were in the process of installing more up-to-date machinery and were beginning to use better-quality ingredients.[64] Al-Dalati, a Damascus sweets and chocolates shop, advertised its wares in 1934 in the Damascus daily newspaper *al-Qabas*, describing an assortment as *mūzā'īk sharqīyya* (Eastern mosaic), emphasizing native production to differentiate its products from more expensive and less familiar imports.[65] This was also a period when Syrian nationalists advocated economic nationalism and buying locally made products, a movement that was typically more visible in textiles and clothing marketing.[66]

Another industry that expanded during the interwar years was the production of sweet biscuits. A box of high-quality imported sweet biscuits cost about £S3.60 per kilogram in 1920.[67] Over 200 tons of biscuits were imported into Syria and Lebanon in 1929, mostly from the Belgian company Social Belge. French and British biscuits were considered the highest quality. A kilogram of British biscuits sold for 80 to 120 piastres in 1934, and French biscuits at 60 to 80 piastres. Biscuits made at the Beirut factory Jabre cost between 37 and 60 piastres per kilogram.[68] Jabre produced 9,000 tons in 1934, and the Lebanese biscuit manufacturer Chelabi made about 5,000 tons. Local biscuits, however, had a difficult time competing with the low-cost Social Belge product or with Palestinian biscuits. Syria and Lebanon imported 774,845 piastres worth of Palestinian biscuits and over 5 million piastres worth of biscuits from Europe in 1931.

Palestinian sweets producers had an advantage over their neighbors when sugar tariffs were eliminated in 1931, enabling them to lower production costs and prices.[69] Syria and Lebanon were the primary export market for sweets companies Lieber and Elite in the Yishuv in the mid-1930s.[70] Confectionary and chocolate were among the few industries that did not suffer during the Great Depression or the Arab revolt in Palestine from 1936 to 1939. In fact, confectionary and candy jumped from 1,489 Palestinian pounds (£P) in total exports in 1934 to £P21,895 in 1937. Chocolate exports rose from £P266 in 1934 to £P4,594 in 1937.[71]

## Conclusion

The growing trade in sugar and sweets between the mid-nineteenth and mid-twentieth centuries offers a window into transformations in the Syrian economy, consumer patterns, and industries. The increase in the use of sugar was part of a larger pattern of the changes in agriculture, technology, trade, and consumption. Worldwide sugar production nearly doubled between 1920 and 1940—from 17 to 30 million tons. The trade in chocolate also grew phenomenally, quadrupling between 1914 and 1940.[72] Imports of foreign sweets increased as well, thanks to falling sugar prices and expanding trade. The gradual mechanization of the sweets industry brought lower-priced candy and chocolates to the local market, making sugar an everyday staple. Syrian sugar consumption grew after World War II and continued this upward trend until 2010, mirroring global patterns. Syrian families consumed an average of thirteen pounds of sweets during the Eid al-Fitr holiday at the end of Ramadan in 2005.[73]

Since the 2011 outbreak of the conflict in Syria, the Damascus branch of Bakdash has continued to sell its specialty, Syrian ice cream made with mastic (a plant resin) and *saḥlab*, which is derived from orchid roots, pounded and stretched with large wooden pestles until it reaches an airy, chewy consistency. The store has faced frequent closures by government authorities, however, including a three-day period in 2018 due to the alleged dirty equipment and contaminated materials.[74] Declining sales resulting from the war led the store's owners to open a branch in Amman in 2013. This has been a bittersweet undertaking: it offers the many Syrian refugees living in Jordan (representing one out of every fourteen people there) a taste of the familiar *būẓa* while reminding refugees of the continued destruction of their country.[75] Other Bakdash outlets have been opened in Lebanon and Dubai in recent years. Members of the Ghraoui family, owners of the famous chocolate company of the same name, were forced to abandon their factory in eastern Ghouta in 2012, as the area has been a stronghold for rebels and a target of government attacks. The family resettled in Hungary, opening a new chocolate factory in 2017, with plans to open a Paris boutique.[76]

Many people who have never been to Syria are learning about the country or at least its culinary history through the growing Syrian diaspora. Across the Middle East, Europe, and the Americas, resettled Syrians have opened numerous small-scale sweets operations or otherwise earn a living in the food industry.[77]

In addition to 6.7 million Syrians living outside of their country, another 6 million have become displaced internally.[78] Many who have remained in the country have faced horrific violence. The death toll had reached approximately 585,000 by early 2020.[79] According to the United Nations, as of April 2019, an estimated 9 million people in Syria require emergency food assistance and 6.5 million of them face starvation. Sugar has become a luxury item in Syria once more.[80]

## Acknowledgments

A few years ago, I met Anny Gaul and Graham Pitts for the first time at the Archives Diplomatiques in Nantes, a serendipitous moment for me. They have both been incredibly generous with their knowledge and contacts within the Middle East food studies community, which has been growing in large part due to their encouragement and hard work. I am so thankful to Anny, Graham, and the staff of the Center for Contemporary Arab Studies at Georgetown University for organizing the conference from which this book evolved. It was one of the most enjoyable academic conferences of my career. I would like to express my gratitude for the invaluable suggestions and guidance on this chapter from Rachel Laudan and Vicki Valosik. I thank all of my fellow participants in the conference not only for offering insight on my paper but for their work on their own chapters and past published scholarship, which have been essential to my understanding of my own research. As always, I am so thankful to have such a supportive and wise dissertation advisor in Dr. Beth Baron at the Graduate Center, City University of New York (CUNY). I would also like to express thanks to my CUNY colleagues and professors for managing to be both gentle and constructive in their feedback on my work.

## Notes

1. The Levant, known locally as Bilad al-Sham, is an area that encompasses Syria, Lebanon, Transjordan, and Palestine.

2. Damascene peddlers were famous for their poetic and musical street cries, signaling their arrival and the goods they were selling. Michel Barbot, "Cris de la rue à Damas," *Bulletin d'études orientales* 25 (1972): 291–318.

3. Records show that ice was brought down from mountains in Mediterranean regions as early as the thirteenth century; the famed Italian ice trade of the fifteenth century is said to have been inspired by the practices and technology of Mamluk royalty; Elizabeth David, *Harvest of the Cold Months: The Social History of Ice and Ices* (Ann Arbor: Viking, 1995); Richard Thoumin, *Géographie humaine de la Syrie centrale* (Paris: Librairie Ernest Leroux 1936), 168.

4. Muhammad Sa'id al-Qasimi, Jamal al-Din al-Qasimi, and Khalil al-'Azm, *Qamus al-Sina'at al-Shamiyya* (Paris: Mouton, 1960), 72.

5. Wadea Kassab, *The Memoirs of Wadea Kassab* (Raleigh, NC: Moise A. Khayrallah Center for Lebanese Diaspora Studies, 1954), 15, lebanesestudies.omeka.chass.ncsu.edu /items/show/13966.

6. Nazik Ali Jawdat, *Remembering Childhood in the Middle East: Memoirs from a Century of Change*, ed. Elizabeth Warnock Fernea (Austin: University of Texas Press, 2002), 25.

7. Ibrahim Alalou, "Arabian Ice Cream: The Road Less Traveled," *Medium*, 11 May 2017, medium.com/invironment/arabian-ice-cream-the-road-less-traveled -82fcfc41828a; Siham Tergeman, *Daughter of Damascus* (Austin: University of Texas Press, 1994), 50–51.

8. Abdul-Karim Rafeq, "The Economic Organization of Cities in Ottoman Syria," in *The Urban Social History of the Middle East, 1750–1950*, ed. Peter Sluglett (Syracuse: Syracuse University Press, 2008), 111.

9. Sa'id al-Qasimi, et al., *Qamus al-Sina'at al-Shamiyya*, 282.

10. Suhayl Sayyid and 'Awn 'Alam al-Din, *al-Dalil al-'Arabi lil-Tijara wa al-sina'a wa al-Mihan wa al-Hiraf wa al-Hatif wa al-Masalih al-'Amma fi Suriya wa Lubnan 1945* (Beirut: Matabi' Sadir Rihani, 1945), 234.

11. Sidney Mintz, *Sweetness and Power: The Place of Sugar in Modern History* (New York: Penguin Books, 1985).

12. Tsugitaka Sato, *Sugar in the Social Life of Medieval Islam* (Leiden: Brill, 2005), 23.

13. Charles Perry, *Scents and Flavors: A Syrian Cookbook* (New York: New York University Press, 2017).

14. Maxime Rodinson, "Recherches sur les documents arabes relatifs à la cuisine," *Revue des études islamiques* 17 (1949): 147.

15. James Grehan, *Everyday Life and Consumer Culture in Eighteenth-Century Damascus* (Seattle: University of Washington Press, 2007), 117.

16. Steven C. Topik and Allen Welles, "Commodity Chains in a Global Economy," in *A World Connecting, 1870–1945*, ed. Emily S. Rosenberg (Cambridge, MA: Harvard University Press, 2012), 754.

17. For consumer practices in late nineteenth-century Beirut, see Toufoul Abou-Hodeib, *A Taste for Home: The Modern Middle Class in Ottoman Beirut* (Stanford: Stanford University Press, 2017).

18. Charles Issawi, *Fertile Crescent, 1800–1914: A Documentary Economic History* (Oxford: Oxford University Press, 1988), 35; Ministère des Affaires Étrangères, La Courneuve, France (MAE-Courneuve), C186/1, "La Syrie commerciale et son avenir," P. Gilly (1920).

19. Akram Khater, *Inventing Home: Emigration, Gender, and the Middle Class in Lebanon, 1870–1920* (Berkeley: University of California Press, 2001), 43.

20. In the case of Germany, the largest supplier of beet sugar, this was due to government policy during the war, which banned exports. This devastated the internal market and led the government to order a 25 percent reduction in acreage for the 1915–1916 harvest. Cultivation was also severely hindered by the shortage of labor, draft animals, and fertilizers. John Perkins, "The Organisation of German Industry, 1850–1930: The Case of Beet-Sugar Production," *Journal of European Economic History* 19, no. 3 (Winter 1990): 566.

21. Topik and Welles, "Commodity Chains," 767–769.

22. Haut Commissariat de la République Française en Syrie et au Liban, *Bulletin économique de l'office commercial pour la Syrie* (Beirut: Imprimerie des lettres J. G., 1924).

23. Topik and Welles, "Commodity Chains," 769.

24. Melanie Tanielian, "The War of Famine: Everyday Life in Wartime Beirut and Mount Lebanon (1914–1918)" (PhD diss., University of California, Berkeley, 2012), 60.

25. Though the primary focus of this project is Syria, most sugar and sweets were imported through Beirut. Lebanon and Syria were treated as one economic bloc under both Ottoman and French Mandate policy, so food products made in Lebanon (most of which were consumed locally) would have been sold in Syria as well. Therefore, Lebanon is included here when relevant.

26. Paul Huvelin, "Que vaut la Syrie?," *L'Asie française* 197 (December 1921): 37.

27. Mohammed Sarrage, *La nécessité d'une réforme agraire en Syrie* (Toulouse: Imprimerie du Sud-Ouest, 1935), 103.

28. "Une raffinerie de sucre en Syrie," *Commerce du Levant* (4 August 1934): 1.

29. Marion Nestle, "Cane Versus Beet Sugar—A Difference?," *Food Politics*, 17 August 2017, foodpolitics.com/2017/08/cane-versus-beet-sugar-a-difference.

30. National Archives and Records Administration (NARA), RG 169, Box 2804a, "Survey of Syria," 1942–1943.

31. MAE-Courneuve, C186/1, Haut Commissariat de la République Française, *Bulletin économique mensuel des pays sous mandat français* (July 1921). In April 1922 there were approximately 54.7 piastres to the dollar, so the cost of sugar was around $0.19 and $0.20 a kilo, respectively. Norman Burns and Allen D. Edwards, "Foreign Trade," in *Economic Organization of Syria*, ed. Sa'id Himadeh (Beirut: American Press, 1936), 264.

32. Ministère des Affaires Étrangères, Nantes, France (MAE-Nantes), Office du Levant 20, "Renseignements sur le régime du travail," 10 May 1927. Almost 21 tons of sugar were imported into the Levant in 1924. The following year, imports jumped to 26 tons, at 2.5 million Syrian pounds. Nearly 32 tons were imported in 1928 for over £S3 million, reaching 34 tons in 1929 at £S3.4 million, indicating a price drop. Prices continued to fall as imports increased, following international sugar production. Worldwide sugar yields grew from nearly 17 million tons to 27 million tons between 1920 and 1935. Prices in Beirut were about 7 piastres per kilo for crystallized sugar in October 1931 and about 9 piastres per kilo for sugar cubes. Crystallized sugar cost 7 piastres per kilo in Damascus at the end of June 1930, and cubes cost 9 piastres per kilo. About 31,000 tons of sugar were imported in 1935 at around £S620,000: George Hakim, "Conditions of Work in Syria and the Lebanon under French Mandate," *International Labour Review*, 513 (1939): 520.

33. The amount of crystallized sugar imported always far surpassed sugar-cube imports; in 1935, for example, fewer than 1,000 kilos of the total sugar imports were sugar cubes. Haut Commissariat, *Inspection Générale*, 45; The National Archives (TNA), Kew, Richmond, UK, FO 371/23279, "Annual Report, Economic (A) for 1938," Consul General Havard to Viscount Halifax, 16 May 1939.

34. TNA, FO 684/9, MacKareth to Eden, 27 January 1936; Robert Parr (Aleppo) to Eden, 29 January 1936; MacKareth to Eden, 10 February 1936; Parr to Eden, 29 February 1936; MacKereth to Eden, 4 March 1936; Philip Khoury, *Syria and the French Mandate: The Politics of Arab Nationalism, 1920–1945* (Princeton: Princeton University Press, 1987), 458.

35. Abdallah Hanna, *Dayr 'Atiyya: al-Tarikh wa-l-'Umran* (Damascus: IFEAD, 2002), 68, 225, 229.

36. Grehan, *Everyday Life*, 118.

37. Saʿid al-Qasimi, et al., *Qamus al-Sinaʿat al-Shamiyya*, 357.

38. Najat Qassab Hassan, *Hadith Dimashqi, 1884–1983* (Damascus: Tlasdar, 1988), 153, 155.

39. Hanna Mina, *al-Mustanqaʿ* (Beirut: Dar al-Adab, 1977), 136–138.

40. The city of Alexandretta in the sanjak of the same name was part of Syria and had a majority Arab population until the French Mandate authorities ceded it to Turkey in 1937. Mina's family was among the 50,000 refugees who fled Alexandretta for Syria after the concession, which is described at the end of *al-Mustanqaʿ*. The province is now part of Turkey and is known as Hatay.

41. Hassan, *Hadith*, 157.

42. Tergeman, *Daughter of Damascus*, 50–51.

43. Tergeman, *Daughter of Damascus*; "al-Dimashqiyin Yahtafun bi Ramadan bi-Anuaʿa Kathira min al-Halwiyat," *al-Bayan* (25 September 2006). A *sāj* is a concave metal pan used on an open flame, often to make single-layer flatbreads common in the region.

44. Hassan, *Hadith*, 153.

45. Norman Burns, *The Tariff of Syria, 1919–1932* (Beirut: American Press, 1933), 218.

46. Many women were employed in textile production in Aleppo, but no women were recorded working officially in food-producing industries from 1926 to 1927. "Activité des industries à Alep durant l'année 1927 et le nombre des travailleurs utilisés durant cette même période," *Bulletin annuel de Chambre de Commerce d'Alep* 16 (31 December 1927): 66–67.

47. MAE-Courneuve, Office du Levant 20, P. Gilly, "Chocolat: Commerce en Syrie," 15 September 1926.

48. Sayyid and ʿAlam al-Din, *al-Dalil al-ʿArabi*, 237.

49. "Le nombre des industries à Damas," *Commerce du Levant* (4 August 1934), 2.

50. Frank Peter, "Dismemberment of Empire and Reconstitution of Regional Space: The Emergence of 'National' Industries in Damascus between 1918 and 1946," in *The British and French Mandates in Comparative Perspectives*, ed. Nadine Méouchy, Peter Sluglett, Gérard Khoury, and Geoffrey Schad (Boston: Brill, 2003), 432.

51. Burns, *The Tariff*, 218.

52. Khoury, *Syria and the French Mandate*, 281.

53. TNA, FO 922/145, "Note sur la situation industrielle des états du Liban et de la Syrie," 1 January 1942.

54. "Marques de fabrique, déposées à l'office de protection de la propriété commerciale et industrielle," *Annexe au Bulletin officiel du Haut-Commissariat de la Republique Française en Syrie et au Liban* (15 February 1929): 1, gallicak.bnf.fr/ark:/12148/bpt6k648684oh/f13.image.r=beurre.

55. "La situation économique au Liban au cours du 1er Trimestre 1934: Rapport des services économiques du gouvernement libanais," *Commerce du Levant*, 21 July 1934, 9.

56. NARA, RG 169, Box 2804a, "Survey of Syria," 1942–1943.

57. Huvelin, "Que vaut la Syrie?," 37.

58. "Toubler Malik al-Shukulata," *Alif Baʾ* (16 August 1923), 3.

59. Ami Ayalon, *The Press in the Arab Middle East: A History* (New York: Oxford University Press, 1995), 206.

60. MAE-Courneuve, Gilly, "Chocolat."

61. MAE-Courneuve, Gilly, "Chocolat."

62. MAE-Courneuve, Gilly, "Chocolat."

63. Joanna Kakissis, "A Syrian Chocolatier's Legend Lives on in Europe—But Stays Close to Its Roots," National Public Radio (31 January 2019), npr.org/sections /thesalt/2019/01/31/686522425/a-syrian-chocolatiers-legend-lives-on-in-europe-but -stays-close-to-its-roots.

64. Marcel Hegelbacher, "Les états du Levant sous mandat français et le commerce des produits sucrés," *Revue de la chocolaterie, confisserie, biscuiterie, confiturerie* 64 (October 1931): 33.

65. "Ist'adad lam yasbaq lahu mithal," *al-Qabas*, 31 August 1934, 7.

66. Philip Khoury, "The Syrian Independence Movement and the Growth of Economic Nationalism in Damascus," *British Society for Middle Eastern Studies* 14, no. 1 (1987): 25–36.

67. MAE-Courneuve, C186/1, "La Syrie commerciale et son avenir," P. Gilly (1920).

68. "La situation économique du Liban au cours du 3ème trimestre 1934," *Commerce du Levant*, 17 October 1934.

69. MAE-Nantes, 1/SL/V 717 CP-3, "Rapport du 2ème Congrès des Chambres de Commerce des États sous Mandat, Beyrouth," 20–22 March 1933.

70. Cyrus Schayegh, *The Middle East and the Making of the Modern World* (Cambridge, MA: Harvard University Press, 2017), 238 n. 87.

71. Sa'id B. Himadeh, "Industry," in *Economic Organization of Palestine*, ed. Sa'id B. Himadeh (Beirut: American Press, 1938), 253.

72. Topik and Welles, "Commodity Chains," 803.

73. Sarah Birke, "Syrian Sweets Becoming an International Sensation," *Christian Science Monitor*, 30 September 2010, csmonitor.com/World/Global-News/2010/0930 /Syrian-sweets-becoming-an-international-sensation.

74. "Muhafazat Dimashq Taghlaq Buzat Bakdash li-l-marra al-thaniyya," *'Inab Baladi*, 13 August 2018, *enabbaladi.net/archives/246378.*

75. Rotem Maimon, "Syria's Famous Ice Cream Is Melting Hearts in Jordan," *Haaretz*, 21 August 2008, haaretz.com/middle-east-news/.premium-syria-s -famous-ice-cream-is-melting-hearts-in-jordan-1.6407892.

76. Kakissis, "A Syrian Chocolatier's Legend."

77. Peter Schwartzstein, "Syria's Beloved Sweet Shops Follow Its Refugees into Exile," *National Geographic*, 16 June 2016, nationalgeographic.com/people-and-culture /food/the-plate/2016/06/syria_s-beloved-sweet-shops-follow-its-refugees-into-exile.

78. UNHCR/The UN Refugee Agency, "Global Trends: Forced Displacement in 2018" (20 June 2019), 3, unhcr.org/5d08d7ee7.pdf.

79. Syrian Observatory for Human Rights, "Nearly 585,000 People Have Been Killed since the Beginning of the Syrian Revolution," 4 January 2020, syriahr.com/en /?p=152189.

80. "Syria's Famed Sweets Bringing Smiles Once More," *Agence France Presse* (2 November 2017), arabnews.com/node/1187036/middle-east.

# CHAPTER 4

# Pistachios and Pomegranates: Vignettes from Aleppo

ANTONIO TAHHAN

The scent of milk simmering on the stove transports me to my grandmother's kitchen in Caracas. I remember sitting on the counter, my feet dangling as she stirred figure-eights in an oversized pot of *ruzz b'ḥalīb*—the Middle Eastern version of rice pudding. She kept her windows open and fans running. The cool touch of the stone counter felt good on my skin.

Once the milk thickened, she would turn off the stove, wait a few moments, then add a splash of rose and orange blossom water to the pot. If you add it too soon, *btrawwiḥ al-ṭaʿmeh*, she used to warn me (you'll dilute the flavors).

Twenty-five years later, I still prepare *ruzz b'ḥalīb* the way my *sitto* did. I add the rose and orange blossom water the way she did. I ladle it into individual cups. I sprinkle a dash of cinnamon on each one and refrigerate them, uncovered. That is how you get the creamy layer on top, she taught me. It was always the most satisfying part to eat. This humble dessert is an expression of my grandmother's affection. It is a tradition that I continue to share with my friends.

I was born in Venezuela to a Syrian family and grew up in Miami. Conversations at home were a mix of English, Spanish, and Arabic. The boundaries between these worlds have always been blurry. It was not rare to wake up to arepas alongside *manāʾish zaʿatar*, a classic flatbread coated with a zesty blend of zaʿatar and olive oil. We celebrated special occasions with oversized batches of stuffed grape leaves and outdated Arabic music—the kind my grandparents listened to in 1950s Syria. As a nine-year old, my favorite singer was Umm Kulthum (she still is).

Our kitchen table was crowded with small plates of mezze that were meant for sharing. When we visited relatives in Venezuela, my mom used to catch up with aunts, neighbors, and my grandmothers over marathon food preparations. Tabbouleh was a team sport. After hours of chopping, I remember the wood cutting boards would be stained green. Chopping parsley was an excuse to gather. Cooking was always a social activity.

There's a saying in Arabic, *baynatnā khubz wa-miliḥ* (between us, there is bread and salt). It recognizes the social role that food plays in bringing people together. This collaborative approach to cooking taught me that food is more than just eating. It taught me that food is a vehicle for passing down traditions and that food is how you take care of one another, both physically and emotionally.

Growing up in an Arab-ish home, if there was an easy way and a complicated way of preparing a dish, my grandmothers insisted on the complicated way. The tastiest stuffed grape leaves were also the tiniest—about the size of your pinky. You could tell the quality of kibbe by how pointy the tips were on each end. The cookies from my childhood were made from semolina soaked in butter, stuffed with dates, flavored with orange blossom water, and individually stamped with hand-carved wooden molds. While these complications may seem unnecessary, they celebrate the collaborative nature of their preparation and the artistry of their makers.

These communal practices are rooted in a long culinary tradition. For thousands of years, the act of preparing a meal has been a collaborative effort. It literally took a village to put food on the table. Harvesting olives, coring vegetables, baking bread—these tasks were as much social as they were practical. This approach is shared across many cultures. From twisting pasta into tiny tortellini in Bologna to stuffing tamales in Puebla, these labor-intensive culinary traditions are meant to be prepared together.

I received a Fulbright research grant in 2010 to study Syrian food culture in Aleppo. I spent nine months in home kitchens, listening to women who taught me the value of an afternoon rolling grape leaves. Mirroring those moments from my childhood, I cored and stuffed, rolled and shaped, alongside home cooks for hours in the day. Conversations that started about eggplants and parsley unraveled into stories of romance and companionship, culture and politics.

On my way to the vegetable market in Aleppo one morning, I realized I was lost. I walked up to a middle-aged man with a graying mustache. He was standing at the corner of a busy intersection snacking on a bag of pistachios. I cleared my throat as I approached him: *Marḥaba* (hello), I said in my distinctly foreign accent. My "h" (*ḥā'*) did not quite carry the bravado of a native Arabic speaker. *Ahlayn* (hello), he replied enthusiastically, as if he was greeting an old friend. For a moment I wondered if I had met this man before. I smiled and asked if he could point me in the direction of the vegetable market.

Before he responded, he extended his bag of pistachios toward me. *Tafaḍḍal* (please, have some), he exclaimed, shaking the bag a few times. My American upbringing taught me not to accept food from strangers, so I declined politely. I made sure to say *shukran* (thank you), so as to not offend. But he insisted. Having lived in Aleppo for a few months, I understood that this was part of an intricate, well-established hospitality dance. When you see it take place between two locals, it is more like a waltz—both sides giving and taking, insisting and declining, before finally accepting. The foundation of this dance is based on the idea of *karam* (generosity). It is ingrained in Syrian culture. Food is a natural way for Syrians to express their *karam*.

We exchanged stories as we walked down the busy street. I mentioned that I was an American Fulbright student studying lunch in Aleppo. While everyone in the Middle East takes pride in their food, Aleppans are famous for their cuisine. There's a saying in Arabic: *Ḥalab imm al-maḥāshī wa-l-kibab* (Aleppo is the mother of stuffed vegetables and kibbes). He assured me that I had come to the right place and referred to Aleppo as the culinary capital of the Middle East.

Over thousands of years Aleppo was conquered and reconquered many times. Under the Ottoman Empire, it established itself as a bustling merchant city, a hub of ethnic and religious diversity. It was the nexus of three continents linking east and west, along the Silk Road. Communities from Armenians and Assyrians to Christians and Circassians to Jews, Kurds, and Muslims claimed Aleppo and its cuisine as part of their collective identity.

Once the conversation shifted to food, the awkwardness of our initial interaction faded. The man was excited to share all the dishes I needed to taste: *hayṭaliyyeh, kabāb b'karaz, sujuq, muḥummara.*[1] As we passed prominent landmarks, he interjected facts about a city he clearly loved. He insisted on walking with me until we reached the suq. Once we arrived at the market, he extended his bag of pistachios another time. I could not say no again: that would be considered *'ayb* (rude).

I reached in the bag and popped a few pistachios in my mouth. They were dry-roasted and salted. I thanked him again—*shukran* (thank you)—and added *ya'ṭīk al-'āfiyeh* (I wish you well). He responded by extending his open hand across his chest, over his heart, saying *yā miyat ahla wa sahla* (you are most welcome, a hundred times over).

Food, especially elements of generosity around eating, is a source of pride and honor for many Syrians. On a trip to Bassouta, we visited a small Kurdish farming village in the outskirts of Aleppo. As we were approaching the village, our van broke down not far from an orchard. Bassouta is famous for its pomegranates, so I took this opportunity to explore on my own. I started weaving through an endless maze of pomegranate trees when I stumbled upon a farmer crouched over a mountain of his harvest. He greeted me with a smile. Without thinking twice, or asking who I was, he grabbed a pomegranate from his pile, cracked it open, and offered it to me. Food remains the ultimate manifestation of hospitality in Middle Eastern culture. Taking care of strangers and sharing what you have is ingrained in the ethos of the region.

During my stay in Syria, I met many people like the middle-aged man and the pomegranate farmer who showed me great hospitality, pride, and kindness. These interactions are the highlights of my time in Syria. From simple gestures of sharing to the many hours spent preparing meals together, my experience in Syria reinforced what I have intuitively understood from my earliest childhood memories—the value of time and generosity in fostering relationships with those we know and those we are still getting to know.

## Sitto's Rice Pudding

Serves approximately 12

### Ingredients

1 cup medium-grain rice*
3 quarts milk (whole or 2 percent)
1 cup granulated sugar
2 tablespoons orange blossom water
1 tablespoon rose water
Ground cinnamon, to garnish

### Directions

1. Rinse rice under cold water (until the water runs clear), then drain.

2. Combine milk and rice in a large pot over medium-high heat. Stir regularly in a figure-eight pattern to prevent the rice from sticking to the bottom.

3. Once the milk reaches a simmer, reduce the heat to medium-low. Continue stirring regularly to draw out the starch from the rice.

4. Cook, uncovered, for about an hour or until the milk thickens. When you run your finger along the back of the spoon, the streak should remain visible. If the milk bleeds into the streak, continue cooking. Note that the milk will continue to thicken as it cools in the refrigerator.

5. Add sugar and cook for five more minutes.

6. Remove from heat and add orange blossom and rose waters.

7. Ladle into individual glass (or other heat-safe) cups, garnish with ground cinnamon, and refrigerate, uncovered,** for a few hours or until ready to serve.

* Calrose and Egyptian rice are ideal varieties of medium-grain rice. Long-grain rice does not have sufficient starch, and short-grain rice tends to have too much, which can lead to a clumpy consistency.

** If you plan to prepare more than a day in advance, cover each cup with plastic wrap to keep the pudding from drying out.

## Note

1. *Hayṭaliyyeh* is a classic dessert that made its way to Aleppo from Asia by way of the Silk Road, which has three components: milk cubes thickened with cornstarch (traditionally wheat starch), milk ice cream, and a milk sauce infused with rose water and orange blossom water. *Kabāb b'karaz* is a classic Aleppan dish of kebabs cooked in a sweet and sour cherry sauce. *Sujuq* is a fragrant Armenian sausage flavored with lots of garlic and seasoned with cumin, allspice, fenugreek, salt, and pepper. *Muḥummara* is a popular Aleppan dip prepared with red peppers and walnuts, infused with pomegranate molasses.

**PART II**

# REVISITING FOODWAYS IN ISRAEL-PALESTINE

# Urban Food Venues as Contact Zones between Arabs and Jews during the British Mandate Period

DAFNA HIRSCH

The dominant paradigm in scholarship on the history of Mandate Palestine until the 1990s was that of a "dual society." In the words of historian Zachary Lockman, this paradigm "has been premised on the implicit or explicit representation of the Arab and Jewish communities in Palestine as primordial, self-contained, and largely monolithic entities ... with distinct and disconnected historical trajectories."[1] The last three decades have witnessed a shift away from this dual society model toward the idea of relational history, which is based on the assumption that neither Arab nor Jewish societies in Palestine can be understood separately from their encounter with one another and the constitutive effects of this encounter for both societies. While relational history need not necessarily focus on actual social encounters, this trend has given rise to many studies focusing on relationships and contacts between Arabs and Jews in various spheres of life.

One of the spheres where contact between Jews and Arabs took place on a regular basis was food and eating. Given the manifold activities involved in the process of producing, selling, preparing, and consuming food, contacts in this sphere took many forms. This chapter focuses on commercial food venues selling local foods during the British Mandate period as contact zones between Jews and Arabs, as well as between European Jews and Middle Eastern Jews.[2] The three "mixed cities" of Haifa, Jerusalem, and Jaffa and the Jewish city of Tel Aviv serve as the chapter's case studies.

Defining food venues as contact zones does not mean that they were spaces of sociability and reconciliation—of "breaking bread." Mary Louise Pratt defined "contact zones" as "social spaces where disparate cultures meet, clash, and grapple with each other, often in highly asymmetrical relations of domination and subordination."[3] While some commercial food venues could function as sites of friendly contact and sociability and serve as channels for cultural transmission, such venues could also be sites of suspicion, animosity, and conflict. Indeed, they were sites where some borders were crossed while others were erected.[4]

Yet Pratt's conceptualization of the contact zone is premised on the assumption of two distinct and clearly demarcated cultures that "meet, clash and grapple with each other," which is reminiscent of the dual-society thesis. Political divisions in Palestine (Jews versus Arabs) did not necessarily coincide with cultural divisions (European versus Middle Eastern or Arab). A central division within Palestine's Jewish society was between European (Ashkenazi) Jews and Middle Eastern (Mizrahi) Jews with ancestral roots in Arab and Muslim countries. For the latter, local Palestinian food, if not always familiar, was not foreign either. Often Mizrahi Jews mediated various local foods to Ashkenazi Jews through the restaurants and food stalls they operated, even when these foods were not part of the fare in the countries from which the sellers hailed.

Using food as a lens for studying intercommunal contact allows us to go beyond conflicting visions and political agendas to examine "the living experience of subjects," including the sensual and affective aspects of European Jewish settlers' encounters with the Levant and its inhabitants.[5] For this purpose, food is a particularly potent lens, given its ability to elicit powerful sensations, ranging from pleasure and longing to a sense of danger and disgust.[6] By this I do not mean to suggest that food in and of itself elicits specific affective reactions; rather, our "gut reactions" to various foods are mediated both by the practical training of our bodies and by more discursive forms of knowledge. One example was the discourse of hygiene, which contrasted salubrious Western modernity to the dirty and dangerous Orient and its foods.[7]

By exploring European Jews' early encounters with Palestinian food in this chapter, I seek to nuance the account of the Israeli adoption of various Palestinian Arab dishes and their presentation as "Israeli food" as "cultural food colonialism."[8] First, this type of account is predicated on the binary division between local Arab and European Jewish settlers, leaving Middle Eastern Jews out of the equation. Second, this concept seems to imply that cultural food colonialism "naturally" follows land colonization. Yet studies on food consumption in colonial contexts show that European settlers' adoption of foods from the indigenous repertoire, if it occurred at all, was hardly a self-evident process.[9] Reconstructing the history of Israeli adoption and appropriation of various dishes from the Palestinian-Arab menu as a sociocultural process requires that we go back to these early moments of (often ambivalent) culinary contact and try to decipher the affective reactions they elicited from European Jews.

In this chapter I draw on archival documents, newspaper and journal articles, autobiographies and memoirs, and interviews. Most materials are in Hebrew, but some are in Arabic and English.[10] While most Arabic-language archival sources on life in pre-1948 Palestine were lost during the Nakba (literally "catastrophe," the Palestinian exodus in 1948),[11] many Hebrew sources contain invaluable information on Palestinian society and ways of life, such as the materials collected by the Jewish paramilitary organization Haganah (Defense).[12]

This chapter opens with a description of the scene of commercial food venues in Palestine's urban centers during the British Mandate period. It then discusses Mizrahi Jews as mediators of local foods to Ashkenazi consumers and finally Ashkenazi Jews' reactions toward these venues and the foods they served, paying special attention to their sensual and affective aspects. As the chapter demonstrates, the most common reaction was rejection, on grounds that were both sanitary and aesthetic. At the same time, for specific groups of (mostly male) consumers, these venues—both "authentically local" and "exotic"—provided a sense of pleasure, adventure, and sometimes also danger.

## Commercial Food Venues in Palestine's "Mixed Cities"

After World War I, Palestine, which was formerly part of the Ottoman Empire, came under British Mandatory rule. According to the mandate system, the administered territories did not become imperial possessions but protected states and were to be governed by the colonial powers until their inhabitants would be "ready" for independence.[13]

In 1917 Britain issued the Balfour Declaration, supporting the establishment of a Jewish "national home" in Palestine. While small-scale immigration and settlement of nationally minded Jews had already begun by the late nineteenth century, the British Mandate period (1922–1948) saw the growth and consolidation of a Jewish national community and national institutions as well as Palestinian Arab resistance to Zionism. Immigration of Jews increased in the 1930s following the Nazi ascent to power, resulting in the Palestinian Revolt of 1936–1939. The Jewish population had reached approximately 600,000 by 1947—about 30 percent of the total population of Palestine.[14] Following the United Nations partition plan of November 1947, violent clashes broke out between the two communities, which developed into a full-fledged war after the British withdrawal in May 1948. This war resulted in the Palestinian Nakba and the establishment of the Israeli state.

The mandate years were a period of accelerated urbanization, in both the Arab and the Jewish sectors. Among Palestinian Arabs, the share of urban dwellers increased from 21 percent in 1880 to 36 percent toward the end of the mandate, mostly due to labor migration from the countryside to towns, while the Jews (both Mizrahi and Ashkenazi) had been a predominantly urban population throughout the period.[15] In both Arab and Jewish societies, a developing middle class exhibited a growing orientation toward consumption and leisure.[16] As a result of these developments, the corpus of commercial food establishments grew and diversified, including street stalls, eateries, and restaurants, which catered to various clienteles—single men seeking to fill their stomachs, recreation-seeking members of the middle class, tourists, British officials and soldiers, and others.

Between the early 1930s and 1948, half of the Palestinian urban population lived in what the British government defined as mixed cities—cities and towns where significant Arab and Jewish populations cohabited. Among the Jewish urban population, the percentage living in mixed cities decreased from 78 percent to 48 percent between 1922 and 1946.[17] Out of the seven mixed cities, it was mainly Jaffa, Haifa, and Jerusalem that exhibited the characteristics of a modernizing, capitalist, and cosmopolitan urbanity. In these cities, trends toward spatial and social segregation, which were exacerbated in the wake of violent clashes, existed side by side with shared neighborhoods, intercommunal interactions, commercial partnerships, and other forms of cooperation.[18] Yet, even in places and periods where trends of separation prevailed, cross-national relationships and encounters still took place.[19] Indeed, food was a realm in which such encounters took place on a regular basis.

The earliest and most common channel for commercial encounters between Arabs and Jews involving food was street vending. Arab vendors sold foods and foodstuffs in commercial spaces populated by both Arabs and Jews, such as Hamra Square in Haifa or, starting in the early 1920s, the Carmel market area in Tel Aviv, located along the municipal border between the two cities. Many also sold their merchandise in Jewish neighborhoods, sometimes announcing it in three or even four languages (Arabic, English, Hebrew, and Yiddish).[20] In some periods, the number of Arab vendors on the streets of Tel Aviv seems to have reached several hundred. According to municipal sources, various unofficial "markets" were formed on the border zone between Jaffa and Tel Aviv.[21]

Vendors sold either raw products such as goat milk (sometimes milked on the spot), eggs, olive oil, tahini, fruits, and vegetables or prepared foods such as falafel, *fūl* (fava beans), hummus, *mashāwī* (roasted meat), *hamleh malan* (roasted chickpea pods), *ka'k* (ring-shaped pastry) with sesame or za'atar, *būza* (ice cream made with resin of *Pistacia lentiscus*), and sweets, including a candy made from thinly crushed chickpeas and sugar. Some sold drinks from big kettles or flasks, like *saḥlab* (a sweet drink made from ground orchid tubers), *sūs* (a sweet drink made from licorice roots), tamarind juice, and lemonade.[22] Most vendors sold products from Arab farms, both in Palestine and abroad, but I also came across cases of Arab vendors selling products produced in Jewish factories.[23]

Restaurants were few and far between in the late Ottoman period and were found only in urban commercial centers. The early restaurants catered primarily to hungry men—bachelors or married men working away from home—as well as to travelers. The main culinary establishment for (male) recreation and socialization in Palestinian society, as in other countries in the Middle East, was the café, where men went to drink coffee or tea, smoke, play dice, read newspapers (or listen to them being read), and (after the mid-1920s) listen to the radio in some establishments.[24] Starting at the beginning of the British Mandate, and most notably in the 1930s and 1940s, the number of cafés and restaurants in major cities steadily increased.[25] In Haifa, alongside the "humble" cafés, which offered coffee, water-pipes, and table games, a fancier variety developed, with the capacity to serve up to several hundred people and space for dancing and artistic performances. The more upscale cafés were visited by women as well (a fact that did not go unnoticed by conservative critics), and there were even cases of women managing cafés.[26] Some of these cafés served alcoholic beverages and foods such as mezze.[27] The simpler cafés did not serve food, but people sometimes bought foods like hummus and *fūl* from other vendors and ate them in the café.

Restaurants of the period can also be categorized as simple eateries, some of which specialized in one or two items like hummus, *fūl*, or roasted meat, versus more elaborate establishments with fuller menus that included a variety of meat and vegetable dishes and stews. In both types, men were in charge of the cooking, in contrast to home cooking, which was the domain of women.[28] A 1927 article titled "Maṭāʿim" (Restaurants) in *Filastin*—the most widespread, nationalistically minded Palestinian newspaper of the time—mentioned the growing number of restaurants in Jaffa. Writing in a modernizing vein, the author reprimanded restaurant owners for their poor hygiene, lack of food safety, and exaggerated prices.[29] He wrote that if Jewish food had been palatable to Palestinians, those who wanted to indulge would undoubtedly have visited Jewish restaurants. This suggests that the notion of eating in restaurants as a form of recreation was already in effect, although it took longer to arrive in smaller towns.[30] Nevertheless, in the mid-1940s recreational restaurant dining was still much more common among Jews than among Arabs.[31]

Haifa became the major city in northern Palestine following the opening of the Hijaz train line between Haifa and Deraa, Syria, in 1905. Many spaces of leisure there were visited by both Arabs and Jews.[32] One of them was the drinks and *būza* shop of Mustafa al-Haj in the northern corner of Hamra Square, which served as a popular recreation spot for Jews on Friday evenings, when Jewish businesses were closed.[33] Sources mention different types of benign or friendly interactions between Jews and Arabs in cafés, including conducting business meetings and playing billiard and card games, as well as less benign ones, like fist-fighting.[34] The city grew in the 1930s and 1940s, following the establishment of refineries and the expansion of the port, and became a cultural center attracting visitors from throughout Palestine and abroad. The number of cafés and restaurants increased: in the early 1940s the Haganah listed seventy-eight cafés and fifty-eight restaurants owned by Arabs in Haifa, mostly downtown.[35] Many of these restaurants were patronized by Jews as well.[36] According to Mordechai Ron, the morning fare was *fūl* with olive oil—sometimes alongside hard-boiled eggs—served with pita bread, a plate of pickles, and a jug of cold water, while hummus reigned during the day. The cook prepared the hummus on the spot and scooped it onto a plate, wiping the edge with his thumb. The dish would be topped with fava beans and olive oil. J. M. (born 1937 in Haifa) noted in an interview how she and her friends used to laugh at Jews who came to eat hummus and *fūl* in the restaurants near the entrance to the port, quoting the Arabic saying "What do donkeys understand about ginger?"[37]

Besides hummus and *fūl*, Ron mentions other dishes that Jewish customers ordered in Arab restaurants, including stuffed vegetables, grape leaves, and vegetables cooked in olive oil or tomato sauce. Some ordered meat, which was often hung on a hook in the entrance to the restaurant. The customers selected their cut, which the owner then chopped with a big knife before adding parsley, salt, and spices and placing the meat on a skewer to be roasted on the fire. Meat was also served in the form of shish kebab or *ṣīnīyya* (meat and vegetables in either tahini or tomato sauce cooked on a brass tray). Some restaurants—especially those that functioned as a meeting place for Muslims, Christians, and Jews—served alcohol and mezze, which could contain a large selection of different dishes.[38]

A café and restaurant culture was also developing in Jerusalem around the same time, particularly in the 1930s, when the presence of the British army led to a growth in the service sector. This attracted both Palestinian and Jewish labor migrants.[39] Many of these food and drink establishments—of both European and Middle Eastern type, either Arab- or Jewish-owned—became sites of intercommunal interaction.[40] According to Salim Tamari, the establishments located at the periphery of the new neighborhoods around the area of Musrara, Jaffa Gate, and the vicinity of the Russian compound provided a particularly cosmopolitan milieu.[41] Yet Jews visited not just these types of establishments but sometimes also simple restaurants in or around the Old City.[42] Journalist Dorothy Kahn Bar-Adon described an "oriental" restaurant inside the Damascus Gate "that displays its wares most temptingly" and serves "humas salad" (prepared without tahini)—at the time unknown to many or most of her readers: "a symphony of color and taste, if it suits your taste. It is made of a bean which is grown in most parts of the country, the beans that vendors sometimes roast on the street. But after the beans are crushed and mixed with oil and lemon and properly garnished in the leisurely Oriental fashion, they are hardly recognizable."[43]

In Jerusalem the Haganah counted sixty-two Arab-owned cafés, restaurants, and canteens and at least nine "hummus kitchens."[44] On the whole, however, eating out as a form of recreation was more prevalent in the coastline cities of Haifa and Jaffa than in more conservative Jerusalem.[45]

A different situation prevailed in the Jewish city of Tel Aviv, which grew out of a neighborhood established by some of Jaffa's Jewish residents who sought to distance themselves from the "Oriental" city and establish a modern and Western "garden suburb."[46] Tel Aviv was home to a third of the county's Jewish population by the late 1930s.[47] The arrival of bourgeois Jewish immigrants in the 1920s and 1930s and the presence of British security forces, which had been growing since the beginning of the Palestinian Revolt, accelerated the development of a vibrant dining scene in Tel Aviv, including restaurants, cafés, and bars—some more fashionable than others. Tel Aviv, with a population of 160,000, had more than four hundred cafés and restaurants by 1939.[48] However, Tel Aviv and Jaffa were never entirely separate: several Jewish neighborhoods, which were part of the Tel Aviv urban sequence, actually belonged to the municipality of Jaffa,[49] while much of the northern Jaffa neighborhood of Manshiyeh, where Arabs and Jews cohabited, was encircled by Tel Aviv's municipal borders. Jaffa remained the urban center for Tel Aviv's residents until the 1930s, but Jews continued to go to Jaffa for governmental, commercial, and recreational purposes even later.[50] In neighborhoods on the border zone between Jaffa and Tel Aviv, inhabited predominantly by Mizrahi Jews, Arab and Jewish stores, workshops, restaurants, and cafés could be found side by side. These were visited by members of the two national groups.[51]

With all due respect to the author of the cited *Filastin* article who implied that Arabs avoided Jewish restaurants, commercial culinary encounters actually went both ways. Arabs, typically those of higher social status, did visit Jewish cafés and restaurants, but to a lesser extent—given Arabs' lower rates of restaurant attendance. Members of the new Palestinian middle class were often attracted to the European cafés and restaurants, with their foreign aura, although Arabs visited Jewish-owned restaurants serving Middle Eastern food as well.[52] Some Jewish-owned establishments that sold alcohol and hosted entertainment shows like cabarets and belly dancing attracted Arabs from neighboring countries. *Filastin* itself published advertisements for Jewish-owned cafés and restaurants, suggesting that they were indeed patronized by Arabs.[53]

Yet these culinary encounters were also impacted by intercommunal tensions, bursts of politically motivated violence, and economic bans from both sides. Starting in the 1920s, and intensifying after the outbreak of the revolt in 1936, an organized Zionist "buy local" campaign, which in effect meant "buy Jewish," put increasing pressure on businesses and customers to boycott Arab produce.[54] Following the violent nationalist clashes of 1929, Arab merchants in Jewish neighborhoods were sometimes beaten and their merchandize damaged.[55] The Tel Aviv municipality played an important role in the campaign, actively encouraging consumers to buy Jewish produce and controlling the influx of products into the city.[56] Produce from Arab farms was usually cheaper than produce from Jewish farms, however, so many Jewish customers continued to buy it. Therefore, Tel Aviv remained an attractive destination for Arab vendors.

The violent nationalist clashes of 1921 and 1929 (followed by an Arab ban on Jewish businesses in Jaffa in 1929) and the Palestinian Revolt, which started with a six-month commerce and labor strike, slowed down intercommunal commerce and promoted greater spatial segregation.[57] Jews and Arabs continued to work side by side in the Carmel market, but any argument could easily turn into a feud.[58] According to the author of a 1946 article on an "Oriental" café near the Carmel market, Mizrahi Jews used to spend time in cafés in Jaffa before the Palestinian revolt, but after the revolt they "transferred the atmosphere [of Jaffa] to the heart of Tel Aviv" by opening establishments of similar style and ambiance.[59]

Nevertheless, many Jews continued to patronize Jaffa in the years after the revolt, especially during the "quiet" years of World War II.[60] Heavy traffic of Tel Aviv residents to Jaffa was noted on days when Jewish cafés and restaurants were closed (such as Saturdays, Yom Kippur, or Passover, when people went to Jaffa to look for bread).[61] Famous Israeli author Haim Gouri (1923–2018) mentions a row of Arab restaurants in the Jaffa neighborhood of Manshiyeh, where he would sometimes eat in the 1930s and 1940s.[62] Future judge Gabriel Strassman (born 1931) wrote that Jews looking for "Levantine dishes" in the

1940s would occasionally go to Wadi Nisnas in Haifa, the Old City of Jerusalem, or Arab Jaffa.[63]

## Middle Eastern Jews Selling Local Food

As Sami Zubaida notes, Middle Eastern foodways, while far from homogeneous, are nevertheless describable in a vocabulary and set of idioms that are "often comprehensible, if not familiar, to the socially diverse parties," within which "differences and boundaries are drawn and redrawn, negotiated and altered."[64] Thus, for the Jews who arrived in Palestine from the Middle East, Palestinian Arab foods and foodways were "comprehensible, if not familiar," even if some of the dishes were previously unknown to most of them. For example, *hummus bi-l-ṭaḥina* (hummus with tahini) was consumed mainly in the Levant, a region from which only a minority came, mostly after the foundation of the state.[65] They found nothing extraordinary or exotic in the consumption, preparation, and selling of foods from the Palestinian Arab kitchen. Therefore, it was often Mizrahi Jews who mediated local foods to Ashkenazi consumers, as street food vendors and restaurant owners.

Jews from Arab and Muslim countries arrived in Palestine both before and during Zionist immigration waves from Europe. The local Sephardic community held political and economic dominance within Jewish society during most of Ottoman rule in Palestine, but their position began to weaken in the second half of the nineteenth century. It further declined with the increase in Zionist immigration from Eastern Europe at the beginning of the twentieth century, especially after the establishment of British Mandatory rule and the foundation of Jewish national institutions. Political power shifted to Eastern European Zionists, who sought to distance themselves from what they considered to be manifestations of the "old" unenlightened and unproductive Jewish culture and from the Orient in general and to shape the new "Hebrew" society and culture along modern and Western lines. Social and spatial segregation along ethnic lines increased during the mandate years. Most Mizrahi Jews were concentrated in the lower and lower-middle classes and were generally unassimilated into Zionist society and institutions, though there were exceptions, mainly among Sephardic groups.

Many Mizrahi Jews made their living by selling local foods on the streets of major cities. Yehoshua Zalivansky, who was born in Tel Aviv in 1919 to an Ashkenazi family, tells in his memoirs about an elderly Mizrahi woman who used to sit on the sidewalk on Tel Aviv's Shabazi Street next to a giant pot on a Primus stove and prepare hummus sometime in the late 1920s or early 1930s. When the chickpeas were soft, she would pound them to a paste in an earthenware dish, add olive oil, lemon, and spices (but no tahini!), and hand it to her customers, who ate standing up. After each customer finished eating, she would wipe the plate, refill it, and hand it to the next customer. Zalivansky first tried the hummus out of curiosity but later ate it whenever he had the chance because it was tasty and he liked the atmosphere in this "standing restaurant for beggars."[66] Other Mizrahi Jewish vendors sold falafel, which by the late 1930s had become quite prevalent and popular on the streets of Tel Aviv. In an article from 1939 titled "Seaside Temptations," nutritionist Lilian Cornfeld described "the filafel [sic] man" as the most popular in the "unending gastronomic procession" along the shore of Tel Aviv: "He seems to give you an almost unlimited amount of food for next to nothing. . . . Unhappy the person who does not know the delights of filafel."[67] Tel Aviv had eight licensed Mizrahi falafel vendors by 1941 and others who sold falafel without a license.[68] Many of the vendors were of Yemenite origins, although falafel was unknown in Yemen.[69]

Jewish immigrants from Arab countries and the Balkans also opened restaurants serving various local and Middle Eastern dishes. Several such restaurants published newspaper advertisements announcing the serving of specific "Oriental foods," sometimes alongside "European foods." The selections of dishes usually included standard restaurant fare such as hummus, *fūl*, falafel, shashlik, and kebab—some of these being dishes that restaurant owners learned to prepare in Palestine.[70] Some of the ads stressed that the food was not only kosher but also clean and fresh, attesting to the common perception of "Oriental restaurants" as dirty and to their desire to distinguish their restaurants from such stereotypes.

Some Ashkenazi consumers seeking to experiment with local food may have opted for Jewish-owned "Oriental" restaurants due to kashrut—the Jewish religious dietary laws. Kashrut is a complex set of rules that stipulate which foods are allowed to be consumed, how they should be prepared (and by whom), and how and when they can be consumed. According to the rules of kashrut, in order to qualify as kosher, meat must be slaughtered in a specific way. Strict observers of kashrut are also forbidden to eat food prepared by non-Jews. In fact, until the 1930s, many Jewish restaurants in Tel Aviv did not observe kashrut. Meat butchered by Arabs, including prohibited animals like camels, found its way into restaurants and homes in Tel Aviv. In the course of the 1930s, nationalist and religious interests coalesced, and serving kosher meat butchered in the Tel Aviv slaughterhouse became the norm in Tel Aviv's restaurants and institutional kitchens.[71] In any case, for the observant non-Orthodox section of the Jewish population, kashrut was a flexible norm centered mostly on meat, while vegetable dishes prepared by non-Jews were tolerated.

Tel Aviv's Mizrahi population had expanded by the late 1930s, due to both migration and Jews fleeing from Jaffa during the Palestinian Revolt. The number of Jewish-owned Middle Eastern restaurants increased.[72] For the refugees, selling food was one of the most accessible options for creating income from small initial investments. Those who were granted permits to open food establishments received some primary financial help.[73] Most of these restaurants were clustered in the southern neighborhoods of Tel Aviv on the border zone between Tel Aviv and Jaffa, where contact between Jews (mostly Arabic-speaking Mizrahis) and Arabs was more prevalent than in other parts of the city.[74] Indeed, restaurants were one public space in which such contacts occurred on a regular basis.

## European Jews' Experience of Arab and Mizrahi Restaurants and Food Stalls

How did European Jewish settlers experience local restaurants and street stalls? What were their attitudes toward the foods they served? While the various sectors of the Jewish population developed different relationships with local foods, including selective (and often temporary) adoption by rural settlers, the following section focuses on the experiences of urban dwellers.

Sources suggest that for the first generation of Ashkenazi settlers, local food sold in restaurants and in street stalls was unappealing. Kahn Bar-Adon reflected this sentiment when she wrote that "[t]he majority of the Oriental restaurants do not tend to stimulate one's appetite."[75] Expressions of repudiation of "Oriental" food and food establishments were usually couched in hygienic and sanitary terms. However, as shown earlier and as the sources make clear, the discourse of hygiene itself reflected nationalist, racial, and cultural assumptions.[76]

Many letters to the Tel Aviv municipality from both residents and merchants complained about various nuisances created by the presence of Arab as well as Mizrahi Jewish street vendors, cafés, and restaurants: litter, shouting, foul odors, and suffocating smoke.[77] For example, in a 1945 letter to the Tel Aviv mayor, one of the city's residents complained that the stench of falafel vendors close to his apartment spread through the surrounding area and deprived neighbors and passersby of the possibility of breathing fresh air. He also mentioned the "many cases" of dysentery, hepatitis, and typhus that befell adults and children after eating the vendors' falafel. He ended with a call to take any measure necessary to preserve the environment of the city and its fresh air as well as the health of residents, especially the younger generation.[78] As this letter suggests, in a city that sought to fashion itself as modern, Western, and Hebrew, the presence of "Oriental" vendors was perceived as out of place.

A popular spot for food vendors was outside schools, where they aroused the concern of teachers, managers, and school physicians. The journal *Hed HaMizrah* (Echo of the East) brought the story of twelve-year-old Rachel, a recent immigrant from Syria who lived in one of Haifa's Arab neighborhoods. Due to her family's dire financial situation, she found work in a restaurant where the owner let her take a hundred falafel balls and sell them on the street. Rachel would sell them to children at small schools. The author of the article, probably a teacher, writes that Rachel was afraid of him because she heard him tell the pupils that falafel was bad for the stomach and they should not eat it.[79] Israeli author David Shacham tells how he used to buy falafel from a Yemeni vendor next to his school in Tel Aviv in secret, because his mother was sure that it was full of germs.[80]

In 1941 the Tel Aviv municipality resolved to eliminate falafel from the streets, revoking all but two permits, but the vendors did not disappear.[81] In December 1944 Haim Halperin, the head of the newly established municipal Department of Supervision, declared a war against falafel vendors, in particular against the selling of falafel, cakes, and sweets outside of schools because they "caused severe stomach diseases like hepatitis, dysentery, and typhoid fever, as well as favism . . . especially among children of 7–8 years." Halperin asked Dr. Eliyahu Rosenbaum, the head of the Education Department of the Tel Aviv Municipality, to see to it that school principals forbade children from buying from street vendors.[82] Vendors who did not comply were fined and their property confiscated; if caught again, they could even be sent to jail.[83] Nevertheless, the vendors always came back. The campaigns targeting school children were unsuccessful too: the pupils continued to buy from falafel vendors.[84] At least part of schoolchildren's attraction to Middle Eastern foods like falafel was probably derived precisely from authority figures' admonitions to avoid it.

The notion that the selling of "Oriental" food in public spaces, especially by Arab vendors, did not fit the Hebrew city was expressed in a 1945 letter to the municipality by several owners of cafés on the Tel Aviv shore. This letter demonstrates particularly well how sanitary discourse could be wedded to nationalist sentiments and economic interests. The writers complained about a person who rented his café to four vendors: one selling salads, another falafel, another soda pop, "and the worst," an Arab selling ice cream, "while none of the Jewish cafés sell ice cream." They wrote:

Like the verse, you should purge the evil from your midst, and besides, they spoiled all the businesses. They have made it into something like a market. It's so cheap, so simple, instead of buying a sandwich at the café, people buy falafel and stuff. Such as kebab, shashlik, etc. It's a shame that we would remain silent about something like this. Both politically and hygienically. It is not nice for the Hebrew city that an Arab sells his merchandise and nobody stands in his way. At night he brings little dirty kids to help him with the business, and he himself has sick eyes, and the entire city comes by to buy his ice cream.[85]

The writers complained further about the smells, the smoke, and the loud shouts and called on the municipality to take action. While the Tel Aviv municipality fought unlawful vending in general, it made a special effort to target Arab vendors, who were defined as "foreigners" in the official documents.[86] Those who were caught were evicted and their property confiscated.[87]

Not only Arab but also Mizrahi Jewish venues were perceived as a piece of Jaffa in Tel Aviv. In May 1939, two months after the end of the revolt, a reporter of the sensational *Iton Meyuchad* (Special Journal) wrote about the restaurant of Yosef Batito, who moved from Jaffa to Tel Aviv after the revolt broke out:

Here the people of Nazareth and the descendants of Albion drink together with the daughters of Tel Aviv, without a hint of racial hatred. Here hatred and anger disappear with the appearance of arak on the tables and everyone drinks to the sounds of a gramophone, which sometimes mix with sounds of a very different kind: smashing of bottles, yelling, swearing, and the sounds of vocal fights.[88]

It is hard to know how the author of this column viewed such interracial sociability. Both the Jewish and Palestinian national movements tried to exert control over various types of national border–crossings, which were perceived as challenging and threatening, and particularly opposed "our women" mingling with "their men."[89] At the same time, this excerpt describes the situation in not entirely negative terms ("hatred and anger disappear"), although it may have been written with a pinch of irony, as the facilitator of this amicable interaction is the bottle. What is clear from this excerpt, though, is that such places were perceived as strongholds of uncivilized behavior ("smashing of bottles, yelling, swearing"), which middle-class Ashkenazim from "good homes" should stay away from.

However, some Ashkenazis, mostly men, were attracted to Arab restaurants specifically for the sense of exoticism, sensuality, and sometimes danger that visits to these restaurants evoked. Judge Gabriel Strassman described how "tahini-hummus-kebab-shashlik meals" at Arab restaurants, albeit cheap, were regarded as festive meals and as a kind of luxury. "Devouring them had something of Oriental charm," he wrote, noting that he and his friends were willing to eat in these restaurants in spite of some of the preparation methods, such as spitting on the roasting meat to improve its taste.[90] As this excerpt shows, the "exotic" allure of Arab restaurants could act as an antidote for potential feelings of disgust. According to writer Menachem Talmi, the restaurant of Abu-Laban in the Carmel market became trendy among Tel Aviv's bohemian circles in the second half of the 1940s.[91] As noted by Pierre Bourdieu, exotic foods appeal to those sectors that are richer in cultural capital than in economic capital and therefore pursue originality at the lowest economic cost.[92]

However, for some men, visiting Arab restaurants apparently involved more than distinction. Yehuda Litani, a journalist and coauthor of a guidebook to Israel's hummus joints and olive oil producers, noted in an interview that in the early 1940s members of the Jewish paramilitary organization Palmach used to visit Arab restaurants as an act of heroism.[93] I end with two literary accounts of Palestinian Arab urban spaces involving food, written by a famous Palmach warrior: Israeli writer and poet Haim Gouri. The first is the poem "A Journey to Haifa's Lower City," which he likely wrote during the war of 1948, shortly before Arab Haifa was destroyed.[94] The second is an account of his visits to Arab Jaffa during the mandate period in *The Crazy Book*, published in 1971. In both of these texts Gouri describes the Arab city in similar terms: full of smoke, smells, noises, shouts, and teeming crowds. It is a space that is decaying, malicious, threatening (Gouri explicitly mentions in his poem a "knife in the back"—obviously intended for the Jewish visitor); but it is also alluring, with its aura of exoticism, historicity, and sensual abundance. At the end of the second stanza of his poem on Haifa, Gouri explicitly mentions an "Oriental" restaurant that "assaults his senses" with the smell of roasting meat. In *The Crazy Book* he provides lengthy descriptions of the food in Jaffa, including the "za'atar powder, which carries the smell of mountains at the end of the summer" and hummus and *fūl* in a puddle of thick olive oil.[95] After the occupation of East Jerusalem, the West Bank, and Gaza in the 1967 war, Gouri described the hummus of Abu Shukri in the Old City of Jerusalem as his "madeleine cookie," which carried him back to the Jaffa and Haifa of his youth.[96]

These descriptions convey particularly well the power of food in producing a "sense of place" tied to specific geographical and human landscapes.[97] For Ashkenazi Jewish settlers, Palestinian Arab places were both threatening and (sometimes because of that) alluring; both "foreign/exotic" and "authentically local." Even as many of these foods were later "Israelized," the sense of locality and authenticity with which they were invested was never symbolically detached from their Arab source.

## Conclusion

Commercial food venues of Ottoman and Mandate Palestine have not yet been studied in depth. I hope that this chapter contributes to the description of these venues—mainly street food stalls and restaurants—by considering their function as spaces of Arab-Jewish encounters. While most of the available sources do not provide in-depth descriptions of the actual interactions that took place in these spaces, they nevertheless offer a glimpse into the burgeoning scene of street food, cafés, and restaurants in Palestine's mixed cities and in the Jewish city of Tel Aviv, where trends of separation and national segregation existed alongside social contacts and cultural exchange.

As demonstrated, it was not only Arab vendors and restaurant owners who mediated local dishes for Ashkenazi consumers. Jews who hailed from various countries in the Middle East also opened restaurants and operated street stalls where they sold local foods, some of which they had learned to prepare from Palestinian vendors and cooks. Both Arabs and Middle Eastern Jews were deemed "Oriental" by Ashkenazi settlers, the majority of whom treated these foods and food establishments with suspicion and sometimes outright aversion. Municipal authorities in Tel Aviv sought to limit the activity of street food vendors and drive Arab vendors off the city streets, but often with little success.

While most Ashkenazi settlers avoided local foods during the mandate period, some did buy from Arab or Mizrahi vendors or visit "Oriental" restaurants. More often than not, they bought products from street vendors, but some also bought prepared foods, especially members of the younger generation. At least for some adults, these venues represented more than the unwelcome presence of the Orient amid Jewish modernity and progress. Both "exotic" and "local," they offered an experience of sensual abundance, culinary pleasure, and sometimes danger. This sense of "exotic localism" or "local exoticism" still seems to accompany the visits of Israeli Jews to various Palestinian culinary spaces to this day.

## Notes

1. Zachary Lockman, *Comrades and Enemies: Arab and Jewish Workers in Palestine, 1906–1948* (Berkeley: University of California Press), 4.

2. There is no simple definition for the food repertoire that is discussed in this chapter. Defining it as "Palestinian," "Levantine," or even "local" seems to suggest a specificity that does not always apply to the foods under consideration, whereas the category of "Middle Eastern" is too broad to refer to a distinct repertoire. Therefore, throughout the chapter I use different designations according to context. Here "local food" is used in a rather descriptive manner, to refer to the food repertoire that is prepared, sold, and consumed by the country's indigenous Arab population.

3. Mary Louise Pratt, *Under Imperial Eyes: Travel Writing and Transculturation* (London: Routledge, 1992), 4.

4. Deborah S. Bernstein, "Contested Contact: Proximity and Social Control in Pre-1948 Jaffa and Tel Aviv," in *Mixed Towns, Trapped Communities*, ed. Daniel Monterescu and Dan Rabinowitz (Aldershot, UK: Ashgate, 2007), 215–241.

5. Ben Highmore, "Alimentary Agents: Food, Cultural Theory and Multiculturalism," *Journal of Intercultural Studies* 29, no. 4 (2008): 392. See also Anat Helman, "European Jews in the Levant Heat: Climate and Culture in 1920s and 1930s Tel Aviv," *Journal of Israeli History* 22, no. 1 (2003): 71–90.

6. Scholars have offered various explanations for why food is so potent in eliciting affect, including the centrality of food to negotiating self and other relationships starting in early childhood and the synesthetic qualities of food that lend it a special mnemonic power. See, for example, Michael Dietler, "Culinary Encounters: Food, Identity, and Colonialism," in *The Archaeology of Food and Identity*, ed. Katheryn C. Twiss (Carbondale: Center for Archaeological Investigations, Southern Illinois University, 2007), 218–242; Highmore, "Alimentary Agents"; David E. Sutton, *Remembrance of Repasts: An Anthropology of Food and Memory* (Oxford: Berg, 2001).

7. Dafna Hirsch, "'We Are Here to Bring the West, Not Only to Ourselves': Zionist Occidentalism and the Discourse of Hygiene in Mandate Palestine," *International Journal of Middle East Studies* 41, no. 4 (2009): 577–594.

8. Lisa Heldke, *Exotic Appetites: Ruminations of a Food Adventurer* (London: Routledge, 2015); Liora Gvion, *Beyond Hummus and Falafel: Social and Political Aspects of Palestinian Food in Israel* (Berkeley: University of California Press, 2012), 130. See also Ahmad H. Sa'di, "Catastrophe, Memory and Identity: Al-Nakbah as a Component of Palestinian Identity," *Israel Studies* 7, no. 2 (2002): 185; Ari Ariel, "The Hummus Wars," *Gastronomica* 12, no. 1 (2012): 34–42.

9. For example, Richard Wilk, *Home Cooking in the Global Village: Caribbean Food from Buccaneers to Ecotourists* (Oxford: Berg, 2006); Cecilia Leong-Salobir, *Food Culture in Colonial Asia: A Taste of Empire* (London: Routledge, 2011); Blake Singley, "'Hardly Anything Fit for Man to Eat': Food and Colonialism in Australia," *History Australia* 9, no. 3 (2012): 27–42.

10. My research assistant, Nisreen Mazzawi, collected Arabic sources and conducted interviews with elderly Palestinian men and women.

11. Manar Hasan, *The Invisibles: Women and the Palestinian Cities* (Jerusalem and Tel Aviv: Van Leer Institute Press and Hakibbutz Hameuchad Publishing House, 2017), 11 (Hebrew).

12. In the second half of the 1940s the Haganah collected detailed information about Palestinian life, settlements, and businesses (including history, social relations, economy, demography, culture, agriculture, and so forth) for intelligence purposes.

13. D. K. Fieldhouse, *Colonialism 1870–1945: An Introduction* (London: Macmillan Press, 1983), 18.

14. Deborah S. Bernstein, *Constructing Boundaries: Jewish and Arab Workers in Mandatory Palestine* (New York: SUNY Press, 2000), 21.

15. Jacob Metzer, *The Divided Economy of Mandatory Palestine* (Cambridge: Cambridge University Press, 1998), 8.

16. Deborah Bernstein and Badi Hasisi, "'Buy and Promote the National Cause': Consumption, Class Formation and Nationalism in Mandate Palestinian Society," *Nations and Nationalism* 14, no. 1 (2008): 127–150; Sherene Seikaly, *Men of Capital: Scarcity and Economy in Mandate Palestine* (Stanford: Stanford University Press, 2015); Amir Ben-Porat, *The Bourgeoise: The History of the Israeli Bourgeoises* (Jerusalem: Magnes Press, 1999), 77–80 (Hebrew).

17. Metzer, *The Divided Economy*, 7–8; Anat Kidron, "The Influence of the Results of the 1929 Events on Haifa and on Jaffa/Tel Aviv: A Comparative Look," *Israel* 22 (2014): 73 (Hebrew). Seven such cities existed: Jerusalem, Safad, Tiberius, Haifa, Hebron and Acre (both until 1929), and Jaffa (officially until 1946, but in effect until 1936).

18. Daniel Monterescu and Dan Rabinowitz, eds., *Mixed Towns, Trapped Communities* (Aldershot, UK: Ashgate, 2007), 2.

19. Mark LeVine, *Overthrowing Geography: Jaffa, Tel Aviv, and the Struggle for Palestine, 1880–1948* (Berkeley: University of California Press, 2005); Bernstein, "Contested Contact"; Tammy Razi, "'Arab-Jewesses'? Ethnicity, Nationality and Gender in Mandate Tel Aviv," *Theory and Criticism* 38–39 (2011): 137–160 (Hebrew); Kidron, "The Influence," 73–109.

20. Mordechai Ron, *Haifa of My Youth: Everyday Life in Haifa in the 1920s and 1930s* (Jerusalem: Ariel, 1993), 79–80 (Hebrew); Tziona Rabau-Katinski, *In Tel Aviv on the Sands* (Ramat Gan: Masada, 1973), 93 (Hebrew); Anat Helman, *Young Tel Aviv: A Tale of Two Cities* (Waltham, MA: Brandeis University Press, 2010), 78–89; Liora R. Halperin, *Babel in Zion: Jews, Nationalism, and Language Diversity in Palestine, 1920–1948* (New Haven: Yale University Press, 2015), 72–82.

21. Tel Aviv Historical Archive (TAHA), Nissim Asulin to Rokach, 10 March 1942, 4/355a; shop owners on the Ba'al Shem Tov street to the municipality, 19 September 1943, 4/356a; A. Litayi, Nachmani 48, to the municipal department of sanitation, 10 July 1944, 4/357b (unless noted otherwise, all documents from TAHA are in Hebrew). See also Helman, *Young Tel Aviv*, 84–86.

22. Shlomo Tiv'oni, *My Friend Had a Vineyard: Musa Al Ful* (Tel Aviv: Hakibbutz Hame'uchad, 1978), 53–54 (Hebrew); Rachel Seri, *A Tree and Its Branches: A History of a Yemenite Family* (Jerusalem: Private Edition, 1988), 59 (Hebrew); Aharon Chelouche, *From Jalabiya to Dummy Hat: The Story of a Family* (Tel Aviv: Private Edition, 1991), 81–84 (Hebrew); Ron, *Haifa of My Youth*, 48–52; Hannah Bezalel, *Lifetimes* (Jerusalem: Private Edition, 2004), 163–164 (Hebrew).

23. TAHA, Head of the Department of Municipal Supervision, Haim Halperin to Mayor Rokach, 9 May 1947, 4/360c. Helperin complained that in recent weeks Tel Aviv was filled with "foreign" lollipop vendors who were hired by "local" (namely, Jewish) factories.

24. Ami Ayalon, *Reading Palestine: Printing and Literacy, 1900–1948* (Austin: University of Texas Press, 2004), 103–106; Bernstein and Hasisi, "Buy and Promote," 131; Maayan Hilel, "Cultural Changes in Palestinian Arab Society, 1918–1948: Haifa as a Case-Study" (PhD diss., Tel Aviv University, 2018), 83, 166–167 (in Hebrew); interview with S. H., Nazareth, 19 April 2012 (interviewer: Nisreen Mazzawi). Some cafés hosted illicit activities such as prostitution and drug dealing, and some functioned as centers for political organization. Haim Fireberg, "Tel Aviv: Change, Continuity and the Many Faces of Urban Culture and Society during War (1936–1948)" (PhD diss., Tel Aviv University, 2003), 275; Hilel, "Cultural Changes," 87–89, 219.

25. According to Hilel, in the second half of the 1940s villagers, too, began appealing to the Haifa municipality to request a license to open cafés and restaurants in their villages. Hilel, "Cultural Changes," 298.

26. Manar Hasan and Ami Ayalon, "Arabs and Jews, Leisure and Gender, in Haifa's Public Spaces," in *Haifa before and after 1948: Narratives of a Mixed City*, ed. Mahmoud Yazbak and Yfaat, Series 6 (The Hague: Institute for Historical Justice and Reconciliation, 2011), 73, 87; Hasan, *The Invisibles*, 97–98; Hilel, "Cultural Changes," 218–219, 232, 248–256.

27. Salim Tamari, *Mountain against the Sea: Essays on Palestinian Society and Culture* (Berkeley: University of California Press, 2008), 181. Mezze is a selection of small vegetable and dairy dishes that are served as appetizers or accompanying alcohol.

28. Liora Gvion, "Cooking, Food, and Masculinity: Palestinian Men in Israeli Society," *Men and Masculinities* 14, no. 4 (2011): 408–429.

29. On the place of hygiene and sanitation in the making of the culture of the middle class, see Seikaly, *Men of Capital*, 53–76. On hygiene and culture building in Jewish society, see Hirsch, "We Are Here to Bring the West."

30. Anonymous, "Mataʻim," *Filastin*, 28 October 1927 (Arabic). See also Hasan and Ayalon, "Arabs and Jews," 69–98; Seikaly, *Men of Capital*, 66; Israeli State Archive (ISA): 5220/13-m, Price Control Office, Galilee District Nazareth, 27 April 1946, Statement of the accused, Sami Haj Said H. Sheikh of Safed. See also interview with S. H.

31. Anonymous, "Palestine Restaurants Are Popular," *Palestine Post*, 5 July 1944.

32. Hasan and Ayalon, "Arabs and Jews"; Hilel, "Cultural Changes," 333–335.

33. Ron, *Haifa of My Youth*, 80; Yaacov Davidon, *Once Upon a Time Haifa . . .* (Tel Aviv: Bitan, 1983), 57–60 (Hebrew).

34. Hilel, "Cultural Changes," 333–334.

35. Hilel, "Cultural Changes," 89.

36. Ron, *Haifa of My Youth*, 92; interview with J. M., Haifa, 26.1.2012 (interviewer: Nisreen Mazzawi).

37. Interview with J. M., meaning "x knows/understands nothing about y."

38. Ron, *Haifa of My Youth*, 92–93.

39. Martina Rieker, "Modern Histories of Jerusalem's Old City: Culinary Practices and Popular Mapping(s) of Palestinian Social Spaces," in *Pilgrims, Lepers and Stuffed Cabbage: Essays on Jerusalem's Cultural History*, ed. Issam Nassar and Salim Tamari (Jerusalem: Institute of Jerusalem History, 2005), 87.

40. Tamari, *Mountain against the Sea*, 176–189; Menachem Klein, *Lives in Common: Arabs and Jews in Jerusalem, Jaffa and Hebron* (Oxford: Oxford University Press, 2014), 130–135.

41. Tamari, *Mountain against the Sea*, 182.

42. Gabriel Strassman, "Oriental Restaurants," *Ma'ariv*, 21 July 1955.

43. Dorothy Kahn Bar-Adon, "Oriental Gourmet: Lamb, Techina, Humas," *Palestine Post*, 10 February 1941.

44. Haganah Archive, "Cafés, Restaurants and Canteens," 1947 (exact date unreadable), 105/24.

45. Hilel, "Cultural Changes," 287. Food shops and restaurants represented a larger share of the businesses (49 percent and 15.4 percent, respectively) in Tel Aviv than in the rest of the Yishuv (47.1 percent and 14.1 percent, respectively). Fireberg, "Tel Aviv," 85.

46. LeVine, *Overthrowing Geography*; Fireberg, "Tel Aviv," 30–31. Tel Aviv gained the status of a township in 1921 and an independent city in 1934.

47. Fireberg, "Tel Aviv," 6.

48. TAHA, "A list of cafés and restaurants in Tel Aviv," 2 July 1939, 1087/2314; Yaacov Shavit and Gideon Biger, *The History of Tel Aviv*, vol. 2 (Tel Aviv: Ramot, 2007), 270 (Hebrew). Shavit and Biger note 254 cafes, bars, and restaurants in 1941 (far short of the number of names listed in the municipal archive dated to 1939) and 422 in 1946. Fireberg, "Tel Aviv," 272. Fireberg notes 254 cafes, bars, and restaurants at the end of 1941 and 422 at the second half of 1946.

49. A disproportionately large percentage of their population consisted of Mizrahi Jews. Fireberg, "Tel Aviv," 26.

50. Fireberg, "Tel Aviv," 2.

51. Bernstein, "Contested Contact"; Klein, *Lives in Common*, 68–70.

52. Hasan and Ayalon, "Arabs and Jews," 75; Tikva Weinstock, "The East Conquers the Stomachs of the West . . . ," *Ma'ariv*, 2 August 1951; TAHA, Shlomo Ajami, letter to Tel Aviv mayor Israel Rokach, 30 November 1942, 2315/4. See also Klein, *Lives in Common*, 82; Hilel, "Cultural Changes," 176, 334.

53. Bernstein and Hasisi, "Buy and Promote," 45; Bernstein, "Contested Contact," 224.

54. Helman, "European Jews in the Levant Heat," 79; Bat-Sheva Margalit Stern, "'Mothers at the Front': The Struggle for 'Buying Local' and the Confrontation between Gender and National Interests," *Israel* 11 (2007): 91–120 (Hebrew); Bernstein and Hasisi, "Buy and Promote"; Hizky Shoham, "'Buy Local' or 'Buy Jewish'? Separatist Consumption in Interwar Palestine," *International Journal of Middle East Studies* 45, no. 3 (2013): 469–489; Yael Raviv, *Falafel Nation: Cuisine and the Making of National Identity in Israel* (Lincoln: University of Nebraska Press, 2015), 52–59.

55. Kidron, "The Influence," 97. See also Haim Gouri, *The Crazy Book* (Tel Aviv: Am Oved, 1971), 89–92 (Hebrew).

56. Shoham, "Buy Local," 479.

57. For example, Ron, *Haifa of My Youth*, 89; Kidron, "The Influence," 73–109; Yaacov Shavit and Gideon Biger, *The History of Tel Aviv*, vol. 1 (Tel Aviv: Ramot, 2001), 99 (Hebrew).

58. Anat Helman, *Urban Culture in 1920s and 1930s Tel Aviv* (Haifa: Haifa University Press, 2007), 112 (Hebrew).

59. "A Short While with the Eaters of Kubbeh and Players of Backgammon: Atmosphere Photographs from an Oriental Café in the Heart of Tel Aviv," *Special Journal* 10, no. 482 (26 July 1946): 5. See also Helman, *Young Tel Aviv*, 127–128; Bernstein, "Contested Contact."

60. Fireberg, "Tel Aviv," 43; Klein, *Lives in Common*, 74. For Haifa, see Hasan and Ayalon, "Arabs and Jews"; Hilel, "Cultural Changes," 334.

61. "A Quick Tour on the Streets of Jaffa on Saturday," *Special Journal* 5, no. 160 (8 March 1940) (Hebrew); "The Joy of Yom Kippur Turned This Year into Mourning for Restaurant Owners in Jaffa," *Special Journal* 6, no. 241 (3 October 1941), 6 (Hebrew); Israel Goldschmid-Paz, "Jaffa As It Is: People among the Ruins," *Al Hamishmar*, 2 January 1953 (Hebrew). Leavened bread is prohibited on Passover and therefore most stores do not sell it.

62. Hagor (Haim Gouri), "Thirty Years," *Davar*, 2 December 1977.

63. Strassman, "Oriental Restaurants."

64. Sami Zubaida, "National, Communal, and Global Dimensions in Middle Eastern Food Cultures," in *A Taste of Thyme: Culinary Cultures of the Middle East* (1994), ed. Sami Zubaida and Richard Tapper (London: I. B. Tauris, 2000), 33.

65. The number of Jewish immigrants from the Levant that arrived in the country during the mandate period was 10,000. Yaron Tzur, "The Immigration from Islamic Countries," in *The First Decade, 1948–1958*, ed. Zvi Zameret and Hanna Yablonka (Jerusalem: Yad Yitzhak Ben Zvi, 1997), 61 (Hebrew).

66. Yehoshua Zalivansky, *Tel Avi, Tel Aviv* (Tel Aviv: Y. Golan, 1994), 88 (Hebrew). All translations are by the author unless otherwise noted. I am grateful to Asaf David for referring me to this text.

67. Lilian Cornfeld, "Seaside Temptations: Juveniles' Fare at Tel Aviv," *Palestine Post*, 19 October 1939.

68. TAHA, 4/355a. The Tel Aviv municipality granted vending license to people who could not make their living in any other way as a form of welfare.

69. Many of the immigrants from Yemen arrived in Palestine via Egypt, so it is possible that they learned to prepare it there and then adjusted the recipe to the Palestinian version, which was made from chickpeas and not from fava beans (*ṭaʿmiya*). Shmuel Yefet, an Israeli falafel maker, tells about his father, Yosef Ben Aharon Yefet, who arrived in Palestine from Aden in the early 1920s and then traveled to Port Said in 1939. There he became acquainted with *ṭaʿmiya*, learned to prepare it, and then went back to Palestine and opened a falafel shop in Tel Aviv: youtube.com/watch?v=nzihYViJFQM (29 January 2017).

70. I have gathered several testimonies from the early 1950s (though no earlier) about Mizrahi Jewish restaurant owners who learned to prepare hummus from Arab neighbors, acquaintances, or restaurant owners.

71. Helman, *Young Tel Aviv*, 121; Alma Igra, "Meatropolis: Tel Aviv's Slaughterhouse and Demarcation of Urban-National Boundaries in Palestine, 1927–1938" (M.A. thesis, Central European University, 2012), 48–50.

72. Weinstock, "The East Conquers the Stomachs"; Kidron, "The Influence," 73–109. Fireberg, "Tel Aviv," 78. According to Fireberg, the Jewish businesses in Jaffa that were harmed during the revolt included twenty-five "drink dealers and restaurant owners."

73. Fireberg, "Tel Aviv," 89, 194. The help was received from a local Zionist fund that was established in the wake of the revolt for social and security purposes. Fireberg, "Tel Aviv," 144–145.

74. Bernstein, "Contested Contact"; Razi, "'Arab Jewesses'?" See also Shavit and Biger, *The History of Tel Aviv*, vol. 2, 238.

75. Kahn Bar-Adon, "Oriental Gourmet."

76. Hirsch, "We Are Here to Bring the West."

77. For example, TAHA, tenants of the Levine House to mayor Rokach, 30 May 1945, 4/357c; a longtime resident of Tel Aviv to the mayor, 10 December 1945, 4/359a.

78. TAHA, a longtime resident of Tel Aviv to the mayor, 10 December 1945, 4/359a.

79. Moshe Rabi, "The Falafel Seller (Everyday Life in Haifa)," *Hed HaMizrah*, 28 January 1944 (Hebrew). When the author asks Rachel what the falafel balls are made of, she answers: chickpeas and dry bread, to which pepper is added in order to make them spicy and tasty.

80. David Shacham, *Requiem to Tel Aviv* (Tel Aviv: Sifriyat Hapo'alim, 2010), 55 (Hebrew).

81. TAHA, the Tel Aviv mayor to the Department of Social Work, 9 November 1941, 4/355a.

82. TAHA, Halperin to Dr. Rosenbaum, 5 December 1944, 4/357b.

83. TAHA, Gabriel G. Ya'acov, in the name of the Organization of falafel vendors to the Tel Aviv mayor, 18 December 1944, 4/357b (vending permits, August 1944–December 1944); Halperin, internal memo to the municipal secretary, 29 January 1945, 4/357c; "Strong Accusations by Falafel Vendors," *Special Journal* 9, no. 401, (22 December 1944): 3 (Hebrew).

84. TAHA, A. Rosenbaum, director of the Department of Education to Haim Halperin, director of the Department of Municipal Supervision, no date, 4/357b.

85. TAHA, several café owners to the municipal department of sanitation, 9 July 1945, 2315/4.

86. TAHA, manager of the license department to the municipal secretary, 29 July 1941, 4/355a. Lacking a centralized welfare system, the Tel Aviv municipality used vending permits as a form of social welfare and granted such permits to people who were unable to make their living in any another way. In 1944, for instance, about 500 licensed vendors were on the streets of Tel Aviv (of whom 386 sold food). Arabs were barred from obtaining such permits.

87. Supervisors were authorized to evict the vendors and issue either a warning or an invitation to court (in the case of vendors who either refused to leave or were caught more than once). In effect, the supervisors often confiscated the property of vendors (both equipment such as carts, trays, and scales and merchandise). While Jewish vendors usually received their property back after reporting to court, Arab vendors were much less frequently sent to court, so their property was not returned.

88. "An Expensive Cheap Love," *Special Journal* 3, no. 126 (21 May 1939), 4 (Hebrew).

89. Bernstein, "Contested Contact"; Boaz Levtov, "'The Same Sea': Jews and Palestinians at the Beach in the Late Ottoman and Mandate Periods," in *Encounters: History and Anthropology of the Israeli-Palestinian Space*, ed. Dafna Hirsch (Jerusalem and Tel Aviv: Van Lear Institute Press and Hakibbutz Hame'uchad, 2019), 76–114 (quotation on 78).

90. Strassman, "Oriental Restaurants."

91. Phone interview with Menachem Talmi, 20 December 2009.

92. Pierre Bourdieu, *Distinction: A Social Critique of the Judgement of Taste*, trans. Richard Nice (Cambridge, MA: Harvard University Press, 1984), 185.

93. Interview with Yehuda Litani, Jerusalem, 16 March 2010.

94. This poem was published in a 1998 collection of Gouri's poems without an exact date, only noting that the poem was written before his 1949 book *Fire Flowers*.

The last two lines of the poem allude to the possibility of destruction, so it seems likely that it was written during the war. Haim Gouri, *The Poems*, vol. 1 (Jerusalem: Mossad Bialik,1998), 20 (Hebrew).

95. Gouri, *The Crazy Book*, 99 (Hebrew).

96. Hagor (Haim Gouri), "Near Herod's Gate," *Davar* 4 June 1971 (Hebrew).

97. Yi-Fu Tuan, *Space and Place: The Perspective of Experience* (Minneapolis: University of Minnesota Press, 1977).

# CHAPTER 6

# The Companion to Every Bite: Palestinian Olive Oil in the Levant

ANNE MENELEY

This discussion of olive oil begins with a rich and unctuous excerpt from Palestinian poet Mourid Barghouti's *I Was Born There, I Was Born Here*, a remarkable memoir of the aftermath of displacement following the establishment of Israel in 1948.[1] He describes in memorable prose how olive trees and olive oil penetrate every aspect of Palestinian life. This quotation provides an anchor, to which we shall keep returning, as the chapter moves through a more conventional anthropological analysis.

> Everywhere you look, huge olive trees, uprooted and thrown over under the open sky like dishonored corpses. I think: these trees have been murdered, and this plain is their open collective grave. With each olive tree uprooted by the Israeli bulldozers, a family tree of Palestinian peasants falls from the wall.
>
> The olive in Palestine is not just agricultural property. It is people's dignity, their news bulletin, the talk of their village guesthouses during evening gatherings, their central bank when profit and loss are reckoned, the star of their dining tables, the companion to every bite they eat. It's the identity card that doesn't need stamps or photos and whose validity doesn't expire with the death of the owner but points to him, preserves his name, and blesses him anew with every grandchild and each season. The olive is the fruit itself (berries that may be any shade of green, any shade of black, or a shiny purplish color; that may be almond-shaped or oblong, oval or spherical) and it is recipes, processes, and tastes (semi-crushed, salted, semi-dried, scored, or stuffed with almonds or carrots or sweet red pepper). Olives are people's social status and what they're good at. The season of their harvest, in the magical autumn, transforms the men, women, and children of the village into bards, singers, and lyric poets whose rhythms turn the tiring work into a picnic and a collective joy. The olive is the pressed oil flowing from the enormous palm-fiber pressing mats, its puzzling color somewhere between shining green and

dark gold. Of the virgin oil produced from the first picking they make each other their most eloquent gifts and in the jars set in rows in the courtyards of their houses they store their peace of mind as well as the indispensable basis of their daily meals. If anyone falls ill, the oil is his medicine, and if they rub their aches with it, the pain goes away (or rather it doesn't, but they believe it does). From its waste, they manufacture soap in the courtyards of their houses and distribute it to the groceries—Shak'a Soap, Tuqan Soap, Nabulsi Hasan Shaheen Soap, and others. From the wood produced by the annual prun-ing, they carve curios, lovely wooden models of mosques and churches, and crosses. With great skill they whittle pictures of the Last Supper, the Manger, and Christ's birth, and statuettes of the Virgin Mary. They fashion arabesque work boxes of various sizes inlaid with mother-of-pearl from the Dead Sea, along with necklaces and rosaries, horses and camel caravans, and carve them to the smoothness, luster, and amazing hardness of ivory. From the crushed olive stones they extract smooth grindings that they use as a fuel for their stoves along with or instead of charcoal, and over whose silent fire they roast chestnuts during the "forty days" of the bitterest cold, leaving the coffee pot to simmer gently, quietly, over its slow heat while outside the thunder mountains collapse, gather, and then collapse again, preceded by lightning at times hesi-tant, at times peremptory. Next to these stoves they exchange their sly humor, make fun of their cruel situation, practice their masterful skill at friendly backbiting, and, when visits of relatives or neighbors bring a boy and a girl together in one house, exchange flirtatious glances that combine daring with shyness. For those who don't like coffee, they bring the blue tea pot, and sage leaves with their intoxicating perfume of the mountains.

These trees have been murdered, I think, and at the same instant, in two different places, stand a peasant with empty hands and a soldier filled with pride; in the same room of night a Palestinian peasant stares at the ceiling and an Israeli soldier celebrates.[2]

Barghouti introduces us to the way olive oil seeps into quotidian life in Palestine, as it does in many other olive oil–producing cultures. Olive oil is a functional food, long established in folk knowledge of the Levant and Medi-terranean as healthy, but it is treasured for far more than its nutritional value. Its material qualities (its luminosity, liquidity, spreadability, durability, capacity to cleanse, capacity to seal or preserve, capacity to insulate, and, notably, lack of miscibility in water) facilitate a range of practices: religious, hygienic, and culinary.[3] The nature of the tree and the collaboration of the human and non-human that is necessary to the practical making of products from it—whether edible substances (olive oil and olives), cleansing substances (olive soap), or combustible substances (fuel for candles)—underpin its imaginary power. It has served as a central ritual substance even prior to the monotheistic traditions: the ancient Greeks imagined the olive tree as a gift from the goddess Athena.[4] Olive oil, unlike fine wine, does not improve with age. There is no point in hoarding it. It must be properly stored to maintain its value. Yet it is seldom wasted. When it declines in quality as it ages, it is often made into soap, and the remains of the pits are fashioned into small logs. These logs are then burned to heat homes or fuel fires, warming people through the "bitterest cold," as Barghouti notes.

The violence that Palestinian olive trees have been subject to under the ongoing Israeli occupation bookends Barghouti's reflection on the olive. In tandem with the radical encroachment of Israeli settlements on West Bank agricultural territory, olive trees and olive oil have become synonymous with Palestine and its contemporary struggle. Yet olive oil is also a valued product all over the Levant. For centuries olive trees and olive oil have been defining features of the Levant and of the Mediterranean more broadly.[5] The olive tree can stand for almost anything: the land, the people, and the evocative cuisine. At the same time, olive trees and olive oil can be incredibly singular and emotionally particular. In *The Golden Harvest* (2019), a documentary about the production of olive oil, filmmaker Alia Yunis traces these tensions between the general and the particular in her travels to Palestine, the homeland of her parents, as well as to other parts of the Levant and Mediterranean. Her documentary explores how people and foods are both bound by the common denominator of olive oil and a Mediterranean geography and also incredibly localized and diverse.[6]

This chapter focuses on Palestine, where the importance of tasting the product of Palestinians' own land and trees has become highly charged as their land, and/or their access to it, disappears. Excerpts from Barghouti's narrative are woven throughout the chapter to explore how the connections between people and their olives are expressed in art, poetry, and literature as well as in the culinary domain. Since my first trip to Palestine in 2006, I have interviewed producers, farmers, chemists, distributors, importers, and consumers of olive oil. My research has tracked what happens when olive-oil processing, standardization, and labeling moves from "techne" to "technoscience"—from local craft to international standards of industrial food science.[7] I have also traced how Palestinian olive oil is transformed from olive oil (*zayt al-zaytūn*) to "extra-virgin" when it travels abroad as a fair-trade product.[8] My understanding of the meaning and politics surrounding the olive tree and its beloved oil has been shaped by my participation as an olive-picking volunteer in seven olive harvests in the West Bank.

## The People and the Tree: Human-Nonhuman Alliances

The olive tree and olives are both referred to by the Arabic word *zaytūn*. It is important to start with the tree itself, though that is not to say that the "olive tree" has exactly the same meaning in other parts of the Levant. Contemporary theoretical moves in cultural anthropology encourage us to incorporate nonhuman life in our interpretations of cultural practices.[9] Cultural anthropology's fascination with human-nonhuman collaboration may well seem like a commonsense truth undeserving of such theoretical elaboration to your average olive farmer: it only takes one bite of a raw olive to determine that the olive fruit is not palatable in its natural state.

The olive tree exists in the wild, but it needs human cultivation to be productive. Olive oil may be touted as a "natural" oil, but it was actually one of the first processed foods. As our archaeology colleagues tell us, ancient olive mills offer enduring evidence of the long-standing human habitation all over the Levant and Mediterranean. In Palestinian imaginaries, the olive tree is understood as an actor, a kind of coproducer of its own product—olive oil—as the result of human-tree co-generativity.

John Hartigan's call to anthropologists to pay more attention to plants is appropriate here, especially his observation that "plants are far more attuned to *place* than humans," becoming "far more exquisite ciphers of 'place' than mammals."[10] The olive trees and the terraces on which they often stand are also testimony to long Palestinian habitation, knowledge, and labor. This capacity of olive trees to mark place and human presence makes them powerful symbolic and material actors in Palestine-Israel. Their longevity and their tenacity undermine the Zionist claim of a "land without people for a people with a land." The most prized cultivar of the olive tree in Palestine is called Rumi (or Roumani). As many will tell you, the tree's name indicates its origin in the Roman period, its centuries of adaptation to Palestine's arid conditions, and its long presence on the land—and, by extension, Palestinian presence there as well. Rochelle Davis notes how in the Palestinian genre of "remembrance"— books that chronicle and record village histories of life before the enormous dispossession and dispersal of the Nakba—the "monumental olive trees," along with olive mills, are invoked as nonverbal testimony of the Palestinian people's long-standing presence on their land.[11]

## Israeli Arboreal Activities in the West Bank

The meaning, practices, and trajectories (and potential trajectories) of olive trees and olive oil in Palestine must be understood in the context of the political economies of Zionism and colonialism since the late nineteenth century, including the radical disruptions of and for Palestinian people in 1948 and 1967. In his lyrical way, Mourid Barghouti asserts that the olive tree in some respects stands in as a metaphor for the Palestinian person. Shoots coming up from the base of an olive tree devastated by a settler's axe or poison provide a material sign of the tenacity and refusal to be erased from memory that is central to the Palestinian concept of *ṣumūd* (steadfastness). This quality may well be why Barghouti suggests that olive trees represent Palestinian "dignity," as they resolutely remain where they belong. Israeli settler attacks against olive trees in the West Bank often proceed as if olive trees are a stand-in for Palestinians, whose presence ought to be (and can be) uprooted from the land.

The uprooted tree is more than a dead tree: it stands for loss of Palestinian life itself. As the olive tree embodies the rootedness of Palestinians in their land, the metaphor of uprooting becomes potent for those who were forcibly displaced from their land with the establishment of the state of Israel. As Palestinian poet and refugee Sharif Elmusa notes, uprooting comes to stand for the refugee:

> I could only imagine the enormity of despair that my parents and the hundreds of thousands of others felt at being uprooted; "uprooted" is still an apt word to describe that event, especially if the tree is old and its roots have spread profusely in the earth, and you can feel the tremendous force that pulled them out and listen to the sound of them tearing.[12]

The processes of rooting and uprooting trees in the Holy Land has long been a part of making historical claims. Trees figure prominently in historian Simon Schama's general argument about history, landscape, and memory in *Landscape and Memory*. It opens with a specific example: the Jewish National Fund's charitable campaign to encourage Jewish schoolchildren to donate their pennies to planting trees, their "proxy immigrants" in Palestine.[13] The trees planted by the Jewish National Fund were primarily pine trees, evoking the landscapes of Europe. As Irus Braverman argues in *Planted Flags*, trees were used as arboreal means of staking claims to land, as surrogate colonialists.[14] Pine trees grow quickly but are short-lived, in contrast to olive trees. While olives bear fruit, pine trees do not. While olive trees are part of orchards, European pine trees are used to establish Israeli nature reserves, which both co-opt Palestinian land and often exclude Palestinians from it. The frequent controversial uprooting of olive trees and the equally controversial construction of the massive separation wall both have been justified by "security" concerns. For Palestinians whose land falls under what is designated as a "closed military area" or a "friction zone"—set up to protect the ever-expanding Israeli settlements in the West Bank—access to their olive trees is cut off through a byzantine system of permits.

I interviewed Palestinian olive-oil producers, farmers, and activists trying to preserve olive trees (some of whom had been imprisoned for their activism by the Israeli military), whereas Braverman, an Israeli lawyer and anthropologist, interviewed Israeli military officials about their understanding of the destruction of Palestinian olive trees. As she indicates, olive trees are sometimes depicted as threatening presences, "as enemy soldiers who need to be cleared out" to make space for Israeli occupiers in the West Bank. She quotes Chief Inspector David Kishik of the Israeli civil administration: "Like children, their trees look so naïve, as if they can't harm anyone. But like [their] children, several years later they turn into a ticking bomb."[15]

The Palestinian interpretation of the relationship between humans and their olive trees is, predictably, different from that of the Israeli military. The Palestinian imagination figures the olive tree as nonhuman kin, expanding the terrain of kinship into the arboreal sphere. In one such personification, Tawfiq Canaan, a Palestinian doctor and amateur ethnographer, describes the olive tree—*al-shajara al-mubāraka* (the blessed tree)—as the nurturer of people, providing them with the olive oil that is so beloved.[16] At the same time, people nurture the olive tree in a spirit of reciprocity that defines their relationship with it. Under normal circumstances, the olive tree can live hundreds of years. This quality of durability has made olive trees central to nationalist discourses, and *the* olive tree (*al-zaytūna*, singular) the symbol of Palestinian nationalism.[17] When Sari Nusseibeh, a member of one of the notable families of Jerusalem and current president of Al-Quds University in Jerusalem, was imprisoned by the Israelis, he was described by a fellow prisoner and nationalist as "the steadfast olive tree,"[18] demonstrating how the qualities of the tree become associated with qualities of persons. The olive tree's capacity to throw up shoots even after it has been cut down also provides a vital mimetic sign of Palestinian tenacity. As Israeli historian Ilan Pappé notes, in Palestinian villages destroyed in the Nakba and planted over with pine trees, the olive trees often reemerged decades later, refusing to submit to the erasure of the Palestinian presence.[19]

### Preserving the Olive, Protecting Palestinian Life

The uprooting of Palestinian olive trees continues in the contemporary West Bank, not in a metaphorical way but in an actual process that Braverman describes as "tree wars." Olive trees continue to be targets of the illegal settlers in the West Bank who cut down, poison, or burn the trees, steal the olives, and harass farmers who are trying to harvest their trees. The destruction of olive trees became a rallying point for Palestinian popular protest against the wall, captured in documentaries like *Five Broken Cameras* (2011).[20] This documentary features activist Eyad Burnat, who says: "We will always be related to our land and our trees because the olive tree is not just a tree to us. It is the symbol of our country, Palestine. It is not just for feeding us. We respect and we love the olive trees because we feel that our relationship with our land is the olive trees." Going further, he implies that the olive tree stands not only for the Palestinians but for the land itself.[21]

Penny Johnson and Raja Shehadeh, famous chroniclers of the disappearing Palestinian landscape, draw together Palestinian authors' reflections on home and exile as refugees or forced economic migrants in *Seeking Palestine: New Palestinian Writing on Exile and Home*.[22] In these essays, as in so much Palestinian writing, olives and olive trees figure prominently. They also provide rich material for Palestinian visual arts. As Davis notes, wild or cultivated plants from their own land or villages become potent visual symbols for artistic representations whereby Palestinians articulate the loss and damage to their people, culture, and land: "These products of the earth—orange and olive trees and cacti—are an essential visual vocabulary in the iconography of Palestinian art, in particular literature and political poster art."[23] Two of these art forms are intertwined in the recent book by Nora Lester Murad and Danna Masad: *Rest in My Shade: A Poem about Roots*. In this poetic work dedicated to "refugees and displaced people everywhere," the olive tree narrates the effect of the onslaught of the occupation for the trees and the Palestinian people.[24] The olive tree's narrative is made viscerally moving through illustrations by Palestinian artists like Rana Bishara, Suleiman Mansour, and Steve Sabella.[25]

Barghouti opens his reflection with the destruction of olive trees that he witnessed on a troubled trip from Ramallah to Jericho. The olive trees are personified: he describes the trees as "murdered," uprooted and discarded like "dishonored corpses." He then describes the centrality of olive oil, including its harvest and milling, in the Palestinian diet and social life. He returns to the olive trees' murder at the end of his reflection by evoking the peasant with "empty hands" staring at a ceiling while a proud Israeli soldier celebrates. In Palestinian arboreal imaginaries, olive trees are kin: their destruction hits at the heart of the family, as a murder would. Lena Jayyusi offers an arresting reflection on the destruction of olive trees in her description of a farmer grieving for his trees, as he would for a child:

> Here, the cutting of the olives is like a visceral blow to him, something extracted and uprooted from his very own life and body. The olive, nurtured in

various ways, courted, sung about and then received as nurture in return, constitutes a corporeal bond of living, of need and sustenance. It is in this that it becomes possible to carry the image or idea of the olive tree farther into other contexts as a symbol of that very life: it begins to function metonymically *as* life itself.[26]

Olive trees are also part of a living lineage of their owners that connects them to their grandfathers and grandchildren, signifying them as holders of wealth, both as inheritors and as those who can grant inheritance. The olive tree for Barghouti is described as a prestigious identity card (unlike the fraught identity card captured in Mahmoud Darwish's famous 1964 poem "Identity Card")[27] that roots Palestinians to their land, establishing them as its rightful owners. Barghouti implicitly contrasts this prestigious olive-tree-as-identity-card to the Israeli-issued identity cards, which are necessary for Palestinian survival but are used—along with permits—to control Palestinian movement in a nightmarish Weberian bureaucratic web.[28]

## Harvesting

The unwilling refugees or involuntary expatriates yearn for the taste of the olive oil of their former land. For diaspora Palestinians, newly harvested olive oil was received as a special gift carrying the scent and the memories of the homeland, connecting them to family members who were able to remain on the land and work it. For those Palestinians working abroad and only able to return to their fields for the harvest, the olive tree is convenient, because it does not require daily attention; pruning, plowing, and grafting can be done relatively quickly.[29] But it is also the harvest season that requires the most intense human-tree labor and human-human labor, although none of the olive producers I spoke with referred to it in those terms. As Barghouti notes in the quotation cited earlier in this chapter, the hard labor of the olive harvest "transforms the men, women, and children of the village into bards, singers, and lyric poets." The rhythm of these antiphonal songs, known all over the Mediterranean, helps ease the hard work. On my first trip to Palestine in 2006, an elderly woman sang one such olive song to me: in one verse, the women picking up olives from the ground mocked the men picking in the trees, who in turn mocked the women in the next verse.

The olive harvest used to be done by extended families, some returning from abroad if they were able, and neighbors swapping labor. But the contemporary olive harvest in Palestine has been refigured as a time of international solidarity, as foreign volunteers deflect the unwanted attention of menacing settlers or the Israeli army. I have participated in seven olive harvest seasons since 2007.[30] We helped farmers whose access to their own land was restricted, who needed to demonstrate that their land was being tended and productive lest it be confiscated by Israel, which does this by invoking an Ottoman law from 1858 about fallow land reverting to the state. Sometimes volunteers with foreign passports have greater access to Palestinian land than the extended families of Palestinian landowners. One man gave me an example: although he got (and paid for) a permit from the Israeli military to pick the olives on his land behind the wall, the Israeli soldier would only grant access to the entire field to his very pregnant wife and aged father, who were physically unable to harvest the field themselves. Hence Palestinian farmers like this man are left in the unenviable position of depending on volunteer migrant laborers like me, whose intentions might be better than their skills.

The owner of the olive field traditionally provided lunch for the pickers, and host farmers today prepare lunch for the volunteers to thank them for their labor. The harvest is hard, with long days of work. As Barghouti notes, however, the shared meal in the fields under the olive trees is often remembered with pleasure as "a picnic and a collective joy." One of the central concerns in olive picking is how to feed the workers so that they can continue the long day's work. Harvesting is great fun, particularly in the morning if the sun is bright. But, as the day progresses, the pickers' bodies are reminded that it is also hard work. Lunches are often served in the field; one of the favorite lunches of the olive pickers in Palestine (certainly this olive picker) is a big pot of lentils and rice or bulgur wheat (*mujaddara*), as is evident in the nostalgic reminiscence of restaurateur Rawia Bishara in *Olives, Lemons & Za'atar: The Best Middle Eastern Home Cooking*:

> As soon as the sun was up, we set out to do the picking, timing it so that lunch coincided perfectly with the hour when the sun was at its most intense. We gathered under a clutch of olive trees, where my mother laid out a delicious picnic. Lunch was always the same—a huge pot of *mujadara*. Stretched out on a lush hillside, blissfully exhausted, surrounded by the people I loved the most and eating that delicious lentil pilaf . . . this image is forever etched in my memory.[31]

Bishara highlights the central qualities of the olive oil in preparing *mujaddara*. The dish can be prepared ahead of time: the olive oil preserves it until the food is served after hours of labor. She describes the dish as "strategic" because it is easy to transport and can be served at room temperature to both nourish and delight the olive pickers with its familiar deliciousness. It provides hearty "fuel," with the healthy fat of olive oil—including a topping of onions fried in the past year's oil—offering a nutritional boost to revive the workers for the rest of the day's picking. Pickers eat the fruit of last year's harvest to enable them to work for this year's harvest, which in turn will feed the harvesters in the following year, if all goes well. The meal holds the laborers until the freshly pressed oil can be tasted, straight from the spout at the olive mill.

## Olive Oil as the Companion to Every Bite

Reem Kassis notes in her cookbook *The Palestinian Table*: "My family produces our own olive oil, so I have rarely had to purchase it."[32] This is what most Palestinians would prefer. Barghouti speaks in *I Saw Ramallah* of his traumatic moment when, as an expatriate, he realized the shame of having to buy olives and olive oil: "the first simple and serious humiliation when I put my hand in my pocket in a grocer's shop and bought my first kilogram of olive oil. It was as though I confronted myself, then, with the fact that Deir Ghassanah [his home village] had become distant."[33]

Olive oil is an important everyday food item: Palestinians, like olive producers everywhere, swear to the importance of olive oil in strengthening the body. One producer described olive oil as the "centerpost" of the house.[34] While the emotional force of the destruction of olive trees—itself visually shocking—is often highlighted, less obvious and publicized is the effect of this destruction on the everyday family food budget. It is not only financially stressful but also humiliating to people to need to purchase olive oil after being used to eating their own oil. Beyond being mere property, olive oil is the foundation for valued social interactions, with the state of the harvest being a topic central to many conversations. Barghouti calls it "their central bank where profit and loss are reckoned," as described at length in historian Beshara Doumani's fascinating account of olive oil as a currency in Ottoman-era Nablus.[35] One former Palestinian landowner who had been reduced to driving a cab for Bethlehem's scarce tourists told me that his family could not afford to buy the local (and expensive) Beit Jala oil after their land had been confiscated. The confiscation of olive trees damages not only the family's budget but also their pride, as everyone prefers the olive oil from the trees of their own family land.

Palestinians talk about olive oil as essential to their survival, a life-giving and life-preserving food, as in the saying: "If we have olive oil, za'atar [a beloved seasoning made of wild thyme, sumac, and sesame seeds] and bread, we can survive anything." These days "anything" usually means the hardship caused by the Israeli occupation. For Gazan Palestinians, olive oil has become so scarce that cookbook author Laila El-Haddad tells us: "They buy olive oil by the shekel's worth, enough for a single dish." She further notes the emotional impact of being deprived of olive oil:

> That olive oil is unaffordable is especially bitter. Olive trees are the most lasting symbol of Palestine. Almost half of Gaza's fertile land lies along its border with Israel. The strip was once thick with olive groves but the Israeli army has levelled well over a thousand acres of them. Most locals rarely use the expensive oil now; they have replaced it with sunflower or soybean oil, doled out sparingly by aid agencies.[36]

Olive oil is a quotidian base for so many dishes in the Levant, yet it is also a luxury good in the sense that it is greatly valued aesthetically. All producers of olive oil seem to believe wholeheartedly that their oil is best. I had found this to be true even in my work with Tuscan olive producers. When I asked a Palestinian olive oil professional about it, he laughed in recognition. Rolling his eyes, he cited one of my favorite Palestinian proverbs: "A monkey in the eyes of his mother is a gazelle." The addition of Palestinian olive oil to Palestinian food elevates it from a mere functional, calorie-providing, "bare-life" kind of food to one that is life-sustaining in providing delicious pleasure. In Barghouti's words, noted in the earlier quotation, olive oil is "the star of their dining tables, the companion to every bite they eat."[37]

The tension between olive oil as a star and as a quotidian companion was evident in one of the many current artistic initiatives designed to preserve Palestinian culture. Mirna Bamieh of the Palestine Hosting Society organizes meals, which she describes as "live art installations," to draw attention to what she feels Palestinians are in danger of losing and what they should try to preserve. Bamieh has hosted several of these dinners, which highlight distinctive Palestinian dishes that go beyond the "hummus and falafel."[38] I attended one such dinner for sixty guests in April 2019, featuring "edible wild plants" at the newly established Palestinian Museum in Bir Zeit, dedicated to reclaiming and preserving Palestinian culture. Nearly all of Bamieh's sixteen courses featured olive oil, demonstrating—as Barghouti noted—that olive oil is "the indispensable basis of their daily meals." Edible wild plants were the star of the dinner, but olive oil was omnipresent, the unspoken glue, a testimony to the embeddedness of olive oil in producing memorable meals. During the meal, Bamieh highlighted a growing concern in Palestine about the loss of knowledge about wild plants, their foraging, and their preparation. The dish that got everyone's attention was *lūf* (arum), a dish that to my eyes resembled Swiss chard; it is full of vitamins but poisonous in its natural state. Bamieh explained to the dinner guests that the leaves would cause the mouth to tingle if eaten raw and, in extreme cases, the throat to close. She explained to me in detail in an interview afterward that *lūf* should be soaked overnight in salt and then cooked slowly in olive oil. Olive oil was the key ingredient in *lūf*'s dramatic transformation from poisonous to healthy, from inedible to edible.

## Extra-Virgin in the Holy Land

As Beshara Doumani indicates, olive oil was central to trade for centuries: it connected Nablus to Damascus, Beirut, and Tripoli in complex and vibrant trade networks of olive oil and olive soap.[39] The way olive oil can travel today is different, to say the least. Israelis control all the contemporary infrastructures of export: airports, seaports, and for the most part highways. The folk pieties about olive oil in general and health are less important as Palestinians move to export their olive oil abroad, where "healthy" olive oil is increasingly identified with "extra-virgin" olive oil. According to international standards imposed by the International Olive Council, extra-virginity is determined by a chemical test, proving that the oil has less than a 0.5 percent acidity level; it should also pass an organoleptic quality test. To travel successfully abroad and gain access to European Union markets and high-end food stores in North America, Palestinian olive oil must be transformed into extra-virgin olive oil.[40] I focus here on a few problems that were related to me by farmers. Many objected to the homogenization of the "Palestinian farmer" and the flattening of the distinctions between regions of Palestine.[41] Extra-virgin olive oil requires a dramatic transformation in production practices.[42] It also has brought a radical refiguration of storing and pressing olives, with many of these transformations being funded by foreign aid.

Palestinian farmers faced another key problem. In order to make extra-virgin olive oil, they need to press their olives collectively each day to ensure that the acidity level does not go up; olives must be pressed as quickly as possible after picking for low-acidity oil. In an interview about collective pressing for the Palestinian Agricultural Relief Committees (PARC), a farmer said that "PARC's collective pressing might produce a technically perfect product, but it takes the heart and connections out of it. People should be allowed to press their olives individually and then take what they want for their own families. They can sell what they don't need and *then* PARC can blend it for export."[43] Many farmers believe that this pooling of everyone's olives means the loss of the distinct taste of their own land and trees. The farmer being interviewed said that the farmers should be allowed to taste their own sweat and their own land. Pooling of olives leaves out the taste of the land, the taste of each farmer's own labor, and the memory of land now inaccessible in favor of a prestigious but homogeneous "extra-virgin" olive oil, where global standards dilute the memory of and longing for the land. What happens in this process is another form of uprooting, a troubling deracination, a removal from the native context, which is unsettling for uprooted Palestinians, as I was told in several interviews. One farmer invoked the kinship metaphor: not letting a farmer taste the first pressing of his own oil is like not letting a father see his newborn son.

For the most part, the market for extra-virgin olive oil is outside of Palestine. When I showed one of my olive farmers a photo I took in April 2019 of a rare example of extra-virgin olive oil for sale to Palestinian customers in Palestine, he had a good laugh. He noted that people wanted their own olive oil, not "extra-virgin," and noted that his own mother would never dream of buying olive oil. The addition of a free bag of za'atar with the purchase seemed to him an even greater shock; he joked that this would question his mom's understanding of herself as a good mother. He explained that she gathered, dried, and prepared her za'atar with her own special recipe of sumac and sesame seeds, for her family in Palestine and for relatives abroad. This exchange of za'atar along with olive oil pressed from the family land was part of creating networks of caring kin, especially with those at a distance. When I told the farmer I had purchased the oil at the Bravo grocery store in Ramallah, he described it as an expensive store. It always had cars lined up in front. Ramallah's new bourgeoisie liked the fact that every product was "modern" (heavily packaged), speaking to a different kind of sense of self.

## Conclusion

Barghouti talks of olive "excess" in Palestinian life. One such "excess" is olive oil's notable spiritual efficacy as a substance coming from the "blessed tree" (*al-shajara al-mubāraka*) and often used in rituals, as well as the way that it is shared as a spiritual offering. As amateur anthropologist Tawfiq Canaan's ethnography of the early twentieth century indicates, both Christian and Muslim Palestinians used olive oil to fuel the votive candles they lit at the saints' tombs dotting the landscape. In this way, they accessed the sacred through vows and left behind oil to be used by others in need, acts of generosity to be rewarded in this life or the next. One farmer in Beit Jala told me that his three priorities were providing oil for his own family, for the poor in his community, and to the Church of the Nativity in Bethlehem for the oil lamps; the remainder would be sold to provide income for his family.

In traditional oil production, every olive is precious, to be pickled or pressed for food or used for ritual purposes. After we novice foreign volunteers had finished picking during one olive season, feeling triumphant after finishing up all the trees in the hot and dusty field, the women in our Palestinian host family quietly moved in. I watched, fascinated, as the women cast their eagle eyes on the branches, quickly plucking the olives we had missed and picking up those we had unknowingly dropped on the ground. This was not simply the commonsense pragmatism of a parsimonious peasant or mere concern with preserving caloric intake; many consider the neglect of olives to be a waste and, to some, a sin. Under the current conditions of occupation, dispossessed Palestinians always face the possibility of losing their land or the permission to stay on their land. When thinking about the loss of the olives that such dispossession brings, we also need to consider how the separation of people and trees might also mean becoming delinked from the sacred, from fellow Palestinians, and also from a beloved and nurturing source of sustenance.

I conclude with an anecdote from a lovely article written by fellow anthropologist Rema Hammami, because it captures how the olive fosters a spirit of generosity, an "ethics of care," that keeps reemerging despite the hardships that people face. Olives and olive oil appear in Hammami's poignant essay about the infrastructures of strangulation—Israeli checkpoints, identity cards, and permits—that heartlessly separate East Jerusalem, where she lives, from the rest of the West Bank, including her place of employment, Bir Zeit University. She recounts how landless peasants from the nearby Palestinian village of Kharbatha continued to gather olives in a garden between her house and another garden confiscated by the Israeli state for the purpose (according to her neighbors) of spying in East Jerusalem.[44] During the Second Intifada, the Israeli army increasingly encroached on the West Bank, causing delays, misery, and the near breakdown of everyday life.

Hammami recounted that one day she snapped, finding herself unable to face the harrowing ordeal of the checkpoints on her way to the university; she turned back to go home but encountered a flying checkpoint set up in front of her house in East Jerusalem.[45] In a fury, Rema barked at the soldier and slammed the door of her gate in his face, only to find one of the elderly olive gleaners cowering in terror in her garden. The poor woman had arisen early to pick the neglected olives, itself a tiring and dusty job, when the Israeli sirens and commotion began. Hunched over her small bag of olives, she told Rema of her fear that the soldiers would pick her up as an "illegal infiltrator."[46] Yet, despite her terror, she had clung to her hard-won olives and even offered Rema a share from her painfully modest bundle. Despite the harrowing cause of this unwanted interaction—the Israeli occupation often seems intent on disrupting quotidian civility and conviviality—the elderly gleaner retains the ethic and obligation of sharing the sustenance of the land. Like the shoots of the devastated olive tree, Palestinian generosity and graciousness emerge, tenacious if shaken, in the midst of the occupation's attempts to erase what Palestinians hold dear.

All of these examples prove that we cannot understand the circulations of Palestinian olive oil or its meanings to its consumers without understanding the context in which it is produced (or prevented from being produced). Barghouti's long reflection on the centrality of the olive tree and olive oil in Palestinian life has been inspirational for my central theme, the deeply moving human-nonhuman relations of co-nurturing between person and tree. The olive tree and its Palestinian attendees are coproducers of their beloved olive oil, which is essential not only to their diet but to imaginaries of time and place: Palestine and its past, troubled present, and future. Like the elderly gleaner, Barghouti reminds us of what the Palestinians might want to preserve—not only the material objects and plants but also the moral precepts of gracious social interaction and co-nurturing—to imagine a positive future for themselves and that which they value.

## Acknowledgments

I would like to thank Rochelle Davis, Anny Gaul, Graham Pitts, and Vicki Valosik for their invitation to the Making Levantine Cuisine conference in Washington, DC, in 2019. I truly enjoyed the fascinating conversations and presentations of all the participants. For years of inspiration on the intertwining of plant and human lives in Palestine, I would like to thank Mirna Bamieh, Farha Ghannem, Rema Hammami, Baha Hilo, Fadi Kattan, Aisha Mansour, Vivien Sansour, and my "olive kin," with whom I have picked olives over the years. I greatly value my conversations about olive trees and olive oil with Omar Qassis and so look forward to his own work on the topic. I thank Alia Yunis for sharing her wonderful film, *The Golden Harvest*, with me. I very much appreciate the careful eye and helpful comments of Vicki Valosik. This chapter is dedicated to the memory of my father, who died shortly before I presented it as a paper. He would have approved of me carrying on and finishing the work I began; I thank the organizers for their kindness. It was with great sadness that I heard of Mourid Barghouti's death on 14 February 2021. His reflections on olive oil have been so inspirational for me.

## Notes

1. Mourid Barghouti, *I Was Born There, I Was Born Here* (2009), trans. Humphrey Davies (Cairo: The American University in Cairo Press, 2014), 10–12. Reproduced with permission of the American University in Cairo Press. This book is the sequel to his equally lovely *I Saw Ramallah* (1995), trans. Ahdaf Souief (London: Bloomsbury, 2005).

2. Barghouti, *I Was Born There, I Was Born Here*, pp. 10–12.

3. Anne Meneley, "Oleo-Signs and Quali-Signs: The Qualities of Olive Oil," *Ethnos* 73, no. 3 (2008): 303–326.

4. Amateur Palestinian ethnographer Tawfiq Canaan noted how oil was donated to the Church of the Nativity in Bethlehem to fuel the candles. "The Christians offer to a church in the name of the Virgin a quantity of the newly pressed oil. Only after such an offering has been given may the freshly pressed oil be used or sold." Canaan, "Plant-Lore in Palestinian Superstition" (1928), reprinted in *Jerusalem Quarterly* 24 (2005): 57–64 (quotation on 58). I discuss the ritual significance of Palestinian olive oil at length in Meneley, "The Qualities of Palestinian Olive Oil," in *Fat: Culture and Materiality*, ed. Christopher E. Forth and Alison Leitch (New York: Bloomsbury, 2014). 17–31. For further discussions of the material qualities of olive oil, see Meneley, "Oleo-Signs and Quali-Signs."

5. Anne Meneley, "The Olive and Imaginaries of the Mediterranean," *History and Anthropology* 31, no. 1 (2020): 66–83.

6. Alia Yunis, *The Golden Harvest* (ZigZag Lawn Productions, USA, 2019).

7. Anne Meneley, "Like an Extra-Virgin," *American Anthropologist* 109, no. 4 (2007): 678–687.

8. Anne Meneley, "Time in a Bottle: The Uneasy Circulation of Palestinian Olive Oil," *Middle East Research and Information Project* 248 (Fall 2018): 18–23; Anne Meneley, "Blood, Sweat and Tears in a Bottle of Palestinian Extra-Virgin Olive Oil," *Food, Culture & Society* 14, no. 2 (2011): 275–292; and Anne Meneley, "Discourses of Distinction in Contemporary Palestinian Extra-Virgin Olive Oil Production," *Food and Foodways* 22, nos. 1–2 (2014): 48–64.

9. Anna Tsing, *The Mushroom at the End of the World: On the Possibility of Life in Capitalist Ruins* (Princeton: Princeton University Press, 2015); John Hartigan, Jr., *Aesop's Anthropology: A Multispecies Approach* (Minneapolis: University of Minnesota Press, 2014); John Hartigan, Jr., "Plants as Ethnographic Subjects," *Anthropology Today* 35, no. 2 (2019): 1–2.

10. Hartigan, "Plants as Ethnographic Subjects," 1 (emphasis added).

11. Rochelle Davis, *Palestinian Village Histories: Geographies of the Displaced* (Stanford: Stanford University Press, 2011), 206.

12. Sharif S. Elmusa, "Portable Absence," in *Seeking Palestine: New Palestinian Writing on Home and Exile*, ed. Penny Johnson and Raja Shehadeh (Northampton, MA: Olive Tree Press, 2013), 40.

13. Simon Schama, *Landscape and Memory* (London: Harper-Collins, 1995), 14.

14. Irus Braverman, *Planted Flags: Trees, Land, and Law in Israel/Palestine* (Cambridge: Cambridge University Press, 2009).

15. Irus Braverman, "Uprooting Identities: The Regulation of Olive Trees in the Occupied West Bank," *PoLAR: Political and Legal Anthropology Review* 32, no. 2 (2009): 237.

16. Taufik Canaan, *Mohammedan Saints and Sanctuaries in Palestine* (London: Luzac,

1927), 31 n. 5. Canaan states: "The Palestinian does not look at the trees simply as plants, but as beings endowed with supernatural powers. The spirits of the upper (and to a lesser degree those of the lower) world, even his local saints, the *awlia*, may live and appear in them. . . . The fellah hangs pieces of cloth on them and uses their leaves for healing purposes" ("Plant-Lore in Palestinian Superstition," *Jerusalem Quarterly* 24 [2005]: 61). Although most of the olive-oil professionals thought this sort of thinking was a thing of the past, some farmers definitely believed it, as I heard at length in several interviews.

17. Nasser Abufarha, "Land of Symbols: Cactus, Poppies, Orange and Olive Trees in Palestine," *Identities: Global Studies in Culture and Power* 15, no. 3 (2008): 343–368.

18. Sari Nusseibeh, *Once Upon a Country: A Palestinian Life*, trans. Anthony David (New York: Picador, 2007), 333.

19. Ilan Pappé, *The Ethnic Cleansing of Palestine* (New York/Oxford: Oneworld, 2007), 227–228.

20. Braverman, *Planted Flags*, cited in Amelia Smith, "Five Broken Cameras: A Picture of Resistance," *Middle East Monitor* (5 June 2015), middleeastmonitor.com /20150605-5-broken-cameras-a-picture-of-resistance. The film *Five Broken Cameras* documents the resistance movement in Bil'in, which started when it became apparent that the Israeli Separation Wall was going to co-opt 55 percent of the village's land and the villagers had to witness the crime of seeing their olive trees destroyed.

21. Emad Burnat and Guy Davidi, *Five Broken Cameras* (New York: Kino Lorber, 2011).

22. Penny Johnson and Raja Shehadeh, eds., *Seeking Palestine: New Palestinian Writing on Home and Exile* (Northampton, MA: Olive Tree Press, 2013).

23. Davis, *Palestinian Village Histories*, 172–173.

24. Nora Lester Murad and Danna Masad, *Rest in My Shade: A Poem about Roots* (Northampton, MA: Olive Branch Press, 2019), 5.

25. For some remarkable visuals, see Jad Dahshan's wonderful article about how the olive tree, olive oil, and even olive soap have been used not only as inspiration but as actual materials for Palestinian artists' work: "Earth, Olive, Stone: Materialities of Palestinian Resistance" (8 June 2020), artmejo.com/earth-olive-stone-materialities -of-palestinian-resistance.

26. Lena Jayyusi, "Iterability, Cumulativity, and Presence: The Relational Figures of Palestinian Memory," in *Nakba: Palestine, 1948, and the Claims of Memory*, ed. Ahmad H. Sa'di and Lila Abu-Lughod (New York: Columbia University Press, 2007), 123.

27. Translated by Denys Johnson-Davies. *Third World Resurgence* 310/311 (June/July 2016): 56, twn.my/title2/resurgence/2016/310-311/poetry1.htm.

28. Yael Berda, *Living Emergency: Israel's Permit Regime in the Occupied West Bank* (Stanford: Stanford University Press, 2018); Helga Tawil-Souri, "Colored Identity: The Politics and Materiality of ID Cards in Palestine/Israel," *Social Text* 29, no. 2 (2011): 67–97; Anne Meneley, "Walk this Way: Fitbit and Other Kinds of Walking in Palestine," *Cultural Anthropology* 34, no. 1 (2019): 130–154.

29. Palestinian olive farmers are not always in agreement about the best way to tend the trees and produce the oil; as I told a few of them on trip in April 2019, they remind me of anthropologists ostensibly working on the same topic, but with a plethora of contradictory opinions and strong opinions on the opinions of others.

30. I describe this experience in Anne Meneley, "The Accidental Pilgrims: Olive Pickers in Palestine," *Religion and Society* 5, no. 1 (2014): 186–199.

31. Rawia Bishara, *Olives, Lemons & Za'atar: The Best Middle Eastern Home Cooking* (Lanham, MD: Kyle Books, 2014), 179.

32. Reem Kassis, *The Palestinian Table* (New York: Phaidon, 2017), 19.

33. Barghouti, *I Saw Ramallah*, 58.

34. Meneley, "The Qualities of Palestinian Olive Oil," 23.

35. Beshara Doumani, *Rediscovering Palestine: Merchants and Peasants in Jabal Nablus, 1700–1900* (Berkeley: University of California Press, 1995).

36. Laila El-Haddad, "How to Eat Well While Living under Siege," *Economist: 1843 Magazine* (15 July 2019), economist.com/1843/2019/07/15/how-to-eat-well-while-living-under-siege.

37. El-Haddad, "How to Eat Well."

38. Bamieh hosted dinners in various cities, including Nablus, featuring the distinctive cuisine of each city. I discuss the wider issue of seed and plant preservation in Anne Meneley, "Hope in the Ruins: Seeds, Plants, and Possibilities of Regeneration," *Environment and Planning E: Nature and Space* 4, no. (1) (2021): 158–172.

39. Doumani, *Rediscovering Palestine*.

40. Being labeled as "fair trade" helps the circulation of Palestinian olive oil as a solidarity product, but it still needs to be classified as "extra-virgin." This juxtaposition of fair trade and extra-virginity is a paradox that I explore elsewhere: Meneley, "Blood, Sweat and Tears in a Bottle of Palestinian Extra-Virgin Olive Oil"; Meneley, "Discourses of Distinction in Contemporary Palestinian Extra-Virgin Olive Oil Production."

41. For instance, making no distinction between Beit Jala oil and Jenin oil is likely to start a quick debate.

42. Meneley, "Time in a Bottle."

43. Interview with author, May 2010, Ramallah. The Palestinian Agricultural Relief Committees was set up in the early 1980s to help Palestinian farmers with agricultural productivity and to help them market their products.

44. Rema Hammami, "Home and Exile in East Jerusalem," in *Seeking Palestine: New Palestinian Writing on Home and Exile*, ed. Penny Johnson and Raja Shehadeh (Northampton, MA: Olive Tree Press, 2013), 118.

45. Flying checkpoints are set up randomly, so Palestinians cannot predict where they will be and try to avoid them.

46. Hammami, "Home and Exile," 132.

# CHAPTER 7

# Even in a Small Country Like Palestine, Cuisine Is Regional

REEM KASSIS

*I am a product of all the civilizations that have passed through the country—Greek, Roman, Persian, Jewish, Ottoman. Each powerful civilization passed through and left something behind. I am the son of all these fathers but belong to one mother. . . . My mother is this land that absorbed them all, and was both witness and victim.*

MAHMOUD DARWISH

"*Maqlūbeh*! Definitely *maqlūbeh*," I told my teta (grandmother) Fatima on the phone. "Mama will make me the stuffed chicken and I'll have the *ḥashweh* at my uncle's house in the Galilee, but it's your *maqlūbeh* that I want to eat first."

I was a freshman at a university in the United States. As my first trip back home to Jerusalem inched closer, my appetite and nostalgia grew, along with the list of dishes that I wanted to eat during my two weeks back. I had taken these dishes for granted growing up. Now I associated them with one side of my family or the other: they reminded me of a childhood I had rushed to discard in exchange for a future of bigger possibilities.

Leaning back into my chair, scribbling down the meals that I so badly wanted to taste again, I thought back to the food I used to eat at our kitchen table in Jerusalem and the food I used to eat at my grandmothers' tables in their villages. It was delicious, it was made with love, and it was our food. But the thought of these dishes making up Palestinian cuisine was an elusive notion back then. It was only when I left home for another country that I understood the importance of food in national identity and the intricacies associated with defining that connection.

During the weekends I spent in the university's library stacks solving economics equations and studying political history, I often thought back to the simple days of my childhood. I remembered red poppies and yellow dandelions leaning into the spring air, the sun barely kissing their leaves, as my family packed up our slew of cars to head out to forage and picnic in the mountains. One car took the dome-shaped iron *sāj*,[1] another the basins of dough, another the coolers with the raw meat and dips and salads, and each a straw mat. I remember the whole family heading out into the surrounding mountains to forage for za'atar and borage leaves.[2] While some foraged, others lit a fire, baked bread, grilled meat, and brewed tea. A similar scene occurred each fall, except that we wore winter boots instead of sandals and the trek was to our olive groves to harvest the season's bounty.

My childhood was the norm, not the exception, because most Palestinian families have a deep connection to the land and its bounty. The leaves, vegetables, and fruits provided by the land are the basis and often main ingredients for many Palestinian dishes. Driving around the country, we see a landscape dotted with olive and fig trees, with grape vines and lemon trees, mountains blossoming with za'atar and sage, and fields filled with dandelions and cauliflower. Families have become intimately familiar with this abundance over time, embracing its unique properties (like the bitterness of dandelion and prickliness of gundelia) and gathering it in season to make the most delicious meals.[3]

Za'atar was folded into a turmeric-spiced dough used to make cheese-stuffed hand pies or dried and ground with sesame seeds and sumac for the condiment that the world has come to know. Borage leaves were stuffed with a rice, meat, and an all-spice mixture then cooked in broth and later served with plenty of lemon. The olives were cured in countless way and shapes, from salt, lemon, vinegar, and chili to cracked, sliced, and whole.

It was these experiences and the ensuing sense of community and connection, so central to my childhood, that ultimately led me from those economic equations into the world of food. The deeper I have gone into the food world, however, the more I have realized two contradictory things. On the one hand, my research has shown me that food is inherently not national (nation-states only came to exist in the eighteenth and nineteenth centuries) but cultural, religious, ethnic, and regional. On the other hand, for Palestinians, who have long been denied an independent and self-sufficient state and whose national identity is constantly undermined, food takes on a greater importance, both politically and emotionally, in defining and preserving a national identity. It becomes a way to reclaim our country at least psychologically and emotionally, if not geographically.

Nonetheless, in spite of the ascent of the nation-state in the late eighteenth and nineteenth century, which gave rise to the idea of national cuisines, food at its core remains a regional and ethnic artifact, at times more closely tied to language and religion than to a defined geography. Think of ethnic or religious groups, such as Armenians, who live across the world but share the same cuisine regardless of where they are. Compare this to people living in the same country, such as India, where the population enjoys vastly different culinary practices and cuisines across the nation. The influence of religion, language, and landscape is undeniable. Looking at the foods that have come to define Palestinian cuisine shows us how instrumental regional influences—like neighboring countries, landscape, climate, and socioeconomic factors—are in defining food.

For example, the Galilee, the northern part of Palestine, shares many eating habits and dishes with Syria and Lebanon. Raw kibbe, *kubbeh niyeh* (lamb and bulgur tartare), for example, is a dish common across Lebanon but only enjoyed in the north of Palestine, near the Lebanese border. In contrast, Gaza, which borders Egypt, has been heavily influenced by Egyptian cuisine, using chili peppers and dill in signature dishes like *dagga* (*daqqa* in written Arabic: tomato and dillseed salsa) or *zibdiyyeh* (tomato, chili, and dill shrimp stew). Jerusalem, Bethlehem, Hebron, and the West Bank, which are closer to the Jordanian desert, have more bedouin-inspired dishes like *mansaf* (dried fermented yogurt and lamb stew).

But food is not just influenced by the surrounding areas. The immediate landscape and its native flora and fauna also have an impact. Take Hebron, for example, a Palestinian city in the southern West Bank recognized for its copious vineyards. Delicacies like *malban* (grape, sesame-seed, and pine-nut fruit roll-ups) and grape molasses are recognized specialties there. The local diet in Palestinian coastal towns like Gaza, Jaffa, Haifa, and 'Akka relies much more heavily on seafood, with specialties like *ṣayyādiyyeh* (onion and cumin spiced rice with fried fish) and *ṭājīn samak* (fish poached in tahini and onion sauce with pine nuts).

Climate and topography also play a role even within the same country. Hebron has the highest elevation in the West Bank and is one of the few places to receive snow, which explains why *buqsuma* (a simple dessert of snow topped with grape molasses) is eaten only there. Jericho, the lowest city on earth, has a dry and warm climate conducive to the growth of hedge mustard, making *ḥwayrneh* (yogurt and hedge mustard dip) a common dish there.

Forces of nature aside, socioeconomic factors also influence cuisine, with marked distinctions between the food enjoyed in cities and rural areas. As historically agricultural and also poorer communities, villages and rural areas relied heavily on legumes and grains such as bulgur and *frīkeh* (*farīka* in written Arabic) as well as seasonal produce and foraged plants. Cities, in contrast, were historically populated more by the elite, who were exposed to trade and foreign visitors, so more expensive rice-based dishes and exotic spices were common there.

Finally, of course, food is influenced by individuals. My great-great-grandmother who came from Syria as a bride brought many trusted family recipes along with her bridal trunk. *Hariseh* (wheat-berry lamb and chicken stew) was one such recipe, a somewhat obscure meal that had never been cooked in her new village or the surrounding ones. By the time I was a little girl, it was eaten throughout our village. When I go back now to visit neighboring towns, this dish is eaten at more and more homes. So food travels in myriad ways across many mediums.

This kind of travel is routine today, due to both easier transportation and easier dissemination of information. Even though we can point to regional specialties within a small country, these differences are becoming less pronounced as food integration and adoption occur not only within countries but across borders as well. In an apparent contradiction, like the ambiguous relationship between nation and region, this process itself has also been a catalyst in the emergence of national cuisines. As people move around the world, through forced or voluntary migration, food becomes a way to hold onto their past and build a sense of identity. Food becomes a proxy for the history and political landscape of an area and its people, creating a sense of connection and a narrative to be recounted and preserved.

In looking at the dishes that are unique to Palestinian cuisine and their fascinating origins, a beautiful story emerges. There is no single Palestinian table. Palestinian cuisine spans our entire geography—from the mountains of the Galilee to the valleys of the south, from the coast of Jaffa all the way to the West Bank. It is scattered across the globe and built around a history situated at a rich geographic crossroads. It is woven with memories of a time when most of us lived together in that land. In spite of our political circumstances and global dispersion, though, what ties all Palestinian tables together is more than just good food. It is the notion of "home," the spirit of generosity, the importance of family, and the value of bringing people together. It is a way to preserve and share a culinary and historical narrative that might otherwise slip through our hands.

### Kubbeh Niyeh

Region: Galilee

*Kubbeh niyeh* (literally, raw kibbe) is the quintessential festive dish in the Galilee. No wedding, holiday, or gathering is complete without a plate of this deep-orange smooth tartare served alongside *ḥawseh* (see the next recipe) and fresh vegetables. The meat was traditionally ground with a giant wooden pestle and stone mortar, creating a sound that signaled a village in celebration. In the face of any death or misfortune, the entire village refrained from making this meal. Animals were historically slaughtered during celebrations. The raw meat was consumed immediately, its freshness guaranteeing safety. Nowadays the best way to ensure safety is to purchase fresh meat from a trusted butcher and grind it at home. It can also be frozen for a few days and thawed halfway in the refrigerator before grinding. Supermarket or preground meat is absolutely not an option for this dish. If you do not want to deal with meat grinding at home, then preorder the meat and have your butcher grind it twice through a fine mincer the very first thing in the morning, on sparkling clean blades.

Serves 4–6

### Ingredients

For the *kubbeh*:

½ pound lean goat, lamb, or beef, completely cleaned of fat and gristle and
    cut into cubes, twice ground through a fine mincer
½ pound very fine bulgur wheat
1 teaspoon salt
1 medium onion, quartered
¼ cup firmly packed fresh herb leaves (any combination of mint, marjoram,
    basil, and thyme)
2 tablespoons red bell pepper paste*
1 teaspoon freshly grated lemon zest
½ teaspoon 9-spice mix (see recipe on page 149 or use Lebanese 7-spice
    blend: *bahārāt*)
½ teaspoon cumin
1 or 2 ice cubes
Olive oil, for drizzling

To serve:

1 recipe *hawseh* (see next recipe)
Fresh vegetables (any combination of scallions, radishes, mint, green chilis, tomatoes, or lettuce)
Lebanese pita bread (optional)
* Note: Red bell pepper paste is a common condiment in most Middle Eastern and Turkish cuisines. It is made of dried bell peppers that have been ground into a paste and can easily be found in Middle Eastern grocery stores. You can substitute 1 teaspoon tomato paste, 1 tablespoon paprika, and 1 tablespoon water.

## Directions

1. Arrange the meat cubes on a plate and freeze while you start on the rest of the dish.

2. Place the bulgur in a large bowl, wash with water, then pour out most of the water. Any remaining water will be absorbed by the bulgur. Sprinkle with the salt and set aside for about 15 minutes. Knead very well with your hands until softened. Taste: if the bulgur still has a bite, add 1 tablespoon cold water at a time and continue to knead (the entire process takes about 10–15 minutes). Set aside. It is possible to skip this step and add the bulgur to the food processor after processing the onion paste and meat, but you will not get the right texture for the dish.

3. Meanwhile, place the onion, herbs, red pepper paste, lemon zest, and spices in the bowl of a food processor and process into a very smooth paste. If necessary, add 1 tablespoon cold water at a time to achieve a paste. At this point, remove the meat from the freezer, place in a bowl or food processor with 1 or 2 ice cubes, and process into a fine paste.

4. Pour the meat mixture over the softened bulgur and mix with your hands until fully combined, about 1–2 minutes. Have a bowl of ice-cold water handy for dipping your hands as you knead to avoid warming the raw meat.

5. When they are combined, transfer the mixture to a serving platter and flatten into a slightly raised dome. Wet your palms with ice water (if necessary) to shape. Drizzle with olive oil and use the back of a small spoon to make indentations in any design you like.

6. To serve, spoon the desired portion onto a plate, flatten it out with the back of a spoon, and top with *hawseh* mixture. Enjoy with fresh vegetables and bread, if desired.

## *Ḥawseh*

Yields approximately 1 pound

### Ingredients

½ cup olive oil
2 medium onions, finely diced
1 pound minced beef or lamb or a combination
1 teaspoon 9-spice mix (see recipe on page 149 or use Lebanese 7-spice blend: *bahārāt*)
1 teaspoon salt
½ cup pine nuts and/or walnut pieces, lightly toasted

### Directions

1. In a medium-sized sauté pan, heat the olive oil on medium-high heat and fry the onions, stirring, until translucent and starting to brown, about 3–5 minutes. Add the minced meat, spices, and salt and fry, breaking up any lumps with a wooden spoon, until liquid has evaporated and meat is nicely browned, about 6–8 minutes.

2. Remove from heat and mix in nuts. At this point, the *ḥawseh* can be used as called for in a recipe or cooled and stored in the refrigerator for up to three days or a freezer for up to one month.

## *Qidreh*

Region: Hebron

*Qidreh*, which literally means "pot" in Arabic, is almost never cooked at home. This hallmark dish of Hebron is prepped at home but then sent to the neighborhood oven, where it is cooked in a special copper pot and wood-fired oven. It is actually quite easy to make but is often reserved for special gatherings because the copper pot and wood fire flavor are hard to replicate at home. It is traditionally made with lamb on the bone, but I use smaller pieces of stewing lamb and cook it in the oven in a cast-iron pot or Dutch oven for an almost identical taste. Try it on a weekend or when you have a large gathering and enjoy it with a side of fresh plain yogurt to contrast with the earthy and well-spiced taste of the rice and meat.

Serves 6 to 8

Ingredients

FOR THE STOCK

3 tablespoons olive oil
2–3 pieces of mastic
2 bay leaves
1 tablespoon 9-spice mix (see recipe on page 149 or use Lebanese 7-spice
   blend: *bahārāt*)
½ teaspoon turmeric
21 ounces boneless shoulder of lamb cut into 2-inch cubes
1 whole onion, peeled
2 quarts water
1 tablespoon salt

FOR THE RICE

2 tablespoons olive oil
2 tablespoons butter
1 large onion, sliced into thin wedges (half moons)
15–18 whole garlic cloves, peeled
1 teaspoon cumin
1 teaspoon 9-spice mix
1 teaspoon turmeric
1 teaspoon salt
1 pound rice (jasmine or medium grain), washed and drained
15.5 ounces (1 can) chickpeas, washed and drained

TO SERVE

Slivered almonds, toasted or fried
Fresh parsley
Plain yogurt

## Directions

1. To make the stock, heat olive oil in a large stockpot until hot but not smoking. Add mastic, bay leaves, and spices and stir until fragrant, about 1 minute. Add the lamb and sear on all sides, about 3 minutes. Add the whole onion, tossing in the spices to coat, then add the water and salt. Bring to a boil, skimming the foam from the surface, then allow to simmer until meat is tender, 60–80 minutes (20 minutes in a pressure cooker). Remove from the heat, strain the stock and reserve, and set the meat aside.

2. Preheat oven to 325 degrees Fahrenheit (160 degrees C or Gas Mark 3). Meanwhile, heat the oil and butter in a medium cast-iron pot. Once the butter has melted, turn the heat to low and add the sliced onion, stirring periodically, until softened and golden, about 10–15 minutes, then add the garlic cloves and sauté for 2–3 minutes. Sprinkle the spices and salt and stir for another minute, then add the rice and toss to coat evenly. Add the chickpeas and give one final toss to combine all the ingredients.

3. Pour 1 quart of the reserved stock over the rice mixture and increase the heat to high. As soon as the stock starts to boil, remove from the heat, arrange the meat on top of the rice, cover the pot, and place it in a preheated oven for 1 hour, until the rice has fully cooked and the meat has browned nicely.

4. Remove from the oven and let sit for 5 minutes. Uncover, sprinkle with toasted almonds and fresh parsley, and serve with fresh yogurt. When the dish is served at large gatherings, the pieces of meat are traditionally removed, the pot is inverted onto a large serving platter, then the pieces of meat are rearranged on top and sprinkled with the almonds. However, it looks just as beautiful served from the pot (especially if you are using a nice Dutch oven) or at a small gathering.

## *Zibdiyyeh*

Region: Gaza

Like several other Palestinian dishes such as *qidreh* (casserole) and *fukhāra* (clay pot), this traditional Gazan dish is named after the vessel in which it is cooked. A *zibdiyyeh* is a glazed terra-cotta pan (similar to cazuelas in Spain and Latin America) that can be used both on the stovetop and in the oven and transferred, sizzling hot, from kitchen to dining table. Regardless of whether you cook this dish in one of these pans or not, the result is astounding, with deeply concentrated flavors from the cooked tomatoes and sweet shrimp against the fiery heat from the chili peppers. I personally cook it an enameled cast-iron braiser for the most authentic flavor and rustic presentation.

Serves 6 to 8

### Ingredients

FOR THE SAUCE

3 tablespoons olive oil
1 large onion, finely diced
3–4 green chilis, finely chopped
6–8 garlic cloves, crushed
8 medium tomatoes, chopped, or 1 large (35-ounce) can of peeled whole
    tomatoes
1 tablespoon tomato paste
1 teaspoon 9-spice mix (see recipe on page 149 or use Lebanese 7-spice blend:
    *bahārāt*)
1 teaspoon ground coriander
½ teaspoon ground cumin
1 teaspoon salt
½ teaspoon sugar
½ teaspoon hot chili pepper (optional)
1 small bunch fresh dill, finely chopped

FOR THE SHRIMP

2 pounds king or tiger shrimp, peeled and deveined
1 tablespoon olive oil
A squeeze of lemon juice
½ teaspoon ground coriander

½ teaspoon ground cumin
Salt
Black pepper

TO SERVE

⅓ cup pine nuts, lightly toasted
Fresh bread

## Directions

1.  Preheat oven to 400 degrees Fahrenheit (200 degrees C or Gas Mark 6).

2.  Heat olive oil in a large oven-proof braiser or frying pan and add the
    diced onion and green chilis. Cook on medium heat until the onions are
    softened and just starting to brown, about 6–8 minutes. Add the garlic
    and cook for another 1–2 minutes. Pour in the chopped tomatoes, tomato
    paste, spices, salt, sugar, hot chili pepper (optional), and dill and bring to
    a boil. Lower heat and simmer until the tomatoes thicken and darken in
    color, about 10–15 minutes. If using canned tomatoes, use a spoon to break
    up as you cook. Taste and adjust seasoning if necessary.

3.  Meanwhile, heat a nonstick frying pan on high heat and mix the shrimp
    with the olive oil, lemon juice, spices, and salt and pepper. Add the shrimp
    to the pan and cook until the shrimp are opaque and pearly pink, turning
    once, about 1–2 minutes on each side. Avoid overcooking the shrimp, as it
    will cook more in the sauce.

4.  When the shrimp are done, add them to the tomato sauce and toss to
    combine. Remove the braiser from the heat, put it into the preheated oven,
    and cook the mixture until it is starting to brown around the edges, about
    5–10 minutes.

5.  Remove from the oven and top with toasted pine nuts. To serve, bring the
    pan to the table, ladle portions into each person's plate, and enjoy it with
    fresh crusty bread.

## *Laḥmeh bi-l-waraq*

Region: Jerusalem

Long before wrapping meat and fish in grape leaves became popularized in the West, it was a technique used across Palestine and the Levant to add flavor and preserve the moisture of meat during cooking. This particular variation, which wraps minced meat patties in the leaves, is considered one of the signature dishes of Jerusalem. It is often reserved for special gatherings or dinner parties because it looks impressive and tastes delicious. Who doesn't love to cut through a little parcel to find a juicy and intensely flavored treat inside?

Serves 6 to 8

## Ingredients

### FOR THE MEAT

2 pounds coarsely ground meat (beef, lamb, veal, or a combination)
3½ ounces (2 loosely packed cups) pita bread or white bread with crust removed, roughly torn
1 onion
1 tomato
1 small bunch of parsley
2 tablespoons olive oil
1 tablespoon 9-spice mix (see recipe on page 149 or use Lebanese 7-spice blend: *bavhārāt*)
2 teaspoons salt
45–50 fresh grape leaves (15–30 if very large), blanched in boiling water for 1 minute (if jarred, soak in cold water for 15 minutes then rinse thoroughly to remove any brine flavor)

### FOR THE SAUCE AND VEGETABLES

2½ cups stock or water
2–3 tablespoons tomato paste
1 teaspoon 9-spice mix (see recipe or use Lebanese 7-spice blend: *bahārāt*)
1 teaspoon salt
1 tablespoon olive oil
3–4 medium potatoes, sliced into ¾-inch thick rounds
3–4 medium tomatoes, sliced into ¾-inch thick rounds

Olive oil, for drizzling
Salt
Black pepper

## Directions

1. Preheat oven to 375 degrees Fahrenheit (190 degrees C or Gas Mark 5).
   Place about a quarter of the meat in a large mixing bowl and set it aside. In
   a separate bowl, cover the bread with water and leave to soak for a couple
   of minutes.

2. Meanwhile, combine the onion, tomato, parsley, olive oil, spice mixture,
   and salt in a food processor and pulse to a coarse consistency. Drain the
   bread, squeezing any excess moisture out with your hands, and add to the
   food processor, pulsing to combine evenly. Alternatively, very finely chop
   or grate everything by hand and mix with the bread, mashing it with a
   spoon as you mix.

3. Pour the mixture over the small portion of meat in the bowl and mix well
   with your hands until fully combined. Add in the remaining meat and mix
   gently with your hands, just until evenly distributed. Avoid overmixing in
   order to retain a fluffy texture when cooked.

4. Divide the mixture into approximately 15 equal-sized portions. On a clean
   work surface, lined with parchment paper for easier clean up, overlap 2–3
   of the grape leaves, vein side up (use only 1 if the leaves are very large), and
   place a portion of meat in the center. Gently shape the meat into a round
   patty and fold in the sides of the leaves around it. Repeat with the remaining meat and grape leaves, making a total of 15 round parcels.

5. In a bowl, combine the stock with the tomato paste, spices, salt, and olive
   oil and set aside.

6. In a 12- × 8-inch baking dish, arrange the grape-leaf parcels upright at an
   angle, with potato and tomato slices between them. Pour the stock mixture
   over, drizzle with some olive oil, and sprinkle with salt and freshly ground
   black pepper.

7. Cover the baking dish in aluminum foil and put it into the preheated oven
   to bake for 40 minutes. Uncover and continue to bake until the potatoes
   have started to brown, about 15 minutes. Remove from oven and serve
   alongside vermicelli rice.

## *Knāfeh*

Region: all over

*Knāfeh* (*kunāfa* in written Arabic) is believed to have originated in the Palestinian town of Nablus. It is quite uncommon to make *knāfeh* at home in Palestine nowadays because it is so readily available at most bakeries and sweet shops across the country. It is available in multiple varieties like *na'ameh* (fine), *khishneh* (coarse), and *malfūfeh* (rolled) and with various stuffings, such as pistachios, cream, cheese, or walnuts. Each is delicious in its own way. People generally have a preference for a certain kind and even a certain place. Since I have been living abroad, however, I often crave the most traditional version of this dessert, which smells and tastes of home. So I make this recipe that was handed down from my father's uncle (who emigrated to the United States over sixty years ago) to my uncle's wife (who emigrated over thirty-five years ago) and now finally to me. It is a very simple dessert: the ingredients really shine, so use the very best that you can find.

Serves 6 to 8

### Ingredients

14 ounces dry/low-moisture mozzarella (mozzarella for cooking)
9 ounces ricotta cheese
16 ounces shredded filo pastry/Kataifi*
6 ounces ghee, melted (or substitute clarified butter), plus more for greasing
1 recipe flavored sugar syrup cooled to room temperature (see recipe below)
¼ cup ground pistachios
* Kataifi (shredded filo pastry) can easily be found frozen at any Middle Eastern or even Mediterranean grocery store. It is also common to find it fresh in Middle Eastern groceries around Ramadan. It can then be frozen for later use. It is much easier to shred the dough if it is still slightly frozen.

### Directions

1. Preheat the oven to 400 degrees Fahrenheit (200 degrees C or Gas Mark 6). Generously grease an 11-inch round baking dish (or a 12- × 8-inch rectangular one) with ghee or butter and set aside.

2. To prepare the cheese stuffing, grate the mozzarella into a large bowl or slice it into thin pieces. Add the ricotta and mix well to combine. Refrigerate until ready to use.

3. Place the shredded filo pastry in a food processor and process until the shreds are roughly ¾ inch in length. If using frozen pastry, you can also crush and shred it with your fingers. Transfer to a large bowl and pour the melted ghee over it. Work with your hands until the pastry has fully absorbed the ghee, feels soft, and has no dry patches.

4. Transfer half the dough mixture into a greased baking dish, pressing it tightly with your hands to cover the bottom. Spread the cheese mixture evenly over the pastry. The easiest way to do this without the bottom pastry sticking to the cheese and coming loose is to drop spoonfuls of the filling evenly over the bottom then lightly press with the back of a wet spoon or your damp hand.

5. Spread the remaining pastry evenly on top of the cheese filling, making sure to fully cover the cheese, then firmly pat down with your hands. Bake in the preheated oven until the crust is a light golden brown, about 25–35 minutes.

6. Remove from the oven, allow to cool for 5 minutes, then flip over onto serving platter. Immediately drizzle with enough flavored sugar syrup to soak the entire cake. Sprinkle the crushed pistachios on top in any design you like. To serve, slice into individual portions and offer extra sugar syrup on the side.

## Sugar Syrup

Yields approximately 2 cups

## Ingredients

2 cups sugar
1½ cups water
A squeeze of lemon juice
½ teaspoon orange blossom water
½ teaspoon rose water

## Directions

1. In a small heavy-bottomed saucepan, combine the sugar, water, and lemon juice and bring to a boil on medium-high heat. Allow to simmer until slightly thickened, about 5 minutes.

2. Remove from heat and add the flavorings. Allow to cool before using or storing in a container in the fridge for up to two months.

## 9-Spice Mix

Makes about 1 cup

### Ingredients

6 tablespoons allspice berries
6 small cassia bark or cinnamon sticks
3 tablespoons coriander seeds
1 tablespoon black peppercorns
1 teaspoon cardamom seeds or 10 whole cardamom pods
½ teaspoon cumin seeds
10 whole cloves
2 blades of mace
1 nutmeg (whole)

### Directions

1.  In a large, dry frying pan, toast all the spices over medium-low heat until you begin to smell the aroma of the spices, about 10 minutes. Stir with a wooden spoon periodically to ensure that the spices do not burn.

2.  Remove the pan from the heat and set it aside to cool completely, about 1 hour. This step is crucial: if the spices are not cooled properly, they will form a paste when ground rather than a powder.

3.  Transfer all the roasted spices to a heavy-duty spice grinder and grind until you achieve a fine powder. Store the spice mix in an airtight container. It will keep for several months, although the aroma will fade with time.

### Notes

1. A *sāj* is a convex bread griddle (cast iron, aluminum, or carbon steel). The dough is spread very thinly across the dome, resulting in the paper-thin bread known as *sāj* bread.

2. Za'atar is an herb in the oregano family native to the Levant, but the term also refers to the condiment made from that herb when dried and mixed with sumac and sesame seeds. The particular variety is known as *Origanum syriacum* or Syrian oregano.

3. Gundelia is a type of thistle with spiny thorns that is cleaned and eaten fried or used in stews.

**PART III**

# LEVANTINE CUISINE BEYOND BORDERS

# Embodying Levantine Cooking in East Amman, Jordan

SUSAN MACDOUGALL

Keen to learn some cooking skills during my fieldwork in Amman, Jordan, I set off from where I was staying in the city's Deir Ghbar neighborhood to my field site in Tal al-Zahra to make *dawālī* (stuffed grape leaves) with my friend Jafra on a Saturday afternoon.[1] We had arranged the appointment in advance—when she announced her intention to make the dish during her weekend break from work, I said I would help her. She greeted me at the door and directed me into her sitting room.

Sunlight came into Jafra's house in the morning, lighting up the sitting room only briefly. Her home was a darkish space for the rest of the day. She often sat in the semilight, happy to enjoy the dusky feeling. I always felt a bit more relaxed at her house. When I arrived that Saturday, she had already made coffee and had her cup set out.

"Sit," Jafra directed me when I stepped into her apartment. "I'll get you a *finjān* [cup]." We sat, drank, and chatted. I told her about my morning, break-fasting on falafel with a friend and his brother. She told me about her morning, cleaning her house and drinking coffee with her husband. "I sat in the house," she told me. "I got ready for *dawālī*." We lingered over the coffee, chatting, until she suggested that we get started.

Jafra brought out a collection of supplies, including a medium rubber bowl filled with the boiled leaves, soft and stuck together in piles. By the time I arrived at her home, she had already purchased, washed, and boiled the grape leaves and allowed them to cool enough for us to fill and roll them. A large rubber bowl was filled with rice and meat, generously flecked with black pepper (*filfil aswad*) and spices (*bahārāt*). We had aluminum dishes to roll the leaves and a big pot for us to fill. Before we started rolling, she quickly sliced tomatoes into the bottom of the pot, holding them in her palm while she moved an old, dull kitchen knife through them. The tomato slices covered the bottom of the pot, creating a protective layer so that the dish could stay on the fire longer, she explained to me. If the tomato burned, that was no problem. But the rolled leaves would split and fill the whole pot with rice if they burned.

Jafra showed me how to make the first few *dawālī*: she peeled a leaf from the pile, spread it out (veins up) on the silver tray she was working with, and placed a small pile of rice and meat in the middle of the leaf. Then she folded both sides of the leaf into the center and rolled up the package tightly, like a cigar. After watching her, I began trying too, and she let me experiment at my own pace. She did not comment on my work, even though the grape-leaf rolls that I made were all different sizes and sometimes not very tight packages. We worked quickly, filling a pot before I even noticed.

While we rolled, we talked about the people we knew. She had a friend from the kindergarten where we had met who no longer called her. Why did she not hear from her? Was this woman frightened of her, or did she just no longer want to be her friend? We talked about our friend Rim and her teaching schedule, which was grueling: she did a morning shift with Syrian refugees and an afternoon shift with the neighborhood's Jordanian children. The time passed. Jafra told me how much she enjoyed this dish, how much she wanted to make it. There was no time to make it when she was working, so it had to happen on a weekend.

When we finished, Jafra put the pot on the fire with water and a Maggi cube, the local brand of chicken bouillon. I said I needed to go.

"No!" She said. "You need to eat *dawālī*. We made it together, so you should stay and eat."

I explained that I needed to visit my landlady and get the keys to my new apartment.

"OK," she agreed. "Go, quickly, while it is on the fire and when you come back we will eat."

I agreed and rushed off to run my errand. When I came back, Jafra moved me right into the kitchen. Musa, her husband, was visiting a friend and would be home later. Her daughter, Aya, was at a friend's and would eat tabbouleh there. Her son, Ayyub, would join us to eat, she said. She handed me two bowls of yogurt to put on the coffee table where we had placed our cups earlier and directed me to the newspaper that she had left on the table outside the kitchen. I unfolded single sheets of newspaper and laid them over the space, then put the yogurt down. When I went back into the kitchen, she asked me to heat the two frozen loaves of Arab bread that were on the round plastic table in the middle of the room. "Sure," I said, "but you will have to light the burner for me!"

Jafra took a cigarette lighter from the table and tipped it close the burner while she turned the knob. A blue flame leapt out. *Tafaḍḍalī* (go ahead), she told me. I stepped into her place and flipped the loaves of bread back and forth on the flame until they softened, heated, and began to puff up with air. Jafra had flipped the pot of *dawālī* over, so that it was bottom-up on top of a large aluminum serving dish and draped with a damp towel. Cooling the bottom slightly made the burned bits at the bottom release, she had told me.

Jafra opened and closed cabinets while we prepared to eat, gathering the soup bowls and spoons. She called to her son: "Ayyub! Ayyub!" He ignored her, remaining in his bedroom.

She lifted the pot off the *dawālī* and shook out the remnants at the bottom before tipping it upright so she could see what remained. Most of it came out easily, with a few bits remaining at the bottom. She took a spoon and scraped off the tomato slices, which were not too burned, piling them on top of the mountain of *dawālī*. She ate the rolled leaves that escaped from the pile, cleaning up the formation with her snacking. "It's so good," she said. "I love *dawālī*." She carried out the platter and placed it on the table. I followed her, ready to eat.

Jafra walked away from the freshly made food to knock on her son's bedroom door, to invite him to join us for the meal. When he refused, she came back. "Ayyub doesn't want to eat," she said. "He says he doesn't want to eat *dawālī*. But you wait: I will leave it in the kitchen, and he will come back and eat it later."

Jafra and I sat down to eat. She sat closest to the pan and spooned generous portions into each of our soup bowls. Then we added yogurt to them. The food was delicious, with the tart taste of the grape leaves and the soft rice and the broth pooled in the bottom of our dishes. We ate quietly and quickly, commenting on nothing but how good the food was. We got full quickly and started eating more slowly, taking the grape-leaf fingers from the platter one at a time, biting them in half in the middle or popping the entire package into our mouths at once.

"I usually just eat once a day," she told me. "But since it's *dawālī*, I will keep eating it. I will keep it in the kitchen and snack on it every time I go by."

"Because it's so good. *Yislamū īdayki, yā Imm Ayyūb*," I told her.[2]

Jafra laughed. "It's good, my *dawālī*, isn't it?" She sat back in her chair, satisfied, and put her hands over her stomach. "Do you want tea now?"

"Not yet," I said. "Let's stay a little bit." And we stayed together for some time in the aftermath of the meal, settled in the relaxed timeline of weekend cooking.

## Embodied Temporalities of Levantine Cuisine

Our session making *dawālī* constitutes a physical embodiment of Levantine cuisine—specifically, the distinct way that time proceeds in the course of preparing an elaborate dish like *dawālī*. Our long day spent with grape leaves, and with each other, emphasized female sociality as a key ingredient of the dish. This example of a leisurely Saturday constructed around a meal shows the role of women's work making food together in the construction of something called Levantine cuisine. When I say "Levantine" here, I mean dishes that were made in the community where I worked—Tal al-Zahra, a working-class neighborhood of East Amman. They were regarded as regional yet further distinguished by national or communal variations. In this usage, "Levantine" is largely an ethnographic term and a translation of *akl bilād al-shām* (the foods of greater Syria), understood in Tal al-Zahra to include Jordan, Palestine, Lebanon, and Syria. Over some three years of fieldwork on domestic life in Tal al-Zahra, I observed that much of women's socializing revolved around cooking and eating. The time and love that they invested in making dishes that they considered part of the heritage of greater Syria infused the cuisine with moral implications. The time and love were anything but abstract: they were evident in the long hours spent working on dishes, time taken away from other activities. Women's work, in short, is fundamental to the concept of Levantine cuisine. The social relations that this work constructs are part of that concept as well.

Levantine cuisine, in all its varied forms, is sensory, embodied, social, and cultural. In their essence, cooking and eating are sensory activities that we do with our bodies. They are equally social, carried out in cooperation with and in the presence of others. Finally, they are cultural, imbued with symbolic meanings that connect us to other times and places as we eat and cook. The women of Tal al-Zahra with whom I worked, mostly descendants of Palestinians and Iraqis, facilitated each of these facets of their cuisine. Their notion of Levantine cuisine emerged from their shared experiences of cooking and eating together and enjoying the time spent in preparation, consumption, and tidying up afterward, experiences like the one I shared with Jafra, making *dawālī*. In addition to producing a regional culinary canon, these sessions also contributed to producing normative conceptions of proper female comportment. As women cooked together, they shared the experience of using their bodies to make food in ways that were time-consuming, laborious, and social. In doing so they cultivated an implied social agreement that women should do this kind of work and that it was particularly female in some way.

Cooking creates the idea of Levantine cuisine and norms for female behavior at the same time. This process has three dimensions. The first dimension is speed: cooking is slow, and the embodied experience of moving at a slow pace while making food at home demands that women who cook arrange their everyday lives in a certain way to accommodate their cooking. The second dimension is historical time and the sense of being connected to the past of a nation where the women no longer live, most often Palestine. The third dimension is knowledge, the accumulation of experience through exposure, practice, and conversation. Each of these dimensions has sensory, embodied, social, and cultural elements. Together, these dimensions suggest that making Levantine cuisine involves a connection to the idea of a geographical place called the Levant and that this connection happens through the body. Each dimension also informs women's ideas of what is desirable, appropriate, and moral for them to do.

The idea of Levantine cuisine attaches in a specific way to the dishes I describe making and eating in this chapter. While the techniques that the women of Tal al-Zahra used were clearly identified as Palestinian, the dishes they made are part of a broader Arab culinary tradition. *Maḥāshī* (stuffed vegetables; singular *maḥshī*), for example, falls under the umbrella of Levantine cuisine, but it takes different forms and names in other parts of the Levant and in Iraq. More a technique than a dish, it has as many variations as there are cooks who make it. Various vegetables can be hollowed out and stuffed, and many others can be rolled into a container for meat, rice, or meat and rice. Yogurt, tomato, and stock can all make up the broth for a dish of stuffed vegetables. Enumerating the different stuffed dishes and their names, and attaching the variations to specific temporalities and geographies, is an endlessly entertaining pastime. Women in Tal al-Zahra were curious about how foods familiar to them looked and what they were called in other parts of the Arab world. The versatility and variability of *maḥāshī*, though, is deemphasized as it is localized and made specific to the historical and cultural lineage of the woman making it as well as to her personal inclinations and tastes. Iraqi dolma, for example, is a dish similar to Levantine variations on *maḥāshī* in that it is composed of vegetables stuffed with rice and meat. Unlike its counterparts in Bilad al-Sham, though, it welcomes vegetables in any combination at all: home cooks stuff whatever vegetable they have in their pantry for the dolma and can throw in a few *fūl* (fava beans) if they like. They stuff tomatoes, potatoes, and onions. When my Palestinian friends ate the dish and asked how to cook it, their experience was one of curiosity and comparison with their own way of making *maḥāshī*. The notion of Levantine cuisine, then, functioned in the Jordanian community where I was working as a frame for broader comparison within which women articulated the uniqueness of their national, local, and personal approach to making the dish.

## A Taste of Amman

During my fieldwork in Tal al-Zahra, I spent time with women in their apartments as they spent their days looking after their homes and families and otherwise attending to the demands of everyday life. In other work, I look at the way they addressed questions of personal freedom, friendship, betrayal, and other weightier dilemmas.[3] Here I examine the question that arose most frequently: what to cook and how to cook it. The conversations at most social gatherings took a detour through cooking, including a recitation of what everyone had made, how they had made it, and whether it had been tasty. Tips on whether to use black or white pepper to season, a knife or a food processor to chop, and almonds or pine nuts to garnish were more prominent than pleasantries.[4]

Tal al-Zahra is not a terribly distinctive section of East Amman. It is far enough west to be upwardly mobile and far enough east to be almost exclusively populated by Arabs. Unlike West Amman, where white foreigners were a common sight, East Amman was known for being more ethnically homogeneous (meaning home to fewer white foreigners).[5] Tal al-Zahra residents had diverse origins—although this distinction between East and West Amman was as much a class division as an ethnic one, with elites almost never residing in the city's eastern part. A largely Palestinian neighborhood since Amman's rapid expansion in 1948, it included residents from Gaza, the West Bank, and what local residents referred to as "[19]48 lands" (*arāḍī tamāniyeh wa-arba'īn*). Within the West Bank and "48" groups, people were often curious to distinguish between villages of origin, even when they themselves had never been there. In addition to people displaced from Palestine, there were also Palestinian people displaced from Kuwait and Iraqis displaced in the aftermath of America's 2003 military campaign. People of other origins existed in speculation: the new apartment buildings being constructed at the edges of Tal al-Zahra were imagined to have owners from the Gulf: whenever rent was increased, the specter of Syrian migrants was blamed for the economic shift. People of "East Bank" Jordanian origin were few but proud.[6]

Tal al-Zahra's designation as a popular (*sha'bī*) neighborhood arose in part from its particular brand of diversity. The moniker *sha'bī* could carry varied connotations in Jordanian Arabic, ranging from praise for authenticity to condemnation for backwardness. As a residential area, Tal al-Zahra carried the full range of associations—among residents and nonresidents alike. Food, though, carried class distinctions slightly differently; home cooking was lauded indiscriminately across classes. Elite Jordanians were inclined to consider "poor" people's home cooking with some nostalgia: it included all of the delicious fats that their grandmothers had used, which they had eliminated from their diets in the name of health. The dishes that people could expect to enjoy in Amman's fanciest home kitchens, though, looked remarkably similar to the ones that appeared in Tal al-Zahra. The well-loved classic dishes were largely the same.

In Tal al-Zahra as elsewhere in Amman, there was a dynamic range of language and opinions for discussing a familiar range of cuisine. Each national origin had a distinctive set of vocabulary for the foods they made: Palestinians had a repertoire of dishes that they considered to belong to their cultural tradition, including *maḥāshī*, *mulūkhiya*, *musakhan*, and numerous other dishes that involved slowly cooking a combination of vegetables and stew meat over a low flame. *Maḥāshī* is an umbrella category that includes anything stuffed with rice and meat; the term means "stuffed" and could include anything prepared using that technique. Zucchinis (*kūsā*) were the staple vegetable for stuffing. Stuffed zucchinis could be in the same pot as either lamb chops and stuffed grape leaves (as in *waraq dawālī*) or stuffed eggplants and a squash-like vegetable called *qarʿa*, also stuffed, and tomato broth. The Iraqi dish dolma, as noted, had some similarities—enough to make it a point of curiosity. The most common homemade sweet was *maʿmūl*, cookies served on holidays (usually Eid al-Adha) when people visit one another to celebrate. The cookies are carefully formed semolina filled with either chopped walnuts and sugar or date paste (*ʿajweh*). Both *maʿmūl* and *maḥāshī* involved the many-step process of stuffing: the outer layer and a filling had to be prepared. Then the stuffing had to be done appropriately, all before the final step of cooking or baking.

Multistep dishes like *maḥāshī* are time-consuming and laborious. For the women I worked with in Tal al-Zahra, having a team of women to assist them and keep them company during the lengthy process was essential both to completing the task and to enjoying it. The feeling of gathering women together to work collectively on assembling big, complicated dishes was part of what those dishes invoked and entailed for the women who knew how to make them. As such, the dishes themselves implied a certain way of life that was marked by a felt experience of drawn-out socializing that accompanied the hard work of making the dish. The luxury of time at home, for one, was a precondition for this kind of work, as was the presence of female neighbors with a similar schedule. The intimacy of these relationships, and the feeling of being with other women up to our elbows in raw meat and uncooked rice, implied a form of social trust and support between women. While it could be fragile, this trust and support connected women to one another. Finally, the time invested in making this kind of food, when other less time-consuming and possibly cheaper options like eggs or falafel could much more easily sate people's hunger, implies an agreement among these women that the food resulting from this time investment was better: more nutritious, more delicious, and more moral.

What emerges around this image of convivial kitchen efforts is a set of positive, community-oriented associations of women, typically mothers, preparing a certain kind of food in a certain way that connects them to a way of life that they consider "moral." I use this word as anthropologist Joel Robbins has used it, in a Durkheimian sense, to describe the morality of reproduction, a comfortably social morality that involves maintaining what already exists and is familiar.[7] In this case, the norms in question have to do with families and women's roles within their families and follow a model of women spending time in looking after everything related to the home, while men socialize outside the home and embody a head-of-household role when at home. This ideal endures in Jordan despite social changes that make it somewhat more challenging to maintain. Many women work outside the home in different ways, and traditional gender roles in the home are up for negotiation as expectations shift toward the ideals of romantic companionship depicted in television series. This pure, uncontested division exists as an ideal type, not as a reality for most people.[8] When women in Tal al-Zahra cooked, though, they could momentarily inhabit the ideal of nourishing mothers; when they discussed cooking together, they also activated the sense of embodying appropriate femininity.

## Bodies Feeling Time: Theoretical Tools

In locating my exploration of Levantine cuisine decisively in embodied experience, I am privileging the sensations of cooking and eating that are likely most familiar to readers. Eating and sharing food are things we do and experience with our bodies: analysis comes afterward, if at all. Gathering data on the embodied and the sensory means allowing some things to be implicit and allowing our own bodies as ethnographers to be a source of information. This type of research entails five key foundational assumptions. (1) It is possible to feel something in our bodies that is shared by other nearby bodies who have the same experience. (2) It is possible to live these shared experiences and understand them as something shared without necessarily naming them as a shared experience. (3) Taste and speed are among these embodied experiences and are both felt. (4) These embodied and felt experiences, including taste and speed, have the potential to connect us to something beyond the present. (5) These embodied and sensory experiences arise in and reflect a context where maternal love is manifested in cooking and serving these well-known dishes. I address each of these foundational assumptions in turn.

First, it is possible to feel something in our own bodies that is shared by other nearby bodies having the same experience. When women sat together to cook in Tal al-Zahra, they moved in similar ways and used familiar physical techniques that allowed them to have a recognizably similar experience. This shared experience involved feelings, both emotional and physical.

Second, all five senses were involved in cooking.[9] This sensory immersion happened without conscious effort.

Third, cooking in Tal al-Zahra included a panoply of sensory experiences, but the ones that concern me most here are taste and timing. Ben Highmore offers a conception of taste as a feeling: rather than being a preconditioned, subconscious choice overdetermined by cultural factors, taste is a cocktail of first-person experiences that build a relationship between the person liking or disliking and the object in question. This approach to taste lets go of the idea that our likes and dislikes are functions of class or group inclusion or at least makes those things secondary. In Highmore's words, "It requires an approach that recognizes that the materiality of taste, as well as what matters about taste, is the feelings through which it is animated."[10] Taste-as-feeling acknowledges a relationship between me and the object that I like and also acknowledges that individual feelings arise in the specific historical contexts that make them possible.[11] In short, this approach says that liking matters and is a real, complex, personal feeling and that its idiosyncratic manifestation in the body exists alongside its shared manifestations in communities of all sizes.

This sort of taste was in question in Tal al-Zahra cooking sessions, where women felt their way into the sorts of spice additions or hand movements that they chose in order to make something more attractive or more delicious. Timing, as well, is a piece of this analysis. The way that women felt time passing in these home environments is contrasted to the way that they experienced speed outside of their homes, which is associated with the modernizing city of Amman and the distinct sort of morality that prevails there. Following Highmore, I suggest that the women experienced feelings of both time and taste as they were making and eating food in Tal al-Zahra. They like some time cadences, which feel good, but they like others less, like preparing food hastily while children hover impatiently or bringing home and serving fried chicken.

Fourth, all the feelings that I describe here were not only ways of connecting to the moment of work and connection with one another but also a way of stirring oneself into the past of a much larger imagined community.[12] Through the embodied encounter of the smells and tastes of mixed spices, ground meat, cinnamon, or shortening, and the remembering of the ways that their grandmothers and mothers prepared the same dishes, the women incorporated themselves into lineages of care and culinary tradition through their own work at cooking. Their work, which connected them to their national pasts, put them in the role of caretakers of that history as well as of the family and guests who ate their food. This work was explicitly gendered, and women were expected to embody the skill of cooking as well as the love of cooking.

The taste of a woman's food was often interpreted as an indicator of her character: *nafas-hā zākī*, women would say of one another, meaning that their delicious soul or breath was infusing the food with good taste. The relational connection between an object and the person who likes it that Highmore describes is manifested in the foods of Tal al-Zahra in two directions, then: through the hand of the cook and the palate of the consumer. For those who ate and enjoyed the food produced, the feeling surrounding its preparation was further linked to the moral character of the woman making it. Her goodness, her deliciousness, translates into her ability to care for those around her by nourishing them. Her food is a form of care, and her particular form of care reflects her character. This close link between the goodness of a woman's cooking and the morality of her character reflects the many layers of assumption underpinning the ways women performed their love for their families and other intimates.

At the base of this stack of assumptions is the ideal of the nuclear family: a husband and wife who divide labor between them and in doing so create a safe environment for their children.[13] The intact nuclear family represents a norm in contemporary Jordan—women's horror stories about married couples who share a home space with the husband's parents reinforce its desirability. This arrangement of family life arrived relatively recently in the region,[14] recorded in the changes that took place among expanding elites of the late nineteenth century and early twentieth century. The ideal of the perfect housewife, secluded in a space that she maintains for her husband, emerged as a dominant ideal during this period and has taken root as an ideal type. Kinship ties remain close in Jordan. It is not uncommon for families to reside in the same building, adding stories or apartments to accommodate sons and their new brides, but the ideal is clearly for one couple to inhabit one household. In current conceptions of middle-class womanhood, sharing home space with another is viewed as compromising to a woman's dignity. Accordingly, one woman's total influence over the domestic space that she cares for represents the achievement of a moral norm.

As the idea of the nuclear family and its association with moral purity has gained purchase in the Middle East, it has been translated into metaphors for the nation. In these metaphors, kings and presidents are the fathers of the nation and women are the mothers, responsible for reproducing its sons and preserving its chastity through their proper comportment.[15] The moral significance of women looking after the kitchen is more political than mere reproduction. A mother's love for her children and a wife's for her husband, manifest in her attention to feeding them well, reproduces the morality of the nation as a collective that includes some and excludes others at the same time that it reproduces the nuclear family. Palestinians are often excluded from the idea of the Jordanian national collective, so the dream of national belonging is particularly urgent. In theorist Sara Ahmed's words, "The reproduction of femininity is tied up with the reproduction of the national ideal through the work of love."[16] Cooking is a work of love that reproduces both ideals of femininity and ideals of the nation through a loving investment of time. At stake in this work of cooking, and the feelings it inspires, is nothing less than the well-being of all the nations that the women of Tal al-Zahra envision themselves as part of. It is infused with sensuality, with sociality, and with love, all of which are folded into ideas about how men and women should contribute differently to making a moral family and an intact nation.

The attempt I make here to read the practice of cooking and eating in Tal al-Zahra relies on these foundational assumptions. These assumptions have a conceptual consequence: namely, that the women making this cuisine did not merely do the cuisine-making as an activity separate from the rest of their lives but rather that they cultivated their bodies in a way that made this kind of cuisine possible. As women's ways of inhabiting their bodies change, the ways that the cuisine is made, experienced, and tasted also change. Different generations of women have varying tastes and embodied relationships with the experience of cooking and eating Levantine cuisine. The idea of a Levantine cuisine includes ideas about how women are encouraged to inhabit their bodies, which have real implications for gender relations in contemporary Jordan. The cuisine itself cannot exist in our shared imaginary without the embodied female labor that goes into making it. This labor underpins not only the consumption of this delicious food by others but also the moral imaginary of the nation and the bourgeois ideal of the intact nuclear family. When we talk about Levantine cuisine, we are also talking about the physical labor of making it. It is women who perform that physical labor uncompensated, in the name of morality and of love.

## Discovering the Familiar

While housework is often conceptualized as routine,[17] and treated as something semiautomated and repetitive, we see in my day with Jafra just how much serendipity, shift, and planning were involved in the act of making lunch for her family. The cadence of the preparation in this case was emergent: Jafra's routine depended on when someone (I) arrived to help her, and the ritual of eating was disrupted and reconfigured at every juncture. Schedules changed, preferences failed to align, and tasks took longer than or not as long as expected. The project of making *dawālī*, in this case, was the response to a desire for this specific kind of well-loved food, the desire for a specific taste. This desire was then lived over an entire day, to be gratified in a short eating session.

The particularity of this experience comes from a contrast with other temporalities—those of the workday or the urban commute,[18] where there are no such time-rich stretches. Jafra, who was working as a teacher during the week, chose to make this dish on a weekend day because her work schedule did not permit another configuration. Her judgment call shows us that this kind of time, required to make the staple dishes in her repertoire, was a scarce good rendered scarcer by engagement in work and in time spent outside of the house. By protecting it, by designating it as a key aspiration of her weekend and enrolling others (myself in this case) in making it possible, she elevated this kind of time to the status of luxury. Passing her day in this fashion was a pleasure for her. Although we worked diligently at making the *dawālī*, which was physically laborious, the flexible, restful cadence made this effort pleasant. In part, the pleasure arose from the taste of the food, its deliciousness and familiarity. It also arose from the anticipation of the dish's goodness, which flavored the work of preparing it.

Of the dimensions mentioned as fundamental to my analysis of Levantine cuisine in Tal al-Zahra, time and knowledge stand out as central to this particular experience. The flexibility of time and the way it unfolded—full of activity, but without the rigidity of a work schedule—distinguished it from professional work and the temporality that prevailed in the workplace. The notion of knowledge transfer also animated our work session. In gently allowing me to experiment with making *dawālī* by imitating her style of preparation, Jafra welcomed me into a manner of learning to cook that reflected her approach with her daughter and the approach that women took with one another when they collaborated to make dishes together. A sort of demonstration followed by a companionable acceptance of varied approaches allowed me to learn about the technique in an embodied fashion rather than in a didactic manner that designated certain movements as "right" and others as "wrong." The third fundamental dimension, historical time, appears in the next vignette.

## A Lifeline to the Land: Connections to the National Past

In sensory and embodied terms, preparing their staple dishes was an avenue for women to inhabit a temporality distinct from that of the workplace or the city and reminiscent of the past. Conversations about food similarly connected women to other times and places by linking them to distinct national spaces. *Maḥāshī* exemplified this connection across places and the implied history of those places. In one case, two friends, Noor (an Iraqi) and ʿAziza (a Jordanian citizen of Gazan descent), were mutually curious about each other's approach to making *maḥāshī*. While ʿAziza adhered to the typical Levantine typology, wherein *dawālī, waraʾ kūsā* (*waraq kūsā* in written Arabic, a combination of stuffed grape leaves and zucchini), and *kūsā maḥshī* served with tomato broth together represented the repertoire of stuffed things, Noor followed the Iraqi tradition of making dolma, a hodgepodge of various different kinds of stuffed vegetables. ʿAziza was fascinated by this variation on a common dish and eager to explain it to her sisters, who were equally curious.

Noor was proud of her cooking and eager to show ʿAziza's sisters ʿAliyaʾ and Safaʾ the technique that she had shown ʿAziza. When the sisters were all together in Amman, she invited them for lunch, making this triumphant dish and laboriously preparing her home to receive them. Mother of four children under ten, she took pains to keep her space as clean as possible. The sisters came on a weekend afternoon and huddled into the small seating area next to the kitchen. While they were drinking juice and making small talk before the meal, Noor enumerated the contents of the dish, going through the things that were stuffed. Zucchini, eggplants, and *siliq* (a leafy plant similar to grape vines) were vegetables they knew as stuffable; carrots and potatoes were less common but still conceivable. Onions, though, were surprising. One of the sisters, ʿAliyaʾ, was incredulous. How do you stuff an onion? Noor explained: you peel the onion, cut deeply enough into the side of the onion so that you can pull the inner layers out, but not so deeply that you cut the onion into two pieces, open up the layers, extract each spherical layer one by one, fill the onion skin with rice, and then fold the cut edges one over another to make a neat package. As the onion cooked, the sides of skin melted into one another to keep the cooked rice inside.

'Aliya' remained confused. Noor continued her attempt to explain, and her sisters tried as well, but the idea remained quite outside of what she could imagine. She remained puzzled until Noor served the lunch.

When Noor triumphantly placed the steaming platter on the table, it contained everything promised: zucchini, eggplants, *siliq*; carrots and potatoes; and onions. It was a pile of cooked vegetables plump with rice stuffing, rolling over each other to rest against the rim of the platter. Before filling her plate, 'Aliya' fished through the selection of vegetables to find an onion. When she found it, she took it in her hand, held it up, and peered at it carefully, like a doctor examining an X-ray. "Now I see," she said. She put the onion back on the platter and allowed Noor to fill a plate and hand it to her.

Noor later shared with me that this was how "Palestinians" reacted. She had never seen a Palestinian successfully stuff an onion. *Mā buḍbuṭ maʿhum* (it doesn't work for them), she said.

This idea of a specific national cuisine emerges in a continual comparison of approaches, recipes, and styles. As the women elaborated recipes and techniques, they made distinctions between what cuisine was associated with each geography and how it was executed in each place. This distinguishing process did not so much develop a hierarchy (as it has in some other contexts) as articulate a clear typology connecting culinary elements to geographical features.[19] This typology allowed women to think of making these foods as a means of participating in their own national communities. Embedded in this idea of a national cuisine is an implied notion of a national history; for 'Aziza and her sister Safa', who had never been to Palestine, the distinction between Noor's rendering of the dish and the rendering that "worked for them" was itself a reference to their heritage rather than to their present. And for 'Aliya', who had returned to Palestine after growing up in Jordan, her inclusion in a group with her sisters implied an uninterrupted continuity in their shared Palestinian identity, erasing the disjuncture that arose from her coming and going.

## Embodied Connection

The act of cooking and eating connected women to a specific kind of temporality that was distinct from the temporality associated with the regimented schedule of the workplace or the hustle of moving about the city. It also connected them with specific cultural imaginaries, like the nation, and distinguished them as members of those groups. Finally, it connected them to an embodied manner of knowledge acquisition that could be inhabited collectively. All of these projects of belonging were holistic, in that they demanded nearly complete immersion in the moments when women performed them, absorbing the entire body's attention. This absorption had the potential to be pleasant, even gratifying. This pleasure and gratification, however, arose from a certain configuration of time, embodiment, and national imaginary that either disrupted or entirely precluded other conceptions of the "good." Insofar as a highly productive professional schedule for women is regarded as desirable, a lifestyle where women spend days together making complex dishes seems less plausible.

Within Tal al-Zahra, both value propositions—moving slowly and being connected to a national past—had their merits: women could plausibly make arguments for the moral validity of both approaches. What I want to emphasize here, though, is that in talking about Levantine cuisine as a concept, we are also talking about the labor of female bodies that produce this cuisine. To reify the cuisine itself without acknowledging how much of its production is enabled and has been enabled by women investing their time, physical energy, and social resources is to erase this very important female contribution from the concept entirely. By attending to the female labor that makes Levantine cuisine a reality, we start to see how "cuisine" means more than food that stands alone on a plate. Cuisine includes the people who make it, the materials they use, and the contexts where they live, cook, and eat. In Tal al-Zahra, this context includes specific ideas about how women use their time and how they fit into a national past, which contribute to notions of what is and is not possible for people of both genders.

### Acknowledgments

Thanks are due to the editors and contributors to the workshop who made this volume possible. Anny Gaul, Graham Pitts, and Vicki Valosik turned a keen editorial eye on this manuscript, and their input improved it a great deal. This project benefited from the support of a Fulbright Scholarship, a Wenner-Gren Dissertation Fieldwork Grant, and funding from the School of Anthropology and Museum Ethnography at the University of Oxford. The writing was aided by help from the British Academy and the Department of Social Anthropology at the University of Cambridge. Christine Sargent contributed to whatever clarity I managed to achieve in it. The magnificent cooks of Tal al-Zahra kept me inspired and well fed during research and continue to be important sources of support.

## Notes

1. All my interlocutors' names are pseudonyms, as is the neighborhood name "Tal al-Zahra."

2. "God bless the hands that did this, mother of Ayyub." The title "mother of Ayyub" is a *kunya*, a common way of addressing married women with children in Jordan and in Tal al-Zahra.

3. Susan MacDougall, "Will You Marry My Son? Ethnography, Culture, and the Performance of Gender," *Journal of the Anthropological Society of Oxford* 8, no. 1 (2015): 25–38; Susan MacDougall, "Ugly Feelings of Greed: The Misuse of Friendship in Working-Class Amman," *Cambridge Journal of Anthropology* (2019): 74–89.

4. I was not alone in this experience: my anthropology colleagues carrying out fieldwork at the same time also noted the constant nature of talk about food. My colleague Christine Sargent took to sending me messages every time she had a conversation about whether or not to wash chicken before cooking it. I heard from her almost daily when she was in the field.

5. I experienced this homogeneity firsthand in Tal al-Zahra when I saw a white foreign couple in the supermarket and found myself staring at them. When I went to visit my neighbor later, she asked me if I had noted the other foreigners in the neighborhood (other than me, that is). We speculated enthusiastically about where they were from and why they would be in Tal al-Zahra.

6. The West Bank was annexed by Jordan in 1948 and lost to Israel in 1967. The current term "East Bank Jordanian" derives its meaning from the contrast with the West Bank and means Jordanian Jordanian, not Palestinian Jordanian. The notion of a distinctly Jordanian bedouin population is not supported by any historical record. It persists as a political reality: Andrew Shryock, *Nationalism and the Genealogical Imagination: Oral History and Textual Authority in Jordan* (Berkeley: University of California Press, 1997).

7. Joel Robbins, "Between Reproduction and Freedom: Morality, Value and Radical Cultural Change," *Ethnos: Journal of Anthropology* 72, no. 3 (2007): 293–314. In Robbins's framework, this is distinct from the "morality of freedom," which involves reflection on what morality means in a context of social change.

8. Mary Kawar, *Gender and Generation in Household Labor Supply in Jordan* (Beirut: International Labour Organisation's Population Council, West Asia and North Africa Region, 2000); Fida Adely, "A Different Kind of Love: Compatibility (*Insijam*) and Marriage in Jordan," *Arab Studies Journal* 24, no. 2 (2016); Mayyada Abu Jaber, "Lifting the Barriers to Economic Progress for Women in Jordan," Washington, D.C.: Brookings Institution, 2014.

9. Teresa Brennan, *The Transmission of Affect* (Ithaca: Cornell University Press, 2004).

10. Ben Highmore, "Taste as Feeling," *New Literary History* 47, no. 4 (2016): 547–566.

11. Raymond Williams, *Marxism and Literature* (Oxford: Oxford University Press, 1977).

12. Benedict Anderson, *Imagined Communities: Reflections on the Origins and Spread of Nationalism* (London: Verso, 1991); Nadia Seremetakis, *The Senses Still* (Chicago: University of Chicago Press, 1994).

13. The role of love between husband and wife in the nuclear family merits its own study. It was a desirable but not essential ingredient in Tal al-Zahra. Several of the women I worked with, in their thirties and forties, had married for love (*zawāj 'an ḥub*), although this was less common than traditional marriage (*zawāj taqlīdī*), where (mostly female) family members brokered marriage agreements without the couple spending much time together prior to the marriage. Young women in Tal al-Zahra regarded both avenues as possibilities, although compatibility (*insijām*) was increasingly regarded as an essential element of a happy marriage, in keeping with nationwide trends. See Adely, "A Different Kind of Love," for a more in-depth treatment.

14. Akram Khater, *Inventing Home: Emigration, Gender, and the Middle Class in Lebanon, 1870–1920* (Berkeley: University of California Press, 2001).

15. Andrew Shryock, "Dynastic Modernism and Its Contradictions: Testing the Limits of Pluralism, Tribalism, and King Hussein's Example in Hashemite Jordan," *Arab Studies Quarterly* 22, no. 3 (2000): 57–79; Esra Ozyurek, "Wedded to the Republic: Public Intellectuals and Intimacy-Oriented Publics in Turkey," in *Off Stage/On Display: Intimacy and Ethnography in the Age of Public Culture*, ed. Andrew Shryock (Stanford: Stanford University Press, 2004), 101–130; Elizabeth Faier, "Looking In/Acting Out: Gender, Modernity, and the (Re)Production of the Palestinian Family," *Political and Legal Anthropology Review* 20, no. 2 (1997): 1–15; Rhoda Ann Kanaaneh, *Birthing the Nation: Strategies of Palestinian Women in Israel* (Berkeley: University of California Press, 2001); Eric Davis, *Memories of State: Politics, History, and Collective Identity in Modern Iraq* (Berkeley: University of California Press, 2005).

16. Sara Ahmed, *The Cultural Politics of Emotion* (Edinburgh: University of Edinburgh Press), 124.

17. Ben Highmore, "Homework: Routine, Social Aesthetics, and the Ambiguity of Everyday Life," *Cultural Studies* 18 (2004): 2–3, 306–327; Bernice Martin, "'Mother Wouldn't Like It': Housework as Magic," *Theory, Culture, and Society* 2, no. 2 (1984): 19–36.

18. Highmore, "Homework"; Center for the Study of the Built Environment, *Basima's Daily Commute to Work (Rihlat Basima al-Yawmiyya ila 'Amaliha)* (Amman, Jordan: CSBE films, 2015); Christopher Parker, "Tunnel-Bypasses and Minarets of Capitalism: Amman as Neoliberal Assemblage," *Political Geography* 28 (2009): 110–120.

19. Arjun Appadurai, "How to Make a National Cuisine: Cookbooks in Contemporary India," *Comparative Studies in Society and History* 30, no. 1 (1988): 3–24.

# CHAPTER 9

# *Shakshūka* for All Seasons: Tunisian Jewish Foodways at the Turn of the Twentieth Century

NOAM SIENNA

The annual survey of the National Restaurant Association in late 2018 declared that one of the "global food trends" of the following year would be *shakshūka*, described as "a globally-inspired breakfast item ... a Tunisian/Israeli dish" of eggs poached in a spicy tomato sauce.[1] The slash in "Tunisian/Israeli" draws our attention to the ways in which the mobility of food links communities across national, regional, and religious boundaries. *Shakshūka* is a stew of tomatoes, onions, and peppers (sometimes with other vegetables), usually topped with eggs poached in the stew.[2] While it originates in North Africa, it has now become a popular "Middle Eastern" dish, especially through its associations with Israeli cuisine. This chapter traces the trajectory of the movement of *shakshūka* from the Maghreb to the Levant through the examination of a rare Judeo-Arabic cookbook, *U-vishalta Ve-akhalta*, published as an eight-page booklet in Tunis around 1907. The cookbook, which presents a mixture of dishes, ingredients, and vocabulary drawn from North African, Levantine, French, and Mediterranean communities, includes some of the earliest known recipes for *shakshūka* and its earliest invocation in a Jewish context, opening a window into the foodways of Tunisian Jews at the turn of the century.

I was first introduced to this cookbook through the work of the late rabbi Dr. Alan D. Corré, longtime professor at the University of Wisconsin–Milwaukee and an accomplished scholar of both Semitic and Romance languages and literatures.[3] While in Tunisia in 1970, Dr. Corré purchased a fragile copy of *U-vishalta Ve-akhalta* in a used bookstore and began translating it before his death in 2017, posting a short summary of the cookbook on his website. The only other surviving copy is located in the National Library of Israel (NLI Rare A5232), where it was accessioned from the collection of Avraham (Robert) Attal. This cookbook was part of a flowering of Jewish books published in Tunisia around the turn of the twentieth century, including Hebrew liturgical texts, Judeo-Arabic folk literature, and translations of French works.[4] Apart from two short-lived attempts to open Jewish publishing houses in the sixteenth and eighteenth centuries, North Africa did not have a Hebrew printing industry until the second half of the nineteenth century.[5] As a result, Maghrebi Jewish authors and publishers generally brought their books to press at printing houses in Europe and the Ottoman Empire or circulated texts in manuscript form. The first Hebrew books printed in the Maghreb—all three by a peripatetic rabbi and printer from Jerusalem named Hayyim Ze'ev Ashkenazi—were published in Algiers in 1853, Oran in 1856, and Tunis in 1861.[6] This initiative was followed by the opening of new presses by the local community in Algeria, but it seems that no further books were printed in Hebrew characters in Tunisia until the 1880s.

At the end of the nineteenth century, three Jewish presses were opened in Tunis in rapid succession. The first was a small press run by the Tunis-born son of a Livornese émigré, Vittorio Finzi, who received a printing license from the bey of Tunis in 1880.[7] The second was the press of Sion Uzan and Joseph Castro (Imprimerie Uzan et Castro), which printed large numbers of popular Judeo-Arabic newspapers, booklets of folklore, and serialized novels, starting in 1885.[8] Finally, Ya'aqov Guedj was the publisher of the 1907 cookbook discussed here. Guedj's family was Tunisian but moved to Algiers, where Guedj apprenticed as a printer and then opened his own press. He moved back to Tunis with his father in 1895 and reopened his press there.[9]

The decades between 1880 and 1920 saw an explosion of Tunisian Jewish books, mostly small booklets of popular literature in vernacular Judeo-Arabic (the Jewish dialect of Tunisian Arabic, written phonetically in Hebrew characters). It is often called al-'arabiyya al-barbariyya (Barbary Arabic) or simply al-yahūd (Jewish).[10] In his 1907 catalog of Tunisian Jewish publishing, the French scholar Eusèbe Vassel lists over 500 such bibliographic items, all printed since 1880.[11] These included translations of European literary works into Judeo-Arabic, such as Alexandre Dumas's *Le comte de Monte Cristo*, printed by Uzan et Castro in 1889, and Daniel Defoe's *Robinson Crusoe*, printed the following year; original compositions in Judeo-Arabic, such as Eliezer Farhi's novel *Sirat Zin al-Tammam*, first published in 1888; collections of folktales, proverbs, and popular songs; and works of geography, history, folk medicine, and dream interpretation. These presses also printed Judeo-Arabic journals and newspapers as well as large numbers of single-page sheets and other ephemera, such as amulets, alphabet posters, and broadsides.

The 1907 cookbook belongs to this genre of popular, ephemeral Judeo-

Arabic publications in early twentieth-century Tunis. The inside cover of the cookbook presents an advertisement for Abraham Touil's bookstore in Tunis, al-Maktaba al-Tunisiyya, which apparently sponsored the printing at Guedj's press. It lists the other items available for sale there: five Judeo-Arabic novellas, three kinds of floral essences used in cooking and as perfumes (orange blossom water, rose water, and églantine water [*mā nisrī*]), and prayer books (*siddurim*) and prayer shawls (*tallitot*).[12] While selling rose water and prayer shawls alongside Judeo-Arabic novellas may seem like an unusual combination for a bookshop, it is typical for Maghrebi Jewish bookstores of this period, which sold stationery, ritual Judaica, and a variety of household objects in addition to books.[13] In fact, throughout the Levant, bookstores advertised a variety of products, including stationery, journals, toys, clothing, and even "superb tea."[14]

The context of bookstores as a source of general household goods might also point us toward the intended audience. The title page presents a mix of languages: first a large title in biblical Hebrew: *U-vishalta Ve-akhalta* (You Shall Cook and Eat); then another title in French: *Livre de cuisines* (Cookbook); and then a subtitle in Judeo-Arabic: *hād l-kitāb yashtamil ʿalā naʿt al-ṭabāʾikh* (this book contains a description of dishes).[15] While knowledge of biblical Hebrew was generally restricted to Jewish men in this period, French was more associated with women, and Judeo-Arabic was shared by both. For example, an 1887 advertisement for a Passover haggadah published by Avraham Boukabza in Algiers explains:

> We have printed a new haggadah for Passover, translated into French . . . since women are obligated in the reading of the haggadah, but the women of our time do not know how to read [Hebrew], and so we have done it all in French. . . . We hope that everyone who buys this haggadah takes great pleasure on the night of the seder meal, whether he understands it all or whether it is his sons or daughters who know how to read in French.[16]

The Alliance Israélite Universelle, a Franco-Jewish philanthropic organization, opened a girls' school in Tunis in 1882, which had an especially strong influence on French literacy among Tunisian Jewish women.[17] It seems likely that the large French subtitle of this cookbook, printed in ornamental Latin characters, was meant to emphasize its modern and sophisticated nature and appeal to a potential audience of modern and sophisticated women. At the same time, its Judeo-Arabic contents indicate that this cookbook was marketed solely within the Tunisian Jewish community.

While there is little direct evidence that Tunisian Jewish women were literate in Judeo-Arabic, some Maghrebi Judeo-Arabic books were aimed at women, with the intention that their husbands would buy them and read them aloud. For example, a Judeo-Arabic household manual with explanations of the dietary laws of kashrut and food preparation (*Dat Yehudit*) was printed in Algiers in 1855 (and reprinted there by Guedj in 1894). The book instructs its readers "to read these laws at all times, and especially women. But since women do not know how to read, and even many men also do not know the Holy Tongue, we have thought to make these [laws] in the Arabic language, so that every man can have it in his house, and can read it to his household at all times."[18] Perhaps this cookbook was similarly intended as a household resource that could be shared by men and women: among Tunisian Jews in this period, women performed the bulk of food preparation tasks, including shopping, cooking, and serving.[19] It is also possible that changing norms in terms of education and the status of women in the community in the early twentieth century led to an increase in Jewish women who were literate in Judeo-Arabic.

*U-vishalta Ve-akhalta* appears to be the earliest modern cookbook printed in North Africa (and the earliest printed cookbook of modern North African cuisine) as well as the earliest printed non-Ashkenazi Jewish cookbook.[20] Thanks to the Arab literary and cultural "awakening" known as the Nahḍa, some printed Arabic cookbooks appeared in the Levant at the end of the nineteenth century, such as the Lebanese cookbook *Tadhkirat al-Khawatin wa-Ustadh al-Tabbakhin* (1885), by Khalil Sarkis. These cookbooks collected local recipes and also drew on Ottoman cookbooks that had been published since the mid-nineteenth century, such as the famous *Melceü't-Tabbahin* of Mehmed Kamil (1844).[21] Cookbooks of North African cuisine, however, were not printed until well into the twentieth century. The next Maghrebi cookbook after *U-vishalta Ve-akhalta* was also produced by a Tunisian Jew, Jacques-Victor Lévy (writing as Jacques Véhel): *La véritable cuisine tunisienne*, printed in Tunis in 1923.[22] Unlike Véhel's cookbook, which is in French and aims to explain (and defend) the value of Tunisian cuisine to French colonial readers, the choice of the author of *U-vishalta Ve-akhalta* to write in Judeo-Arabic indicates his (or her) primary commitment to a Jewish audience.

*U-vishalta Ve-akhalta* assumes a high degree of culinary knowledge on the part of its audience. Following the advertisement for the bookstore, the cookbook contains six pages of suggested dishes, each with a short list of ingredients. The "recipes" are closer to simple descriptions of each dish's contents: it gives no quantities and almost no cooking instructions. The dishes do not seem to be listed in any particular order. The book includes four recipes for soup or stew, twelve recipes for meat dishes (beef, lamb, chicken, and duck), one recipe for fish, twelve vegetable-based recipes, and twenty-two dishes called tagine. "Tagine" usually refers to a kind of egg-based frittata in modern Tunisia, rather than the stew more familiar from Morocco. I suspect that the Tunisian version is meant in this cookbook.[23]

The majority of these recipes are typical of modern Tunisian cuisine shared by Jews and Muslims. Many scholars have pointed out the ways in which cuisine is a central arena for cultural contact and cooperation for Jews and Muslims in the Maghreb. Joëlle Bahloul, for example, describes the similarities in what she calls the "Maghrebi Judeo-Muslim diet," with a shared range of fruits and vegetables, grains, and spices.[24] Mohamed Snoussi has even shown that in Tunisia at the turn of the century Jews and Muslims would buy meat from butchers of each other's community, sometimes in direct opposition to the protests of their religious leaders.[25] Snoussi writes, "It is certain that the Muslim and Jewish women of the Hara [Jewish quarter], where the poor families of both communities knew no partitions and rubbed shoulders daily in that open space, exchanged not only recipes but also dishes and meals."[26]

*U-vishalta Ve-akhalta* contains dishes that are specifically Maghrebi in flavor, such as tagine, as well as foods shared across the Arab Levantine world, such as *mulūkhiya* (jute mallow), *fūl* (fava beans), okra (here called *ganāwiyya*, rather than the Levantine and Turkish *bāmiya*), and, of course, several different recipes for eggplant (*bridjān* or *bītanzāl*). Bahloul's "Maghrebi Judeo-Muslim diet" is well represented in this cookbook's portrayal of Tunisian Jewish cooking.

The recipes in *U-vishalta Ve-akhalta*, however, also show another stream of long-standing influence—the interaction with European communities (both Jewish and non-Jewish), particularly those from France, Italy, and Spain. The Jews of Tunis had a close relationship with Italy and even included a group known as the Grana or "Leghorn Jews": families of Livornese origin who had settled in Tunis, beginning in the seventeenth century.[27] Several recipes in the cookbook use loanwords from European languages, such as *stūfadū* (Italian *stufato*, Spanish *estofado*) and *brūdū* (Italian *brodo*) for stew or *brūklū* for cauliflower (Italian *broccolo*).[28] Especially noticeable in this cookbook is the prevalence of tomatoes and potatoes, introduced to North Africa in the seventeenth century after Spain brought these vegetables and their names—*ṭamāṭim* (Spanish and French *tomate*) and *bāṭāṭa* (Spanish and Italian *patata*)—from its colonies in the New World.[29]

Other aspects of the cookbook embed it in its Jewish context. All the recipes conform to the Jewish dietary laws, avoiding nonkosher meats and the mixture of meat and dairy. In fact, none of the recipes indicate the use of dairy products at all. This is to be contrasted with Véhel's 1923 Tunisian cookbook, *La véritable cuisine tunisienne*, which includes recipes that combine meat with dairy and call for nonkosher meat: hare, camel, and pork. In fact, as Yassine Essid notes, at no point does Véhel's cookbook explicitly describe itself as presenting Jewish cuisine. Some French writers therefore criticized it for misrepresenting itself.[30]

Several dishes in *U-vishalta Ve-akhalta* are to this day specifically associated with the Tunisian Jewish community, such as *bānātāj* (banatages, a frittata of meat and potato, sliced into diamonds), *mīnīna* (a terrine of chicken and hard-boiled eggs), and *bqayla* (slow-stewed greens with fried chickpeas, today usually made with spinach). Interestingly, *U-vishalta Ve-akhalta* does not explicitly include one of the most famous of all Tunisian Jewish foods, the Shabbat stew known as *tfina* (called *dafina*, *skhina*, and *ḥamin* elsewhere in North Africa), although it does include slow-cooked dishes like *bqayla* that were traditionally served on Shabbat and holidays.[31] Perhaps *tfina* was so well known that it hardly needed to be mentioned. Similarly, while the title indicates that the foods are suitable "for holidays and other days," no recipes are singled out for any particular holiday, such as Passover, with its special dietary stipulations, and the High Holidays, which also carry a number of food-related traditions. Nonetheless, it is clear that the diet described by this cookbook is deeply rooted in the Jewish community; as noted, its use of the Judeo-Arabic language is an indication that its intended audience was Jewish.

This brings us back to where we began: *shakshūka*. As shown by Anthony Buccini, *shakshūka* is one member of a widespread family of "western Mediterranean vegetable stews" developed after the introduction of tomatoes and peppers in the early modern period; it is related to the Turkish *menemen* and more distantly to the Provençal ratatouille.[32] While Gil Marks suggests that it was introduced to the Maghreb from the Ottoman Empire, it is more likely that the Maghrebi *shakshūka* and the Turkish *menemen* share a common ancestor, along with similar dishes like the Basque *piperade*, Spanish *pisto con huevos*, and Italian *uova in purgatorio* (Neapolitan *ova 'mpriatorio*).[33] The word *shakshūka* itself derives from an onomatopoeic verb in the Maghrebi dialects of Arabic related to mixing or chopping.[34]

Two recipes for *shakshūka* are presented in *U-vishalta Ve-akhalta*, one for winter and one for summer. The one with summer vegetables is more recognizable as the *shakshūka* of today, including tomatoes and peppers, cooked with a base of fried onions, and topped with poached eggs: "Winter *Shakshūka*: this is [made] with green fava beans, carrots, potatoes, and cauliflower. Summer *Shakshūka*: this is [made] with peppers, tomatoes, onions, *margāz* [merguez sausage], and cracked eggs."[35]

A comparison with the recipe for *shakshūka* in Jacques Véhel's 1923 cookbook readily demonstrates the different intended readerships. While *U-vishalta Ve-akhalta* assumes that the reader is already familiar with *shakshūka* and its method of preparation and thus only indicates which ingredients are preferred in its seasonal variations, Véhel first introduces his readers to *shakshūka* itself and gives detailed instructions on how to prepare it. While he also offers two versions, he does not associate them with seasonal preparations, calling them simply "varieties":

> The word chakchouka corresponds to what is called in French "salade russe," but there is not much similarity. There are two different types of chakchouka, and they are prepared as follows:
>
> Variety I: finely chop onions and brown them in frying oil, stirring them occasionally. Pour two glasses of water over them. Coarsely chop peppers, tomatoes, and potatoes, place them in the pot, and break a few eggs over them. Add salt and pepper. Remove the pot from the fire as soon as it is found that the eggs are cooked to perfection. Optionally, add pieces of sausage.
>
> Variety II: the same preparation as before, but adding chopped cauliflower, slices of carrot, fava beans (fresh or dried), and one or two cloves of garlic. If you want to supplement this with small sausages, it is best to add them at the beginning with the oil. Optionally, add eggs.[36]

While *U-vishalta Ve-akhalta* is the first published Maghrebi cookbook, this is actually not the first published recipe for *shakshūka*. Marcelin Beaussier's 1871 Arabic dictionary defined *shaqshūqa* as a term in Tunisian Arabic referring to "a dish composed of tomatoes, fresh peppers, and onions, with eggs on top."[37] Several recipes for this popular dish appeared in the French press in the 1890s; *Le Gaulois*, for example, describes *shakshūka* (*chakchouka*) as "very suitable for breakfast" and perfect "for housewives in search of exotic preparations." It recommends adding "a slice of smoked ham to replace the strips of sun-dried lamb" of the original.[38] Interestingly, *shakshūka* first appeared in the French press as "Oeufs à la tunisienne" (Tunisian-style eggs) but over the course of a few years was described as generically North African, then Egyptian, Arabian, and Turkish.[39] This may testify to the movement of *shakshūka* into the Levant but more likely represents a homogenizing Orientalism in the French colonial empire that did not bother to differentiate local cultures or contexts. Long before *shakshūka* was a "global food trend" or sold at Trader Joe's, this dish was already being touted in colonial France as "the dish of the season ... that can be appreciated by even the most delicate European palates."[40]

The initial recipe introducing the dish to "European palates" makes no mention of its connections with Jewish foodways, although the dish is included in two French Jewish cookbooks of the 1920s, which presented Jewish recipes from both Western and Eastern Europe as well as from the French colonies in North Africa. A tomato-and-pepper *shakshūka* appears in Édouard de Pomiane's *Kasher: Cuisine juive, ghettos modernes* under the title "la chep-chouka d'Alger," described as a Shabbat dish "much better than 'tchoulend'" (the Ashkenazi bean stew known as *tsholnt* or *cholent*). It is also mentioned as "chekchouka" in Suzanne Roukhomovsky's *Gastronomie juive*, which includes a long section of Tunisian Jewish recipes.[41] The appearance of *shakshūka* in *U-vishalta Ve-akhalta* and in these French cookbooks affirms Tunisian Jews' particular affection for it.

It is therefore no surprise that Tunisian Jews brought *shakshūka* with them when they immigrated to Israel in the 1950s (following the establishment of the state of Israel in 1948, and especially after Tunisian independence in 1956) along with many other Maghrebi Jews.[42] While many new immigrants from the Islamic world faced discrimination, racism, and anti-Arab sentiment in Israel, certain aspects of their culture, including food, were valorized as contributing to the harmonious mosaic of new Israeli ethnicity and validating the emerging sense of locally rooted Levantine identity.[43] It appears that *shakshūka* was among the foods adopted by the general Israeli public in the late 1950s; unlike hummus or falafel, however, it had not been previously associated with Palestinian or Levantine cuisine.

The earliest mention of *shakshūka* in an Israeli context is in Lilian Cornfeld's 1962 cookbook *Israeli Cookery*, which presented Jewish foods from Yemen, Iraq, North Africa, and the Balkans, alongside the foods of Eastern, Western, and Central Europe, all as part of the "harmonious, healthy balance of nutritional, climatic, and economic needs" of the new Israeli menu. Cornfeld (1901–1995), a Montreal-born Israeli nutritionist known as the "mother of modern Israeli cuisine," was a leading advocate for incorporating Arab dishes into the Israeli Jewish diet as part of creating a new national cuisine: "with the blending of food habits in Israel, the national preferences seem to be mostly for oriental foods. . . . This is sound ecology: foods which have been eaten here for centuries and on which countless generations have survived and thrived, are low in cost, highly nutritive and well balanced foods."[44] Cornfeld's recipe for "Schiksuka (Vegetables with Eggs)" appeared in the section on dishes from "Tunis and Tripolitania." Cornfeld notes that Maghrebi Jewish cuisine uses vegetables "profusely and in many delightful and interesting ways."[45] *Shak-shūka*, in its tomato-pepper-eggs form (the summer *shakshūka* of *U-vishalta Ve-akhalta*), quickly became a popular food in Israel, as a quick, flexible, healthy, and easy-to-prepare meal. The prevalence of tomatoes and peppers in Israeli agriculture solidified that particular version of *shakshūka* as the preeminent one (some Israeli *shakshūka* makers even replaced the fresh vegetables with tomato puree), and other seasonal varieties were forgotten.[46]

In recent decades, *shakshūka* has been reexported as an Israeli food and/or a specifically Maghrebi Jewish food to Europe and North America and has also been adopted by Palestinians and other Arab communities in the Levant. It is now frequently described as a generically Levantine or Middle Eastern dish, often to avoid the politicized implications of "Israeli" food. A green tomato *shakshūka* appears in Rawia Bishara's Palestinian cookbook *Levant*, for example, while a red *shakshūka* is featured on the cover of Yotam Ottolenghi and Sami Tamimi's celebrated cookbook *Jerusalem*, and two versions of *shakshūka*, described as "the signature breakfast of the Middle East," appear in Sami Tamimi's Palestinian cookbook, *Falastin*.[47] When Melissa Clark featured a recipe for *shakshūka* in the *New York Times* cooking website in 2013, describing it as Israeli, the *Times* Facebook and YouTube pages received hundreds of comments calling for corrections and protesting that it was Tunisian, Egyptian, Palestinian, Libyan, or Arabian—but certainly not Israeli.[48] Numerous recipe blogs and cooking websites continue to speculate about the true origins of *shakshūka*, their guesses ranging from Morocco to Yemen.

As Buccini notes, *shakshūka* is a perfect symbol, through both its mobility and its harmonization of diverse ingredients, of the "jumble and ultimate harmonization of the culinary efforts of humble people of distinct ethnic backgrounds" across the Mediterranean.[49] In fact, according to one linguist, the phrase "parler chakchouka," "to speak *shakshūka*," is used by young North Africans today to refer to the "code-switching" common in their casual speech, alternating between Maghrebi Arabic and French.[50] Through *shakshūka*, and many of the other recipes in *U-vishalta Ve-akhalta*, we can see conversations happening through food, connecting Tunisian Jews with Western Europe, the Ottoman Empire, and the Levant. In their introduction to *Global Jewish Foodways: A History*, Simone Cinotto and Hasia Diner argue that Jewish foodways demonstrate "the centrality of food in the everyday life and identity of mobile people, [and] the vital importance of mobile people in promoting food exchange."[51] In Tunisia, Israel, France, and every other area of the Jewish diaspora, food connected communities through trade and exchange, preserved histories of migration, and reflected changing social and cultural norms. While there is still much to discover about this cookbook, its few pages open a precious window onto Tunisian Jewish foodways at the turn of the twentieth century.

**Notes**

1. Mollie O'Dell, "New Proteins, Ethnic Breakfasts Are What's Hot in 2019," RestaurantNews.com (19 December 2018), restaurantnews.com/new-proteins-ethnic -breakfasts-are-whats-hot-in-2019-association-research-shows-121918.
2. The name of the dish is often also spelled with French-inspired orthography as

*shakshouka.* While the underlying Arabic is often written *shaqshūqa*, it is also sometimes spelled (and usually pronounced) *shakshūka.*

3. See the university's description of the website of Alan D. Corré (17 April 2017), minds.wisconsin.edu/handle/1793/76383. Dr. Tsivia Tobi, a renowned Israeli scholar of Tunisian origin and a specialist in Tunisian Jewish women's culture, has begun to prepare a new edition and translation of the cookbook with commentary, to be published in 2021.

4. Yosef Tobi and Tsivia Tobi, *Judeo-Arabic Literature in Tunisia, 1850–1950* (Detroit: Wayne State University Press, 2014).

5. Noam Sienna, "Making Jewish Books in North Africa, 1700–1900" (PhD diss., University of Minnesota, 2020).

6. Avraham Attal, "'Al ha-defus ha-'ivri ba-magreb," *Mi-mizraḥ Umi-ma'arav* 2 (1980): 123–124.

7. Silvia Finzi, "Elia Finzi, imprimeur de père en fils," in *Métiers et professions des Italiens de Tunisie* (Tunis: Éditions Finzi, 2003), 278–284.

8. According to Attal ("'Al ha-defus ha-'ivri ba-magreb," 124), the Uzan-Castro press opened in 1891. But the bibliographies of Eusèbe Vassel and Daniel Hagège as well as the listings of the Bibliography of the Hebrew Book (BHB) project at the National Library of Israel demonstrate that they were printing Hebrew and Judeo-Arabic material starting in 1885. See Eusèbe Vassel, *La littérature populaire des israélites tunisiens* (Paris: Ernest Leroux, 1907), 104, 242; and Michal Saraf, "Daniel Ḥagège ve-ḥiburo 'al toldot ha-sifrut ha-'aravit-yehudit be-tunisia, 1862–1939," *Pe'amim* 30 (1987): 45.

9. Attal, "'Al ha-defus ha-'ivri ba-magreb," 124. Guedj is also mentioned briefly by Daniel Hagège: see Tobi and Tobi, *Judeo-Arabic Literature*, 244. Attal claims that Guedj moved to Tunis in 1890, but numerous examples of books printed by Guedj in Algiers from 1890 to 1895 can be found. According to Vassel, Guedj printed a Passover haggadah in 1895 that was begun in Algiers but finished in Tunis (Vassel, *La littérature populaire*, 83), although no examples appear to have survived.

10. For more general background on Judeo-Arabic, see Geoffrey Khan, "Judeo-Arabic," in *Handbook of Jewish Languages* (Leiden: Brill, 2015), 22–63; and Esther-Miriam Wagner, "Judeo-Arabic Language or Jewish Arabic Sociolect? Linguistic Terminology between Linguistics and Ideology," in *Jewish Languages in Historical Perspective* (Leiden: Brill, 2018), 189–207.

11. Vassel, *La littérature populaire.* Vassel does not list *U-vishalta Ve-akhalta,* so it seems to have been published toward the end of 1907 or perhaps in early 1908.

12. The novellas, written by Yosef Bijawi and Y. Mamo, are listed as *Tales of Zina the Beautiful, Tales of Zudar ibn 'Umar, Tales of the Hunchback, Tales of the Most Precious of the Worlds,* and *Tales of Muhammad the . . . ?!* This last one, which was published in 1907, is listed as being "in press," which helps confirm the dating of this cookbook to late 1907 or early 1908. On these books, see Tobi and Tobi, *Judeo-Arabic Literature.* All translations are the author's unless otherwise noted.

13. See, for example, the catalog of Avraham Boukabza, which advertises books, *tallitot,* tefillin, mezuzot, and illustrated birth amulets: *Sefer Ma'ase Bustinai* (Algiers: Boukabza, 1886), 282–283, and the catalogs of Sion Uzan from 1910 and 1920, which advertise books, music, *tallitot,* and alphabet posters: NLI 2009.L.12 and 2010.L.220.

14. Ami Ayalon, "Arab Booksellers and Bookshops in the Age of Printing, 1850–1914," *British Journal of Middle Eastern Studies* 37, no. 1 (2010): 80–81.

15. The biblical quotation "And you shall cook and eat" is from Deuteronomy 16:7.

It is not clear whether the Hebrew or the French title is intended to be the main title. The full Judeo-Arabic subtitle reads "This book contains all types of foods, appropriate for rich and poor, for holidays and other days. The composer of this book is F. I." I have not yet been able to identify this author; Tsivia Tobi has suggested it might be Eliezer (Lazzero) Farhi, a well-known Tunisian Jewish writer and publisher in this period (Tobi, personal communication, June 2019). It is also possible that the cookbook author was a woman.

16. Printed in the margins of *Daniel Ha-kuzari* (Algiers: Abraham Boukabza, 1887), 14–20.

17. Joy A. Land, "Corresponding Women: Female Educators of the Alliance Israélite Universelle in Tunisia, 1882–1914," in *Jewish Culture and Society in North Africa*, ed. Daniel Schroeter and Emily Benichou Gottreich (Bloomington: Indiana University Press, 2011), 239–256.

18. Avraham Laredo and Yiṣḥaq Hakohen, *Dat Yehudit* (Algiers: Cohen-Solal, 1855), 1. This book was first composed in Judeo-Spanish (Haketía) and printed in Livorno in 1827. It was translated into Judeo-Arabic by Yaʿaqov Ankawa in 1855 and republished by Guedj.

19. Joëlle Bahloul, "Flavors and Memories of Shared Culinary Spaces in the Maghreb," in *A History of Jewish-Muslim Relations: From the Origins to the Present Day*, ed. Abdelwahab Meddeb and Benjamin Stora (Princeton: Princeton University Press, 2014), 1052–1061.

20. While many Sephardi recipe collections must also have circulated in manuscript, few have come to light. Regarding the medieval documents of the Cairo Geniza, S. D. Goitein wrote, "I have repeatedly asked my colleagues who work on the literary Geniza texts to watch for fragments of Judeo-Arabic cookbooks; for the time being, none has come to my attention": *A Mediterranean Society*, vol. 4 (Berkeley: University of California Press, 1983), 432. Rudolf Nunes Ferro has published a Dutch Sephardi recipe book (ca. 1800), from a manuscript in the University of Amsterdam: *Suasso's Kookrecepten: Een Portugees-Joods kookboek uit de 18e eeuw* (Amsterdam: Amphora Books, 2002). Nicholas Stavroulakis and Esin Eden published a cookbook based on two manuscript cookbooks from the 1890s, written in Ottoman Turkish (Osmanli) by Dönmeh families, descendants of Sephardi Jews who had converted to Islam under the influence of Shabbetai Sevi in the seventeenth century: *Salonika: A Family Cookbook* (Athens: Talos Press, 1997). See Marc Baer, *The Dönme: Jewish Converts, Muslim Revolutionaries, and Secular Turks* (Stanford: Stanford University Press, 2010). The nineteenth-century Anglo-Jewish cookbook of Judith, Lady Montefiore, *The Jewish Manual, or Practical Information in Jewish and Modern Cookery: With a Collection of Valuable Recipes & Hints Relating to the Toilette* (London: T. and W. Boone, 1846), also shows some influence from the western Sephardi (Spanish-Portuguese) community. On the history of Ashkenazi Jewish cookbooks in Europe and America, see Barbara Kirshenblatt-Gimblett, "Kitchen Judaism," in *Getting Comfortable in New York: The American Jewish Home 1880–1950*, ed. Susan Braunstein and Jenna Weisman Joselit (New York: Jewish Museum, 1990), 75–105; and Barbara Kirshenblatt-Gimblett, "Cookbooks," *YIVO Encyclopedia of Jews in Eastern Europe* (2010), yivoencyclopedia.org/article.aspx/Cookbooks.

21. Maxime Rodinson, "Recherches sur les documents arabes relatifs à la cuisine," *Revue des études islamiques* 17 (1949): 106–110; Ami Ayalon, "Private Publishing in the Nahḍa," *International Journal of Middle East Studies* 40, no. 4 (2008): 561–577; Özge Samancı, "The Cuisine of Istanbul between East and West during the 19th Century,"

in *Earthly Delights: Economies and Cultures of Food in Ottoman and Danubian Europe, c. 1500–1900* (Leiden: Brill, 2018), 77–98. See also the contribution by Graham Auman Pitts and Michel Kabalan in this volume.

22. See the reprinted edition by Yassine Essid, *La véritable cuisine tunisienne* (Tunis: MediaCom, 2003). I am grateful to Anny Gaul for calling this to my attention and sharing it with me.

23. Carol Helstosky, *Food Culture in the Mediterranean* (Westport, CT: Greenwood Press, 2009), 95–96.

24. Bahloul, "Flavors and Memories," 1055. See also Guy Chemla's reminiscences on Tunisian Jewish cuisine in "La cuisine judéo-arabe de Tunisie," *La pensée de midi* 3, no. 13 (2004): 32–38. A similar description of Egyptian and Iraqi Jewish cuisine is presented in Nancy Berg, "Jews among Muslims: Culinary Contexts," in *Global Jewish Foodways: A History*, ed. Simone Cinotto and Hasia Diner (Lincoln: University of Nebraska Press, 2018), 70–88.

25. Mohamed Larbi Snoussi, "Viande cacher et viande trîfa chez les juifs tunisiens: Rituel ou politique?" in *Alimentation et pratiques de table en Méditerranée*, ed. Yassine Essid (Paris: Maisonneuve et Larose, 2000), 139–148.

26. Mohamed Larbi Snoussi, "Tolérance et intolérance en Tunisie au début de la colonisation: Le cas de la situation des juifs tunisiens (1881–1914)," *Revue d'histoire maghrébine* 30, no. 109 (2003): 86. Compare also the theatrical sketch of Jewish, Muslim, and Christian customers in a Tunisian Jewish restaurant, ca. 1940, analyzed by Yosef Tobi: "Judeo-Arabic as Reflected in Jewish Theatrical Arts in Tunis during the 20th Century," *Quaderni di Semitistica* 28 (2012): 363–380.

27. The Grana formally separated their communal institutions from those of their Tunisian coreligionists, known as the Twansa, in 1710. On the relationship between the Grana and Twansa of Tunis, see Jacques Taïeb, "Les juifs livournais de 1600 à 1881," in *Histoire communautaire, histoire plurielle: La communauté juive de Tunisie* (Tunis: Centre de Publication Universitaire, 1999), 153–164; Yaron Tsur, "Haskala in a Sectional Colonial Society: Mahdia (Tunisia) 1884," in *Sephardi and Middle Eastern Jewries: History and Culture in the Modern Era*, ed. Harvey E. Goldberg (Bloomington: Indiana University Press, 1996), 146–167.

28. On Tunisian Arabic *brūklū* for "cauliflower," see *Wortatlas der arabischen Dialekte: Band I: Mensch, Natur, Fauna und Flora*, ed. Peter Behnstedt and Manfred Woidich (Leiden: Brill, 2010), s.v. "Blumenkohl," 165–166. Another dish that I have not yet been able to identify, *bolido* or *būlidū*, also seems to have emerged from southern European foodways, based on its name.

29. Ellen Messer, "II.B.3: Potatoes (White)," in *The Cambridge World History of Food*, ed. Kenneth Kiple and Kriemhild Coneè Ornelas (Cambridge: Cambridge University Press, 2000), 187–201; Janet Long, "II.C.9: Tomatoes," in *The Cambridge World History of Food*, 351–358. While tomatoes are known as *banadūra* (from Italian *pomodoro*) in many Levantine dialects, this cookbook uses the Spanish-derived *ṭamāṭim*, as do most Maghrebi dialects. This word seems to have entered Maghrebi Arabic in the seventeenth century: "besides the Sallad ordinary in other Countreys, they have one sort rarely to be met with in Europe, which they call by a word, sounding Spanish *Tomátos*." Lancelot Addison, *West Barbary; or, a Short Narrative of the Revolutions of the Kingdoms of Fez and Morocco* (Oxford: John Wilmot, 1671), 80–91 (quotation on 80). On Arabic terms for tomato, see *Wortatlas der arabischen Dialekte*, s.v. "Tomaten," 157–158.

30. See Yassine Essid's introduction in *La véritable cuisine tunisienne* (Tunis:

MediaCom, 2003), 10–11; and E. G. Gobert, "Usages et rites alimentaires des tunisiens," *Archives de l'Institut Pasteur de Tunis* 29 (December 1940): 482.

31. Joëlle Bahloul, "The Embodied Republic: Colonial and Postcolonial French Sephardic Taste," in *Global Jewish Foodways: A History*, ed. Simone Cinotto and Hasia Diner (Lincoln: University of Nebraska Press, 2018), 147. There are three recipes for "dfina" in Suzanne Roukhomovsky: *Gastronomie juive: Cuisine et pâtisserie de Russie, d'Alsace, de Roumanie et d'Orient* (Paris: Flammarion, 1929), 195–196.

32. Anthony Buccini, "Western Mediterranean Vegetable Stews and the Integration of Culinary Exotica," in *Authenticity in the Kitchen: Proceedings of the Oxford Symposium on Food and Cookery 2005*, ed. Richard Hosking (London: Prospect Books, 2006), 132–145 (quotation on 132).

33. Gil Marks, *Encyclopedia of Jewish Food* (Boston: Houghton Mifflin, 2010), 547–548.

34. See the entries for *sh.q.sh.q* and *sh.k.sh.k* in Marcelin Beaussier, *Dictionnaire pratique arabe-français contenant tous les mots employés dans l'arabe parlé en Algérie et en Tunisie* (Algiers: A. Bouyer, 1871); Reinhart Dozy, *Supplément aux dictionnaires arabes* (Leiden: Brill, 1881); and Hans Stumme, *Grammatik des tunisischen arabisch nebst Glossar* (Leipzig: J. C. Hinrich, 1896).

35. F. I., *U-vishalta Ve-akhalta* (Tunis: Guedj, ca. 1907), 7. It is spelled *saksūka* in the cookbook. This demonstrates a common feature of Maghrebi Judeo-Arabic dialects: namely, the lack of differentiation between *sin* and *shin* ("sibilant merger"); see Jeffrey Heath, *Jewish and Muslim Dialects of Moroccan Arabic* (London: Routledge, 2002), 132–133.

36. Reprinted in Essid, *La véritable cuisine tunisienne*, 32–33.

37. Marcelin Beaussier, *Dictionnaire pratique arabe-français* (Algiers: Imprimerie Bouyer 1871), 341.

38. "Mondanités: Chronique de l'élégance," *Le Gaulois*, 11 July 1896.

39. "Chatchouka: Oeufs à la tunisienne," *L'Art culinaire* 12 (1894); "Ménage," *Le rappel*, 12 August 1896; "La cuisine à travers le monde: Arabie," *Le petit journal*, 30 August 1896; "Un plat turc: Le chakchouka," *Le petit Troyen*, 18 June 1899. See also the recipe for "un vrai checkchoucka arabe" in "Boujadi," *Ma première étape: Journal de route d'un soldat sud-tunisien* (Paris: privately printed, 1885), 244.

40. "Mondanités," *Le Gaulois*.

41. Édouard de Pomiane, *Kasher: Cuisine juive, ghettos modernes* (Paris: A. Michel, 1929), 191; Roukhomovsky, *Gastronomie juive*, 211. The sources for the North African recipes in de Pomiane and Roukhomovsky are not clear, although it is possible that one or both of them used Véhel's cookbook as a source, probably alongside recipes collected from Maghrebi Jews living in France. On these cookbooks, see Valérie Assan and Sophie Nizard, "Les livres de cuisine juive: À la recherche d'un monde perdu?," *Archives juives* 47 no. 1 (2014): 113–131.

42. On the immigration of Maghrebi Jews to Israel, see Michael Laskier, *North African Jewry in the Twentieth Century: The Jews of Morocco, Tunisia, and Algeria* (New York: NYU Press, 1994), 117–344. It is possible that some of those immigrants also brought with them their copies of *U-vishalta Ve-akhalta*. The copy currently in the National Library of Israel was from the collection of Avraham (Robert) Attal (1927–2011), who grew up in Tunis and immigrated to Israel in 1956. Attal, who worked as the librarian of the Ben Zvi Institute in Jerusalem, amassed an unparalleled collection of rare

Hebrew and Judeo-Arabic publications from North Africa (especially Tunisia) during the course of his life. After his death, his book collection was acquired by the NLI, while his papers and other ephemera are held by the Ben Zvi Institute. See Rachel Simon's entry in *Encyclopedia of Jews in the Islamic World* (Leiden: Brill, 2011), s.v. "Attal, Robert (Hatal, Avraham)."

43. Dafna Hirsch, "'Hummus Is Best When It Is Fresh and Made by Arabs': The Gourmetization of Hummus in Israel and the Return of the Repressed Arab," *American Ethnologist* 38, no. 4 (2011): 617–630; Yael Raviv, *Falafel Nation: Cuisine and the Making of National Identity in Israel* (Lincoln: University of Nebraska Press, 2015). See also Dafna Hirsch's contribution to this volume.

44. Lilian Cornfeld, *Israeli Cookery* (Westport, CT: Avi Publishing, 1962), vii. For more on Cornfeld, see the biography by her son, Giveon Cornfeld: *Lilian: Israel's First Lady of Cuisine* (Bloomington, IN: Xlibris, 2012); and also Ronald Ranta and Claudia Raquel Prieto-Piastro, "Does Israeli Food Exist? The Multifaceted and Complex Making of a National Food," in *The Emergence of National Food: The Dynamics of Food and Nationalism* (New York: Bloomsbury Academic, 2019), 119–129.

45. Cornfeld, *Israeli Cookery*, 37. She writes that the Tunisian and Libyan recipes were prepared for her by "Dia Hasson and Inez Pelach, cooks of Pardess Katz Hospital." Cornfeld also included a *shakshūka* recipe in her Hebrew cookbook, describing it as originating in Libya (Tripoli): *Ha-bishul Ha-ṭov mizraḥ u-ma'arav* (Tel Aviv: privately printed, 1967), 49. For other examples of early recipes for *shakshūka* in the Israeli press, see "Ma mitbashel?" *Haboqer*, 28 July 1965, 4; "Sir Ha-sirim," *'al Ha-mishmar*, 6 July 1967.

46. See, for example, Rafram Haddad's account of *shakshūka* in Israel: "Eikh nadeda ha-shaqshuqa mi-kfarei drom tunisia le-ṭafritei aruḥot ha-boqer be-jenin?," *Siḥa Meqomit*, 13 April 2014, mekomit.co.il/shakshuka.

47. Rawia Bishara, *Levant: New Middle Eastern Flavours* (London: Kyle Books, 2018), 20; Yotam Ottolenghi and Sami Tamimi, *Jerusalem: A Cookbook* (Berkeley: Ten Speed Press, 2012); Sami Tamimi and Tara Wigley, *Falastin* (New York: Ten Speed Press, 2020), 28–29.

48. See, for example, "Shakshuka Recipe: A Traditional Baked Egg Dish—Melissa Clark" (9 May 2013), youtube.com/watch?v=RPQBbm-2K-0.

49. Buccini, "Western Mediterranean Vegetable Stews," 142–143.

50. Foued Laroussi, "50 ans de recherches sur le code-switching arabe-français au Maghreb: Où en est-on aujourd'hui?" in *Algérie, 50 ans de pratiques plurilingues: Les cahiers du laboratoire de recherches en sciences du langage, analyse de discours et didactique* 9 (Constantine: Université Frères Mentouri Constantine 1, 2017), 187.

51. Simone Cinotto and Hasia Diner, "Introduction: Jewish Foodways in Food History and the Jewish Diasporic Experience," in *Global Jewish Foodways: A History* (Lincoln: University of Nebraska Press, 2018), 9.

# CHAPTER 10

# Unmaking Levantine Cuisine: The Levant, the Mediterranean, and the World

HARRY ELI KASHDAN

Arianne and Scott Bennett opened the Amsterdam Falafelshop in the Adams Morgan neighborhood of Washington, DC, in 2004, offering typically Levantine falafel sandwiches: fried chickpea patties with an array of self-serve vegetable toppings and sauces, folded in hot pita. A common street food in the Levant, falafel has been propagated by Levantine migrants around the world. Amsterdam Falafelshop's corporate website explains the restaurant's genesis: "Inspired by the falafel shops throughout Amsterdam, [the Bennetts] have brought the exciting flavors of Europe and the Middle East first to Washington DC, then the Greater Boston Area and Dallas, Texas. Believing that food can be both quick and delicious, the Bennetts have set out to perfect the Falafel Experience."[1]

Any one of these phrases might well serve as the starting point for an analysis of the circulation of Levantine food culture, but my primary interest in this chapter lies in the two introductory clauses. The Bennetts were inspired by the falafel shops of Amsterdam, not the Levant, and the flavors that they claim to offer are therefore rooted not only in the Middle East but in Europe as well. An article published in the *Washington Post* soon after the Falafelshop's opening informs readers that the space is decorated with an "Amsterdam motif," including some signs in Dutch. No mention is made of Middle Eastern decor, though we do learn that the chef is a Palestinian Jerusalemite, whose falafel recipe was learned at his father's side.[2] I do not intend to quibble over the authenticity of such manifestations of Levantine food as the Bennetts' Palestinian-Dutch-American falafel in the following pages. Instead, my aim here is to examine the discourses by which local Levantine cuisine is globalized and the processes that render culinary ideas like "Dutch falafel" legible.

Drawing on research trips to Levantine restaurants across southern Europe and the United States, a collection of products found in American grocery store aisles, and a number of popular Anglophone cookbooks, I argue that the culinary culture of the Levant is subsumed first within the broad and flattening discourse of the Mediterranean and then within a denatured global food culture that lacks reference to the histories and contexts of particular recipes. Consequently, the geographical terminology by which we might attempt to locate a specific dish becomes semantically muddled. In other words, the Levant embodied in the falafel made in Washington, DC, by a Palestinian working in a restaurant opened by two Americans who were inspired by vacations in Amsterdam is—by virtue of this falafel's mixed origins—something quite different from the Levant whose borders we might sketch on a map. It is not more or less real but definitely distanced from a specific physical place. This mobile culinary Levant, in its dispersal through the Mediterranean and global frames, is a signified without a signifier, a definite geographic and cultural space that is never labeled or clearly described.[3] In other words, we often eat "Levantine food" without it being described as such. The term is largely absent from restaurant names and menus and from the titles of regional cookbooks. Similarly, the falafel at Amsterdam Falafelshop inescapably evokes the Levant without ever speaking its name. What is falafel? Levantine food, unquestionably. By virtue of the erasure of the label "Levantine" from descriptions of falafel and similar foods, however, it becomes possible for these dishes to be inscribed within alternative epistemologies that privilege far broader "Mediterranean" and even global frames in lieu of a specifically Levantine identification.

The idea of "Amsterdam falafel," despite its hybridity, is relatively straightforward. We can easily trace the migration patterns from the Levant and the tourist routes from America that led to the Amsterdam Falafelshop's opening in Washington, DC, in order to understand whence and how this manifestation of falafel emerged. A more complicated example, taken from the menu of a fast-food stall I visited in Milan, elucidates the difficulty of characterizing culinary objects whose roots are further obfuscated. At this Milanese food stand, customers have the choice of falafel, a meat-filled calzone kebab or panino kebab, a sweet calzone Nutella, samosas, *riso* basmati (a fried rice dish, judging from the picture next to the menu item), pizza margherita, *alette di pollo* (chicken wings), calamari, and *patatine fritte* (french fries). This assemblage, almost absurd in its variety, tends to denature each one of its elements. The juxtaposition of falafel and kebab is readily understood, and the pairing of both with pizza makes sense in the Italian context, but the accretion of other elements alongside these dishes makes the menu as a whole difficult to explain. Judging by the food alone, we cannot begin to guess who owns this establishment or who does the cooking. Restaurants like this one rarely have websites with corporate biographies that we can parse for histories and identifications.

We might proceed via ethnographic interviews with the cooks and proprietors, but such a methodology would distract from, if not entirely overwhelm, the stories inherent in the foods themselves. Failing such an exercise, this group of foods resists geographic analysis. To understand the menu, we must turn away from questions of its production and instead imagine the conditions under which such an array of offerings might be consumed.

The dishes that appear on this menu in Milan are convenience foods, snacks that satisfy a craving for salt and fat but do not quite meet the requirements of a full meal. Many of the options are deep-fried, suggesting that the foods of convenience also present opportunities for self-indulgent or even hedonistic eating. Not incidentally, this menu might also be described as being made up of dishes that appeal to the unsteady hungry, making their way home after a night of drinking and clubbing. The falafel on this menu is less readily understood as Levantine food than as "drunk food" or as a snack without any particular cultural baggage. The history and geographical origins of the recipe are irrelevant to this Milanese manifestation of it, where the context of samosas, pizza, french fries, and Nutella works to equally de-locate each dish. In fact, to return to the example of the Amsterdam Falafelshop, the 2005 *Washington Post* article about the restaurant's opening is written entirely from the perspective of whether and how the Falafelshop has impacted business at the many late-night pizzerias in the Adams Morgan neighborhood, where a "big slice" is the traditional meal of the drunken hungry.[4] The article posits that falafel has been incorporated into a local culinary landscape and culture and is best understood not under the rubric of "Amsterdam"—let alone "Palestine"—but within the context of late-night snacking.

Complicating this suggestion that falafel be categorized as a fast-food option like any other is the revelation that the falafel and pizza clienteles in Adams Morgan rarely overlap. One interviewee in the *Washington Post* article smugly observes: "Frankly, people who come for falafel are usually a different kind of drunk than the pizza drunks. There's no fights here."[5] This distinction undermines the idea that falafel and big-slice pizza have come to fill the same niche; they may be foods eaten under similar circumstances, but they are not, in this context, eaten by the same people. I posit several reasons for this split, drawing first on Pierre Bourdieu's *Distinction*, which would suggest that the choice between pizza and falafel in this instance is a function of habitus.[6] The "different kind" of drunks who choose falafel certainly seem to imagine themselves superior to the ones who choose pizza, primarily on the axis of class. Falafel is a less familiar food to American consumers than pizza (even more so in 2005 than now), so we might imagine that consumers who pick falafel over pizza already have some degree of familiarity with Levantine cuisine, from personal heritage, from travel experience, or because their habitus ascribes cosmopolitan value to any food of the other. Some of the clientele may also be drawn by the impression that a falafel sandwich with its various vegetable ingredients is a healthier choice than a slice of pizza, even though falafel itself is fried. Falafel and pizza, while satisfying the same late-night craving, remain distinguished by the apparently divergent self-understandings of their customers.[7]

According to Bourdieu's concept of distinction, a significant portion of falafel eaters at the Amsterdam Falafelshop might seek out falafel because its foreign cachet reinforces their own self-conceptions of belonging to a particular class and culture. It remains unclear, though, whether these values are derived from the dish's Levantine origins or from the Dutch identification suggested by the Falafelshop in both its name and decor.[8] What has occurred is a kind of doubling of falafel's totemicity, in the sense suggested by Roland Barthes in *Mythologies*. Barthes argues that food can carry the soul of the nation: steak frites are the physical embodiment of France and Frenchness; milk is both Dutch and an avatar of Holland; tea signifies the very core of what it means to be English.[9] Falafel could easily be said to serve a similar role in Palestine (and more recently in Israel), where its status as the national snack endows it with a piece of the nation's soul. But in the Bennetts' presentation, falafel carries the soul not of Palestine but of Amsterdam: in its evocation of the memories of their travels there it serves them most saliently as a totem food of that city. Its Dutch valence is reinforced by the restaurant's physical environment, which offers diners a cosmopolitan vision of Amsterdam without any references to the Levant beyond those encoded, for knowledgeable consumers, in the food itself.

This doubled totemicity makes clear the stakes of the circulation of Levantine cuisine outside the Levant: the Levant itself can seem to disappear within foreign affiliative structures, and its cuisine is consequently remade under other categories of identification. Food is always imbricated with complex histories, meanings, and narratives. When food travels, further layers of complexity are added to these stories, whether through the branching narrative trajectory suggested by Dutch falafel made by a Palestinian in America or through the complete fragmentation of meaning on a globalized Milanese fast-food menu. To call the falafel offered by either of these establishments "Levantine" elides a rich array of additional and alternative narratives through which we might understand their production and consumption. These dishes demand a new method, what we might call culinary close reading. Such a method entails treating any recipe, and any specific manifestation of a recipe, as a story unto itself. "Amsterdam falafel" in Washington, DC, tells two stories. The first is of an encounter between Western tourists and Eastern migrants and the attempt to memorialize that encounter by serving it, as food, to others. The second is how consumer choices evidence distinction. The Milanese fast-food menu, in contrast, narrates a different kind of culinary globalization. This leads to gastronomic juxtapositions that are readily legible from a consumer's perspective but—beyond the market's imperative to satisfy a wide range of consumer preferences—incoherent from the production side.[10]

These two examples outline the borders of my inquiry: the displacement of Levantine food in the Mediterranean and its resulting global displacement. These dynamics of displacement come into focus if we step away from the particular cases of these two restaurants to examine some of the broader patterns by which Levantine food is characterized in non-Levantine Mediterranean spaces. The wild variety of the Milanese fast-food menu is an unusually extreme variation of a much more common phenomenon: the pairing of döner kebab (a Turkish meat dish prepared on a vertical rotisserie spit) and pizza. Countless shops across southern Europe are marketing these two items together. These establishments almost always serve french fries in addition to their flagship products and occasionally provide a selection of sandwiches. The core offerings of döner and pizza, though, remain the same. On the consumption side, these shops seem to cater to the same clienteles as in my earlier examples: those looking for a convenient snack to satisfy cravings induced by alcohol or sudden hunger. On the production side, however, the pairing of döner kebab and pizza is peculiar in its repetition. As the Milanese menu suggests, hundreds of foods might satisfy these cravings. Why specifically these two, döner kebab and pizza, over and over again? To put it more trenchantly, what does the repetition of this pairing suggest about the culinary links between the Levant and the Mediterranean?

The word "pizza," on one hand, has come to operate as a capacious linguistic descriptor. A New Mexican restaurant in my Virginia hometown offers a crunchy "Mexican pizza"; the English-language menu of a Turkish restaurant that I visited in Istanbul explains that a *pide* is a "Turkish Pizza." It seems that any flatbread with toppings can be, and frequently is, designated a "pizza." The range of the term is enormous. In his *Mediterranean Diary*, an account of ten years of travel around the Mediterranean Sea, the Italian journalist Raffaele Nigro observes that this semantic expansion tends to dilute what he understands to be the essential, original, or authentic character of Italian pizza. Sitting in a public square in Rabat, he remarks, "Two steps from us there is an Italian restaurant that offers, by now, of Italian food, only pizza, the most international food in the world, more diffused than Coca-Cola and McDonald's."[11] The implication is that "international" or globalized pizza is not, and cannot be, the same thing as Italian pizza. In Barthesian terms, pizza's spread decreases its totemic power. Distress over this weakening of Italian claims to pizza as a part of the nation's patrimony motivated the country's successful petition to have "The Art of Neapolitan Pizzaiuolo" (pizza-making) inscribed on the Representative List of the Intangible Cultural Heritage of Humanity by the United Nations Educational, Scientific and Cultural Organization (UNESCO). Italian pizza, epitomized in its Neapolitan form, in an almost legalistic sense *cannot* travel. The globalized pizza that Nigro scorns in Morocco is, under this scheme, not really pizza at all—at least not any more than Turkish *pide* is. Instead, it is a kind of denatured global dish, divorced from the places and spaces that lend it meaning. As a consequence, it becomes possible to replace a static or idealized concept of "pizza" by a range of translations making use of the same signifier. *Musakhan* is Palestinian pizza; *lahmajun* is Armenian pizza; *pissaladière* is Provençal pizza; and "pizza," in a bizarre linguistic twist, becomes "Neapolitan pizza," the adjective having become a necessary means of distinguishing the linguistic "original" from a horde of what are not imitators but independently developed variations of the obvious culinary theme of adding toppings to flatbread. The Platonic ideal of a pizza, in many minds, may be the pizza margherita, but the necessity of pointing to such an ideal highlights the enormous variety of foods and food cultures that now make use of the term "pizza" as a matter of convenience, especially in translation.

The relationship of the term "döner kebab" with the dish described by that label is the reverse. The dish itself seems to manifest quite stably: a vertical rotisserie of self-basting meat, shaved to order and usually served with vegetable accompaniments in a type of wrap or folded sandwich. The descriptor, however, varies fluidly, from döner to gyro to shawarma, depending on both the location of the restaurant and the national origin, ethnicity, and linguistic background of its owners. The material of the dish changes more significantly in its guise as the Mexican *al pastor*, a taco made with pork prepared on the same roasting apparatus, which was imported to Mexico by Levantine immigrants. The diverging expressions of the dish raise two questions. First, should we conceive of *al pastor* as a type of Mexican shawarma, or do the changes in meat and spicing so significantly alter the dish that we must consider it separately from its progenitor? In other words, is *al pastor* Levantine food? From the perspective of culinary history, the answer is clearly yes. While efforts to pin down the origins of a dish are always fraught both historically and politically, in this case it seems fairly clear that *al pastor* directly descends from the signature Levantine culinary innovation of the vertical spit and is thus inscribed in the genealogy of Levantine cuisine, in spite of the radical—in the Islamic Levantine context—switch from beef and lamb to pork.[12] From a consumer's perspective, though, the answer might differ. A diner looking for a halal snack, for example, might recognize the similarity of döner and shawarma but find *al pastor* completely alien despite the shared history of the dishes. Isolating *al pastor* because of its use of pork effectively erases the Levant from the dish and obscures a history of migration that has led to ongoing innovations within a globalized Levantine cuisine.

Leaving the extreme case of *al pastor* aside for the moment, the second question raised by these dishes is subtler: are döner, gyro, and shawarma the same thing? And which is the more salient factor: the extremely similar materiality and overlapping histories of these dishes or their divergent nomenclature? When labeling and classifying a recipe, which matters more? The importance of these questions becomes clear if we consider the better-known case of the beverage known variously as Turkish, Greek, or Arab coffee, which is the subject of furious debates over ownership throughout the Levant. National and ethnic pride are at stake in these contests. A contemporary example of the same kind of disagreement comes from Yotam Ottolenghi and Sami Tamimi's *Jerusalem* cookbook. *Jerusalem* often makes the case that food is not only an indicator of a shared culture but even a potential starting point for peace and understanding between Palestinians and Israeli Jews. Describing one characteristic dish, they write, "Everybody, absolutely everybody, uses chopped cucumber and tomatoes to create an Arab salad or an Israeli salad, depending on point of view."[13] The point that Ottolenghi and Tamimi are trying to make is one of commonality, rooted in Jean Anthelme Brillat-Savarin's oft-quoted dictum about diet determining identity. All Jerusalemites eat the same things, so, in some way, they are all the same. I maintain, however, that "depending on point of view" is a terrifically reductive gloss on a question of ownership that is, to many people, a matter not just of nomenclature or even pride but of national sovereignty. Are an Arab salad and an Israeli salad the same thing? Are Turkish, Greek, and Arab coffee the same thing? Are döner kebab, gyro, and shawarma the same thing? How much does the name of a thing matter? If we are served meat shaved from a vertical spit, we should be attentive to the fact that we know what it is in a material sense but may not necessarily be sure what to call it. Accordingly, significant parts of its history remain opaque. The narratives of these dishes are elusive.

The cases of pizza and döner arrive at complementary semiotic disunity. We might call a wide array of things pizza, and we might call shaved meat from a vertical spit by several different names. "Pizza" and "döner" are fractured signs. This fracture is perhaps an inevitable function of the dishes' spread. A visitor who approaches the restaurant Las Torres de Quart: Döner Kebab-Pizzas-Sandwich in Valencia, or Resto-Rapid L'Oasis: Pizzas-Kebab-Sandwiches in

Nice, or the simply named Pizza e Kebab food stall in Venice, or the Ali Baba Kebab House in Lisbon, where signage advertises both döner and pizza, is immediately entangled in a semiotic mystery. Is the food the same at all of these places? Are the owners and cooks from the same places? We might answer the first question via the expensive but not impossible method of research trips to conduct repeated blind taste tests. And the second question can be resolved with ethnographic inquiry. But the way that most consumers usually encounter this juxtaposition involves neither taste tests nor interviews, but instead the mere happenstance of proximity and the kind of casual decision-making driven by cravings.

An attentive visitor might notice a Turkish flag on the corner of the counter in one of these establishments or a poster of Damascus on the wall in another. Perhaps a Lebanese cedar decorates the door, or the name itself provides a clue, as in the very first of these restaurants I encountered: Estambul: Doner Kebap-Pizzeria in Valencia.[14] There are too many of these establishments, spread over far too large an area, to be able to confirm precisely what percentage of them are operated by persons of any particular national origin. Evidence from my own experiences at dozens of similar restaurants suggests that in most cases these are Levantine restaurants serving pizza as an item added to a menu of Levantine street food. What strikes me most, however, is the general absence of culinary storytelling in these establishments. Their menus do not include histories of the owners or dishes and the decor is largely anonymous. Occasional small visual indications aside, these eateries are a naturalized part of Mediterranean Europe's urban culinary landscape, as opposed to restaurants categorized as foreign or "ethnic." The addition of pizza seems to authorize and explain their profusion, and the customer easily understands döner's culinary niche in light of the more familiar role that pizza plays in the context of southern European (and international) street food. The pairing is obvious and inevitable. The globalization of one food authorizes the globalization of the other, first within the Mediterranean context and subsequently in the world. "Pizza Kebab" restaurants now are found in Cliffside Park, New Jersey, and East Elmhurst, Queens, New York.

This type of fast food provides instructive examples from the frontlines of culinary globalization and a brilliant site for understanding how certain kinds of dishes travel. But Levantine food has also capitalized on the gourmet cachet often attributed to the foreign and "exotic," as demonstrated in the case of the recent astounding commercial success of hummus. Hummus, at first, seems mainly subject to dynamics that overlap with those influencing the diffusion of pizza and döner. Like pizza, hummus travels via a process of linguistic spread that leads to semantic bleaching. In its Levantine context, hummus, like döner kebab in the Levant and pizza in Italy, is often a convenience food, served from a profusion of hole-in-the-wall eateries, each with its ardent devotees. Unlike döner, however, the origins of hummus are impossible to determine with any certainty. Instead, like pizza, it is the subject of irresolvable debates over the precise time and location of its invention.[15] These debates aside, it can be said with a high degree of certainty that the dish has Levantine roots and is certainly characteristic of the region today. Unlike both pizza and döner, however, global manifestations of hummus have rapidly multiplied outside the context of fast food, along several contradictory axes.[16] Hummus provides us with a clear case of the transformations that a single dish undergoes in moving through Levantine, Mediterranean, and global frames.

"Hummus" has evolved from a specific Mediterranean product into a catch-all label for a wide variety of dips and spreads that bear little relationship to the original dish. The Arabic word *hummus* means simply chickpeas and refers to both the beans and the dip made from them. The circumstances under which the dish spread beyond the Arab Levant are murky, presenting a chicken-or-egg conundrum of transmission. Hummus frequently appears on the menus of Greek restaurants in the United States, alongside more recognizably Greek dips such as tzatziki and taramosalata. But did hummus first arrive on the Greek table on these menus as part of the flattening of Levantine cuisine into an indistinguishable, generic Mediterranean foodway, or did it travel first through Greece as a naturalized part of Greek national cuisine and make its way from there onto Greek menus in the United States?

To understand the relevance of this question to the present discussion, it is useful to pause for a moment over the idea of "Mediterranean cuisine." For perhaps obvious reasons of politics and prejudice, many Levantine restaurants in the United States label themselves as "Mediterranean" rather than Arab, Lebanese, Palestinian, and so forth. In discussions with restaurant owners in Ann Arbor, Michigan, however, this labeling was repeatedly explained to me as a function not of geopolitics but of a desire to capitalize on the healthy associations of Mediterranean food. A colleague of mine who owns one of these "Mediterranean" restaurants put it more bluntly, explaining that the word "Arab" is offputting, whereas the term "Mediterranean" draws in a wide clientele by virtue of its political blandness and its cultural capital. The name of this colleague's restaurant, like so many others I have visited, includes the word "Mediterranean." Its website explains that the restaurant serves "Levantine cuisine" but also prominently features a description of the food as "healthy Mediterranean." The owners have Syrian heritage; hummus is, naturally, the first item on the menu. They also serve chicken shawarma, but their grilled beef dish is labeled a "gyro," borrowing from the Greek, for unclear reasons.

Neither the chicken nor the beef is prepared on a vertical rotisserie. From the perspective of a consumer, this distinction between gyro and shawarma is elusive, the labeling haphazard and illogical. Except for the Greek gyro and an Egyptian *fūl* (fava beans) dish, the menu is entirely Levantine in origin. Many other "Mediterranean" restaurants focus on the same set of dishes, occasionally augmented by tzatziki (itself often a generic label for any garlic and yogurt dip), Yemeni stir-fry, or pizza. In these cases, the label "Mediterranean" is clearly replacing the label "Levantine" or "Arab" and simultaneously authorizing some minor examples of fusion cuisine on menus that are less interested in fetishizing "authenticity" than in attracting as many customers as possible. Furthermore, the process seems to go both ways: a Mediterranean restaurant can, in culinary fact, be a Levantine Arab restaurant with a few Mediterranean additions, but a Greek restaurant can also serve hummus and falafel. None of this is necessarily strange until customers like my students, whom I regularly poll on this question, begin assuming that hummus is a dish of Greek origin. At this point the Levant has been subsumed within a generalizing Mediterranean frame. Commercial decisions to blur certain culinary borders have a direct impact on how people conceive of those foods. In the process, Levantine food disappears.

"Greek hummus" does not seem to be used as a convenient translation for a dish with different origins, like "Turkish pizza," but instead simply refers to hummus served at a Greek restaurant. "Italian hummus"—a dish that I have seen on several menus—might be a standard hummus served at an Italian restaurant (perhaps with Italian herbs as a garnish, though the question of what separates Italian herbs from Greek or Levantine herbs presents yet another puzzle). But it might also be a convenient translation for an Italian white bean dip, which, not being made with chickpeas, is not hummus at all in the linguistic sense. This has generated the dramatic profusion of hummuses that we now encounter both on restaurant menus and in grocery stores. I am not speaking of chickpea dips with unusual additions or garnishes, which are products of culinary fusion and the demand for novelty (spinach and artichoke hummus, for example). A new labeling practice has led to a bewildering array of products, including green "soybean hummus" and yellow "lentil hummus," in my grocery store's refrigerated section. "Black bean hummus" is found on increasing numbers of Mexican restaurant menus, indistinguishable in taste and presentation from any other black bean dip, sitting alongside salsa and guacamole.[17] By virtue of these processes, what was a typically Levantine food becomes a category label: first, for dishes with no connection to the Levant except via the seaways of the Mediterranean, and, second, for any kind of bean spread at all. As with pizza, hummus becomes a way of making an entire category of dishes legible to Western consumers. This is strange in that "bean dip" is hardly difficult to parse as a culinary label. But hummus is more viscerally associated with an idea of the gourmet foreign. "Bean dip," however delicious, may not sound as appetizing.

Levantine dishes and Levantine culinary terminology therefore both travel, but in ways that are often discrete from one another. As the space between these two dimensions of Levantine food broadens, an increasing array of gastronomic improvisations fills the gap. Consequentially, Levantine food itself loses its distinctiveness. First, it becomes part of a broad Mediterranean assemblage, either via repeated pairings like döner with pizza or on menus that blur the distinctions between the origins of dishes like tapenade, tzatziki, and hummus. Acts of translation then diffuse the Levant even further, into products like soybean and black bean "hummus" that borrow Levantine nomenclature to make a global food culture legible to consumers. These processes are not at all unique to Levantine cuisine. Similar distortions have afflicted sushi, egg rolls, and tacos, to name just a few (including, on one memorable menu, the bold invention of "ahi tuna sushi tacos"). The curious feature of the Levant's culinary heritage, though, is how actively Levantine food seems to seek its own denaturing. As "hummus" replaces "bean dip," "Mediterranean" exerts an irresistible influence over the cuisines of the sea's eastern half. The consequences of this influence are readily apparent in web searches for material on these cuisines. A search for "Middle Eastern food" on Google returns a political map of the Middle East, while the results page for "Mediterranean food" is topped by a map showing the locations of nearby Mediterranean restaurants. The Middle East's political importance overshadows the word "food" in the search. Mediterranean food is so recognizable as to be located not in the Mediterranean zone but wherever that American searcher happens to be located. A search for "Levantine food" returns far fewer results than either "Middle Eastern food" or "Mediterranean food."

The disappearing signifier of the Levant and the corollary displacement of Levantine cuisine to the Mediterranean tends to erase the idea of a distinct Levantine culinary culture. "Levantine" itself is a term weighted with negative baggage, a pejorative shorthand for a region—and its peoples—looked down upon as uncivilized, unclean, and untrustworthy by Western European travelers in the modern period. Western European colonial and imperial descriptions of the Levant's inhabitants evoke a perilous hybridity and suspect morality, notwithstanding the efforts of writers like Jacqueline Kahanoff, an Israeli of Egyptian Jewish descent, to reclaim the term as a space of possibility. "Levantine" has unsavory connotations, while the contemporary replacement "Middle Eastern" (a term already less precise, embracing a far larger swath of territory) carries political freight.[18] A Mediterranean affiliative turn offers the opportunity of capitalizing on what Peregrine Horden and Nicholas Purcell call "the romantic Mediterranean," constituted by "more or less explicit allusion to a wide repertoire of images and commonplaces about life in the region—always positive, sometimes near-idolatrous."[19] This is the Mediterranean of sun, sex, and sea. In a word, the Mediterranean sells.

My contention throughout this chapter has been that the Levant dissolves in the Mediterranean, but this dynamic might be more precisely described as one of inverse synecdoche: the whole stands in for the part. More than the Levant disappearing within a flattening Mediterranean rubric, it seems that the Mediterranean itself has seen its culinary meaning shrink to its Levantine aspect. Levantine cuisine is not unmade so much as remade under a Mediterranean label. Precision aside, we more or less know what we expect from a Mediterranean menu. Empirically, Mediterranean food is Levantine food, with some additions from elsewhere around the basin. What is altered here are the stories, not the foods themselves, which are remarkably resilient in the face of the discursive obfuscations described thus far. The falafel at a "Mediterranean" restaurant does not need to suffer in flavor from the owners' affiliative decisions. Even in the extremely distanced case of the Amsterdam Falafelshop, I must acknowledge that the Dutch framing does not at all diminish the taste of its excellent falafel. Granted that the food itself remains delicious, it is doubly incumbent on scholars of the culinary to remain attentive to the contexts in which Levantine food is presented and the stories suggested by such framing.

Three strands of discourse thus emerge from the displacement of Levantine food. Alongside the inverse synecdoche in which the Mediterranean stands in for the Levant are the globalized Levant embodied by Amsterdam falafel and soybean hummus and the silent Levant suggested by the pairing of döner and pizza in countless restaurants across Mediterranean Europe. These divergent manifestations of Levantine food have in common an expedient relationship with Levantine histories and geographies, which they are quick to dismiss in favor of frameworks of identity with greater commercial potential. This holds true whether the target consumer is motivated by health-consciousness, tipsy cravings, prejudice, or simple ignorance of the foreign. Such discourses create a predicament for the scholar, who can easily slip into the uncomfortable position of insisting that falafel is "really" Levantine even when it declines to frame itself as such, being actively presented as pan-Mediterranean, Dutch, something else entirely, or completely without geographical context. Our attention must be directed both to the histories of these dishes themselves and to the narrative frames in which we encounter them today.

A cuisine gains geographical distinction through one of two methods. The first involves its recognition and categorization by foreign travelers. The second occurs when the cuisine itself travels and, in doing so, takes up a geographical marker tied to its place of origin. Under the first rubric, Levantine cuisine was invented from the outside. The label itself is a somewhat outmoded and definitely disparaging description of a region (and its people) that today's travelers would more likely recognize as the Middle East. Under the second, Levantine cuisine never really existed at all: the term, with its obviously pejorative overtones, was never taken up by most of the peoples to whom it referred. Indeed, an English-language search for keyword "cookbook" and title "Levant" or "Levantine" in Worldcat (an unscientific but highly suggestive corpus) produces a total of only 6 results, while substituting "Middle East" or "Middle Eastern" shows 196 volumes.[20] National cuisines are somewhat better represented: 346 for Turkey/Turkish, 111 for Lebanon/Lebanese, and 81 for Syria/Syrian. But to speak of Levantine cuisine demands a regional not national framework. Indeed the framing of this volume pursues the utility of a Levantine turn as opposed to the national siloing of the study of the Eastern Mediterranean. Among cookbooks, however, Levantine cuisine, with its meager 6 volumes, is nearly an absent object.[21]

The unwritten corpus of Levantine cookbooks parallels the missing "Levantine" restaurants of the Levantine diaspora. Even more than the unlabeled culinary assemblages found in southern European fast-food restaurants, the preference for the term "Mediterranean" in restaurants demonstrates that avoidance of a Levantine marker is not merely a function of the substitution of "Middle East" for "Levant" in contemporary political geography. The region's foodways are widely dispersed but rarely spoken of as such. I do not intend to suggest that nomenclature is, in itself, dispositive and delimiting of the entire range of possible culinary identifications for Levantine dishes; nor do I think that these choices are entirely without consequences for our understanding of the region's foodways. To call the dishes discussed here either Mediterranean or Middle Eastern suggests an effort to affiliate with a broader, less specific regional identity and may even reflect an active avoidance of the particularities of the Levantine zone. The effect of such avoidance is the unmaking of Levantine food culture and its remaking under other geographical—and necessarily cultural—categories. When such enterprises are successful, the Levant is remade under the guise of the Mediterranean or the Middle East. At other times, the Levant disappears, replaced by Amsterdam, or, as in the case of the döner-and-pizza shops dotting southern Europe, by a globalized anonymity that makes of this identificatory void a global nonplace in which foods exist without history. A new food culture emerges from this void: a global cuisine of convenience foods. In this cuisine, falafel sits comfortably alongside pizza. When I was an undergraduate, I frequented a late-night campus eatery that offered a falafel sandwich in addition to a menu of pizzas, fries, and smoothies. But most customers' favorite dish was a fusion item created from disparate pieces of the menu: a falafel pizza, which consisted of five falafel patties crushed on top of a cheese pizza. Neither the falafel nor the pizza was particularly good. But the combination definitely satisfied a craving.

## Acknowledgments

My thanks to Anny Gaul, Graham Pitts, and Vicki Valosik for their shepherding of this volume and to everyone at Georgetown's Center for Contemporary Arab Studies for hosting the fabulous conference where this project took shape. Thanks as well to the many friends and colleagues who continue to send me photographs of restaurants and menus from their travels in the Mediterranean and beyond.

## Notes

1. "Company," Amsterdam Falafelshop, falafelshop.com/company (accessed 11 April 2019).

2. Allan Lengel, "Adams Morgan Acquires Late-Night Jones for Falafel; Shop Caters to Pocket of Fans in Big-Slice Country," *Washington Post*, 15 August 2005, Factiva.

3. In semiotics, the "signified" is the actual thing (the very concept of the Levant itself), while the "signifier" is the word or image we use to describe that thing ("the Levant").

4. Lengel, "Adams Morgan Acquires Late-Night Jones for Falafel."

5. Lengel, "Adams Morgan Acquires Late-Night Jones for Falafel."

6. Pierre Bourdieu, *Distinction*, trans. Richard Nice (Cambridge, MA: Harvard University Press, 1984).

7. On "self-understanding," see Rogers Brubaker and Frederick Cooper, "Beyond Identity," *Theory and Sociology* 29, no. 1 (2000): 1–47.

8. Brubaker and Cooper, "Beyond Identity," on "identification."

9. Roland Barthes, *Mythologies*, trans. Annette Lavers (New York: Noonday Press, 1989), 58–64.

10. I realize this is a bit cynical. Though I was unable to sample the entire menu, I must acknowledge that it is perfectly possible that both the chicken wings and the falafel are entirely delicious. A globalized food culture need not necessarily be unappetizing. Samosas and kebabs sound like a wonderful combination.

11. Raffaele Nigro, *Diario Mediterraneo* (Rome: Laterza, 2001), 247 (my translation).

12. Mark Miller, *Tacos* (Berkeley: Ten Speed Press, 2009), 76.

13. Yotam Ottolenghi and Sami Tamimi, *Jerusalem: A Cookbook* (Berkeley: Ten Speed Press, 2012), 10.

14. This restaurant also advertises an *auténtico bocadillo* (real sandwich), though it is unclear whether that indicates a sandwich that is authentically Turkish or authentically Spanish.

15. On these debates and their stakes, see Dafna Hirsch, "'Hummus Is Best When It Is Fresh and Made by Arabs': The Gourmetization of Hummus in Israel and the Return of the Repressed Arab," *American Ethnologist* 38, no. 4 (2011): 617–630; and Ari Ariel, "The Hummus Wars," *Gastronomica* 12, no. 1 (2012): 34–42.

16. None of this is to say that gourmet pizza does not exist, but I maintain that gourmet pizza is still an exception to its general status—in the global frame and in the Mediterranean frame—as a fast food.

17. Journalist Sara Yasin often highlights similar products on her Twitter account, @sarayasin.

18. For deeper analysis of the connotations of "Levantine," see Gil Hochberg, *In Spite of Partition: Jews, Arabs, and the Limits of Separatist Imagination* (Princeton: Princeton University Press, 2008), 45–50. On Jacqueline Kahanoff's reclamation of the idea of the Levantine, see Deborah Starr, *Mongrels or Marvels: The Levantine Writings of Jacqueline Shohet Kahanoff* (Stanford: Stanford University Press, 2011).

19. Peregrine Horden and Nicholas Purcell, *The Corrupting Sea* (Oxford: Blackwell, 1999), 28.

20. For comparison, using the keyword "cookbook" and title "Mediterranean" returns 436 results.

21. One of these volumes, on closer inspection, is in fact a book of Japanese recipes written in French, recipes from the "pays du soleil levant" (land of the rising sun).

CHAPTER 11

# Fine Dining to Street Food: Egypt's Restaurant Culture in Transition

SUZANNE ZEIDY

The mid- to late nineteenth century witnessed a surge in cultural exchange between the Levant and Egypt. Normally discussed in terms of intellectual and political history, these exchanges also had a profound influence on Egyptian food culture. People and publications circulated between Beirut and Cairo, promoting and participating in a new set of culinary practices and modern lifestyles.[1] In Naguib Mahfouz's classic depictions of interwar Cairo, Egyptian men dined on Levantine-style mezze during their nights out, in marked contrast with the local, traditional fare that their wives prepared at home.[2] Egypt's most popular mid-century cookbook author, Nazira Nicola, better known as Abla Nazira, infused her cookbooks with recipes gleaned from Cairo's restaurants and bakeries—many of which featured Levantine dishes.[3] In other words, mezze have long had a place in Egypt's food and restaurant culture. But these small appetizers, which are designed to share, and the patterns of sociability that go with them took on new meaning in Egypt after the 2011 revolution.

As a restaurateur in Cairo for twenty years, I have witnessed the changes in Egypt firsthand. Using my restaurants as a window into Egyptian society from 1999 to 2019 illustrates how the Egyptian restaurant scene evolved from a predominantly Western-oriented style to a more locally inspired setting. Just as Egypt's political and economic situation influenced local society and food culture in the 1970s and 1980s, recent events in Egypt have brought about a trend toward *baladī* (literally meaning "local") food culture—a form of gastronationalism that for the first time is seeing Egyptian food culture truly reflected in Cairo's restaurants.

## Egyptian Restaurants in the 1970s

During the rule of Gamal Abdel Nasser in the 1960s, Egypt went through a period of Arab nationalism, an ideology that strove to stand up against Western exploitation. Nasser promoted industrialization and expanded social services in an attempt to improve the standard of living of the masses. When Anwar Sadat took power in 1970, he instituted an *infitāḥ* (open-door policy), which aimed to open up the Egyptian economy by privatizing industries that were previously nationalized by Nasser, reducing subsidies, and welcoming foreign investment and imports. These privatization schemes did open up business opportunities, but they also contributed to a "crony capitalism" culture, wherein a small circle of well-connected business owners was able to benefit massively.

All this meant that the upper class prospered during the 1970s, while the poor suffered a deterioration of their standard of living, including soaring food prices. This dichotomy in society was vividly displayed in Egypt's restaurant culture in the 1970s. Cairo's street-food carts provided easy, cheap meals for laborers: *kusharī* (a layered dish of rice, macaroni, lentils, fried onions, spicy tomato sauce, and chickpeas), *fūl mudammas* (slowly simmered fava beans mashed and seasoned with olive oil, lemon, and parsley, usually eaten with *'aysh baladī*: subsidized whole-wheat pita loaves), and *ṭa'miya* (the Egyptian version of falafel made from fava beans and mixed herbs). Street food was more about basic nourishment than about eating out. It was a cheap solution, whether eaten for breakfast or lunch, and was made up of local ingredients.

Meanwhile, five-star hotels like the Nile Hilton were home to the lavish European-styled restaurants as well as nightclubs that appealed to the upper classes. Some simple local restaurants also existed with the addition of service and seating and offered salads and grilled meats in a casual setting. These provided a place where families could enjoy various mezze such as tahini (a dip made of sesame-seed paste seasoned with lemon, salt, and cumin), baba ghanoush (a tahini dip mixed with roasted eggplant), *salaṭa baladī* (a finely diced salad of tomato, cucumber, and onions in a tart vinegar dressing), and flatbreads, followed by a main course of grilled lamb kebabs or *kofta* (minced meatballs). It was also in the 1970s that fine-dining restaurants first started to appear—but they were always Western in style.

As the upper class continued to prosper in the economic boom of the 1980s and Egypt increasingly opened up to the world, more restaurants were established to meet the new demand for Western-style dining. They were mostly located in hotels, partly because they were aimed at tourists but also because it was easier to obtain the necessary liquor and operational licenses under the umbrella of a five-star tourist entity. With time, fine-dining restaurants also started to spring up in the different neighborhoods of Cairo. In line with international trends at the time, French restaurants were the most prestigious and admired.

Two close friends and I set up La Bodega in 1999 on the first floor of Baehler's Mansions, a residential building in upmarket Zamalek—a district home to embassies, expats, and well-to-do Egyptians. Over the years the restaurant became a home away from home for expats and locals alike. In creating La Bodega, we wanted to stay away from the fussiness of the French-style restaurants popular in Egypt in the 1980s while providing a high level of food and service. Some of La Bodega's favorite dishes in earlier years included filet au poivre, baked sea bass amandine, and Pernod-flambéed prawns.

## A Shift Occurs

Tourism was booming and La Bodega was flourishing in the early 2000s. The restaurant hosted a steady clientele of diplomats, expats, and tourists, along with Egyptians from the middle and upper-middle classes. The view of Egypt from inside La Bodega was of a thriving economy and prospering population. But this was not the case for the majority of Egyptians. Economic-reform policies largely benefited the upper classes, while those living close to the poverty line experienced little or no improvement in their standard of living. Despite economic growth on the surface, a large part of society was neglected. Disgruntlement started to brew. Global food shortages and Egypt's high inflation caused food prices to soar in 2002. The extreme shortages of bread once again affected the lives of the poor, echoing the "bread riots" of 1977, while the spending habits of the rich remained unchanged.

High levels of corruption, the wide gap between the rich and poor, and the loss of dignity of millions led to the January 2011 revolution. Egyptians across all social levels, led by the youth, took to the streets to regain their dignity and to take charge of their own lives.

Starting in 2011, a national pride and interest in the country and its politics was felt in Egypt in a way that many had never seen before. As a result, rather than consider their own cuisine backward or unsophisticated, people started to look to their heritage for culinary inspiration. A revival of food traditions started to take place.

## *Baladī* Food and Mezze

As Egypt navigated through its political turmoil in the months following the revolution, a sense of chaos dominated. Entrepreneurs set up food stalls and cafes on sidewalks, serving local dishes and *shisha* (a traditional tobacco pipe where smoke is cooled by passing through water). Crowds of people, ever more interested in gathering and discussing current events, would frequent these cafes. There was also a surge in the *baladī* food culture, in both traditional and contemporary presentations. The word *baladī* literally means "my country," but it also refers to rural rather than urban and indigenous rather than international—fundamentally Egyptian in nature. Interestingly, back in the 1980s and 1990s, *baladī* had a derogatory connotation. This has become much less the case since 2011.

The popularity of *baladī* foods was bolstered by the lower costs of the local ingredients and the comforting familiarity of the tastes—but also by their provenance, thanks to the new sense of nationalism that was being felt everywhere. The *baladī* revival entailed giving a contemporary twist to traditional Egyptian foods: restaurant design took on a new representation of traditional Egyptian features. This juxtaposition of classic Egyptian features with modern aspects in both architecture and menus is illustrated perfectly by two restaurants: Cairo Kitchen, which I opened in 2012, and Zooba, which opened around the same time. Zooba's vibrant cement brick tiles and brightly colored vintage doors give their space a traditional look with a modern flair, while their menu fuses local dishes, such as *fūl* and *ṭaʿmiya*, with contemporary presentations. Cairo Kitchen, with its façade and interior resembling an abstracted *kusharī* cart, was a canteen-style eatery specializing in home-style Egyptian food as well as *kusharī*.

In the spirit of this *baladī* revival, diners might satisfy a craving for a McDonald's burger with Zooba's spicy *ḥawāwshī* sandwich (a meat patty with harissa raisin hot sauce, orange carrot slaw, and tahini) as a mark of nationalist gastronomic pride. Similarly, Cairo Kitchen's "well-being" *kusharī*, a twist on the traditional dish made from brown rice and without pasta to eliminate gluten, provided a health-conscious, locally inspired alternative to a home-cooked meal.

Nationalism was not the only factor that contributed to the surge of *baladī* food culture. Political instability brought tourism to a standstill, and uncertainty reigned. In the years following the revolution, Egypt faced pressure to follow International Monetary Fund regulations that proved to be financially painful for the Egyptian people. Reduced subsidies, increased prices, and the devaluation of the Egyptian pound in 2016 dealt a financial blow to all levels of society.

Consumption habits began to change. Although socializing plays an important part in most Egyptians' lives, expensive dinners were increasingly out of reach. A more frugal lifestyle was inevitable for most. We could see that people were making changes in their spending patterns simply by looking at La Bodega's sales records. We saw a reduction in foreign wine sales in favor of affordable locally produced wines and fewer orders for expensive dishes like pappardelle with truffles or saffron-sautéed scallops in favor of value-for-money dishes: most commonly, mezze platters to share.

### Mezze

With dinner outings becoming more of a luxury than in earlier years, Egypt's restaurant scene saw a renewed interest in traditional mezze-style offerings. Mezze is nothing new to Egyptian diners. Not only is the concept shared with the nearby Levant, but the offering of mezze in the home is deeply rooted in Egyptian culture and highly valued, showcasing the generosity of the host.

Historically, mezze was ordered in local restaurants as a *taṣbīra*: something to "give you patience" while waiting for the next course to come. More recently, however, there seems to have been a widespread shift away from Western-style dinners in favor of mezze as a meal in itself. Part of mezze's popularity can be attributed to the fact that it requires less "commitment" in terms of both money and time. In a group outing, people can easily contribute the amount they choose to the overall bill and also come and go at any time. Moreover, this style of dining is more conducive to the Egyptian tendency to socialize in a *shilla* (social group). The concept of going out for mezze rather than dinner thus gained momentum and started to appear on menus even in Western restaurants, including La Bodega. In recent years, all of La Bodega's menus included a substantial selection of "Foods to Share," giving guests the opportunity to forego the traditional dinner altogether in favor of mezze-style dishes. These are often a mix of Egyptian recipes and recipes adopted from Levantine cuisine, as the recipes included at the end of this chapter demonstrate. One of my favorite dishes with Levantine roots that has been widely embraced in Egypt is *kubayba*, known as kibbe in Lebanon and Syria and *bulgur köftesi* in Turkey. For both home and restaurant gatherings, a platter of *kubayba* served with carrot and beetroot tahini dips, both contemporary twists on the classic Egyptian dip, is an appetizing addition to a mezze spread.

Members of Egypt's overwhelmingly young population are now looking for their own interpretation of a restaurant culture, with a character that is specifically suited to their lifestyle. In its later years La Bodega was forced to reinvent itself, adapting its food and offerings to accommodate a shift in society and an ever-changing set of parameters. Mezze and *shīsha*, two local traditions that had been put aside in the past in favor of a Western-style dining culture, were newly embraced for their Egyptianness. After twenty years in business, La Bodega closed its doors in 2019. It is now time for a new generation to take over this evolving food culture, for this chapter to end, and a new one to begin.

### Kubayba

With roots in Levantine cuisine, *kubayba* has become a mainstream mezze dish in Egypt. More widely known as kibbe in the Levant and often made with lamb instead of beef, this dish can be made in a pie form as a main dish or as teardrop-shaped meatballs as mezze. *Kubayba* has been widely embraced in Egypt and is often served with a bowl of tahini for easy dipping. To add a contemporary twist and splash of color, I serve it with two vibrant tahini dips made with carrot and beetroot.

Yields 14 *kubayba*

### Ingredients

7 ounces bulgur wheat
9 ounces minced beef, chopped
1 onion, finely chopped
1 teaspoon ground allspice
Pinch of freshly ground black pepper
2 teaspoons salt
Vegetable oil for deep frying

### For the filling

1 tablespoon pine nuts
2 tablespoons olive oil
½ onion, finely chopped
9 ounces minced beef
1 tablespoon chopped fresh coriander
1 tablespoon chopped fresh parsley
½ teaspoon ground allspice
½ teaspoon ground sumac
1 teaspoon salt
Freshly ground black pepper

### Directions

1. To make the *kubayba*, soak the bulgur wheat in cold water for 20 minutes then drain, pressing down to remove any excess water and squeezing the grains dry in your hands.

2. Place the beef and bulgur wheat in a food processor and mince to a fine paste. Put the beef, bulgur wheat, onion, allspice, pepper, and salt in a large bowl and mix together, adding water if needed to keep it moist. Set aside.

3. To prepare the filling, toast the pine nuts by placing in a dry frying pan over medium heat and stirring for 2 to 3 minutes until they turn golden brown.

4. Heat the olive oil in a pan, add the onion, and cook over medium heat until soft. Add the beef, stirring until browned, then add the pine nuts, coriander, parsley, allspice, sumac, and salt and pepper to taste, and cook for about 5 minutes.

5. Shape the *kubayba* mixture into about 14 golf ball–sized rounds using damp hands. Hollow out the centers using your thumb and place a rounded teaspoon of the filling inside the hole. Close the balls up and shape the *kubayba* into teardrop shapes. Leave to rest in the refrigerator for about 20 minutes or in the freezer for about 10 minutes to firm up before frying.

6. Fill a saucepan three-quarters full with vegetable oil over high heat, then deep fry the *kubayba* until browned on all sides and cooked through. This takes about 10 minutes. Serve hot as mezze.

## Beetroot Tahini Dip

Tahini is made from ground sesame seeds and is an omnipresent dressing on the Egyptian table. It is eaten as a sauce with meat, chicken, or fish or on its own as mezze, dipped with *'aysh baladi*, the whole-wheat pita loaves. This recipe is a contemporary version, adding beetroot for sweetness and a deep red color.

Serves 4 as a part of a mezze selection

### Ingredients

1 pound beetroots
5½ ounces tahini paste
4 garlic cloves, crushed
Juice of 1 lemon
2–3 ice cubes
Salt

### To serve

Olive oil
Handful of crushed walnuts

### Directions

1. Wash the beetroots and trim off the stalks and roots.
2. In a large pan of boiling water, simmer the beetroots for about an hour or until tender, then peel when cool enough to handle.
3. Puree the beetroots in a food processor or blender until very soft. Add the tahini paste, then add the garlic and lemon juice. While blending, add the ice cubes to prevent the dip from becoming too oily. Season to taste with salt.
4. Serve with a drizzle of oil and a scattering of crushed walnuts.

## Carrot Tahini Dip

The orange color of this dip contrasts nicely with the deep red of the beetroot tahini dip. A platter of *kubayba* with a bowl of each makes an attractive mezze platter combining a classic dish from the Levant and the flavors of Egypt.

Serves 4 as a part of a mezze selection

### Ingredients

1 pound carrots
5½ ounces tahini paste
4 garlic cloves, crushed
Juice of 1 lemon
2–3 ice cubes
Salt

### To serve

Olive oil
A sprinkle of pomegranate seeds

### Directions

1. Wash and trim the carrots. Cook in boiling salted water for about 10 minutes until slightly softened.
2. Puree the carrots in a food processor until smooth. Add the tahini paste, then add the garlic and lemon juice. While blending, add the ice cubes to prevent the dip from becoming too oily. Season to taste with salt.
3. Serve with a drizzle of oil and a scattering of pomegranate seeds.

### Notes

1. Christian Saßmannsausen, "Eating Up: Food Consumption and Social Status in Late Ottoman Greater Syria," in *Insatiable Appetite: Food as a Cultural Signifier in the Middle East and Beyond*, ed. Kirill Dmitriev, Julia Hauser, and Bilal Orfali (Leiden: Brill, 2019), 33–40.

2. Sabry Hafez, "Food as a Semiotic Code in Arabic Literature," in *A Taste of Thyme: Culinary Cultures of the Middle East*, ed. Sami Zubaida and Richard Tapper (London: Tauris Parke, 2000), 268.

3. Omar Taher, "Abla Nazira: Sanai'ayat Matbakh Masr," in *Sanai'ayat Masr: Mashahid min Hayat ba'd Binat Masr fi al-'Asr al-Hadith* (Cairo: Karma, 2017), 124–125. Taher describes Nicola's research in local bakeries and restaurants, where she sought to learn "Eastern" recipes like baklava as well as meat and vegetable dishes.

# Conclusion: Writing Levantine Cuisine

ANNY GAUL WITH POETRY BY ZEINA AZZAM

*To apply what one learns out of a book literally to reality is to risk folly or ruin.*
EDWARD SAID, *ORIENTALISM*

The contributors and editors of this volume—an assembly of food writers, historians, anthropologists, and literature scholars—gathered for a workshop on its contents in June 2019. Sitting in a seminar room at Georgetown University, we shared and discussed our group of essays on Levantine food in a relatively conventional format. But our conversation also delved into the practical matters of cooking. We talked about the difference between writing recipes for home use versus for a restaurant kitchen and rolled in a table for Antonio Tahhan to explain and serve *hayṭaliyya*, a milk pudding served with rose ice cream and pistachios, placed in porcelain bowls and passed down the conference table from person to person after lunch (see also chapters 3 and 4). We cooked dinner together at the end of the day, remarking on the differences between conversations that take place in an academic setting and those that unfold while working together in the kitchen—even among the same people talking about the same subjects on the same day.

As we talked and ate throughout the workshop, our discussions often turned to the difficulties of putting food into words. We heard stories about migrant cooks who found themselves in new places, able to communicate through food but not language, and talked about the untranslatability of some Arabic culinary terms. We considered cooking instructions that can only really be conveyed through gestures or sensory cues, the way a single word might signify a range of meanings across regions or Arabic dialects, and kitchen commands that are expressed with one word in vernacular speech and an entirely different word in a cookbook written in formal Arabic. From the morning until late in the evening, we confronted the challenges of collectively "making" Levantine cuisine in the kitchen and on the page.

Putting food into words can present other challenges. In one of her poems, Palestinian American poet Zeina Azzam responds to an experience she once had at a writing workshop when a panelist advised the audience to avoid using food as a device for conveying Arab cultural identity. "We are advised not to write / anymore / about tabbouleh and hummos," she writes, before unleashing a litany of Levantine delectables that defies the panelist's admonition, transforming it from proscription to provocation. In the very notion that food as a theme is too easy, too clichéd, or too reductionist, Azzam's poem reveals a strong pull to translate food into text, as an act of preservation, celebration, or dissent.

At the Workshop on Identity and Ethnicity

We are advised not to write
anymore
about tabbouleh and hummos,
baba ghannouj,
lemony grapeleaves stuffed with
rice and meat.
Our culture is larger
than the life of the chick pea
from sprout to table
or the time it takes to eat
a bowl of minted yogurt,
rolled cabbage with garlic cloves,
stuffed baby squash.

Mujaddara with caramelized onions
is beyond the pale now.
Let's not talk about eggplants
and pine nuts, or ground pistachios
ornamenting baklawa in sweet syrup.
Orange blossom water in lemonade.
Cardamom-infused coffee.
And should we mention
the special foods served when
a baby is born, a tooth appears,
someone dies, the moon a thin crescent

at the start of Ramadan,
Easter's arrival.

A baklawa backlash is unfolding
and I am starved
for metaphors.

Azzam's words also suggest that the lyrical rhythms and invitations of poetry may well be the most apt means for expressing the culinary ineffable. Each line creates meaning not only by signifying but by affecting—inducing a sensory response that calls the reader's body back into a world beyond text. The *leh* at the end of "tabbouleh" evokes the sound of colloquial Levantine Arabic (ironically, easier to spot in written English than in Arabic script, which typically omits the short vowel sounds that communicate so much of Arabic's regional nuances). The sour acidic tinge of "lemony" grape leaves prompts the reader's mouth to water. The poem summons the sharp freshness of "a bowl of minted yogurt," the aromas of "cardamom-infused coffee," the sticky feel of syrupy baklava on our fingers, and the mouthfeel of eggplant flesh against pine nuts. It also reminds us of the way that food expresses commensality in material terms, tying communities together as they mark milestones and holidays with the products of communal labor. In short, it reminds the reader in a dozen ways how culinary knowledge and sensory memories are embodied somewhere beyond the written text. In doing so, Azzam's poetry fulfills what Nadia Seremetakis explains as the potential of sensory experience to offer a "counterpoint to any linguistic discourse," a way of generating meaning that is "not mere repetition but transformation," not just communication but creation.[1]

Following from this, Seremetakis highlights the political stakes of considering sensory engagement as a means to understand the world. The senses, she writes, mediate between the personal and the collective, the past and the present. They are a means to understanding what has been alienated or excluded from "public culture, official memory and formal economics." Performing or prompting sensory experience thus represents a kind of "*poesis*, the making of something out of that which was previously experientially and culturally unmarked or even null and void."[2] In conjuring worlds of personal experience in the present and collective memory of the past, Azzam's poem shows rather than tells us why taking food seriously as a subject is not only generative but important, a subject that can stand up against a will to silence.

The day after holding a workshop on the chapters in this volume, we gathered in the auditorium of the Freer and Sackler Galleries, the Smithsonian's National Museum of Asian Art, to present talks and a tasting to a bustling public audience. The productive tension between food and writing came up once more. Contributor Reem Kassis spoke about leaving her childhood home in Jerusalem to study in the United States, telling a series of stories about food and memory that culminated in her cookbook *The Palestinian Table*. Kassis related how her mother had helped her re-create her family's recipes even as she cautioned that "cookbooks can only get you so far." She insisted that, beyond written measurements and instructions, good cooking requires "this thing called *nafas*." During the question-and-answer period, Azzam—who happened to be in the audience that day—asked Kassis to expand on the concept of *nafas*. Responding at length, she described it, among other things, as "part of you that goes into cooking that's not something that can be captured in a recipe."[3] The exchange inspired Azzam to write a poem:

Nafas in the Kitchen
*For Reem Kassis*

The Palestinian chef
says nafas is like a spirit,
an undefined knowing
that lives in the act of
preparing food

as if ancestors
reside in the knives
that chop and slice,
the parers and the
juicers, the measurers
and the tasters.

Nafas flows from the scents
of spices from childhood,
the deep colors of
beets and saffron,
the memories of how
to stuff a grapeleaf
just so,
pick mallow leaves
from their stalks,
grate nutmeg resolutely
with a coarse metal shield.

You can't teach nafas,
she stresses,
just like you can't implant
a memory, a presence.
It seeps into generations,
forming something bigger
than both the pinch of salt
and the generous stewing pot.

Nafas is the sigh
that emanates from
the core, the inhale
and exhale into air,
to share.
Even zaatar, she says,
breathes between cultures,
travels thousands of miles
to bring nafas
to new homes,
kitchens in exile.[4]

If Azzam's first poem concludes with a plea, "I am starved / for metaphors," then her second answers with an extended comparison. The poem's opening does not promise to tell us what *nafas* is but rather to describe what it is *like*: "a spirit," "an undefined knowing." It goes on to narrate what it *does*—*nafas* "reside[s]" in tools and in bodies and "flows" from sensory memories; it is something that "seeps," "breathes," and "travels." Simultaneously embodied in people and things, something that is shared with others through food and yet impossible to fully capture or teach, *nafas*, in Azzam's rendering, epitomizes both the pull of writing about food and the limits of doing so. Against the backdrop of the Palestinian experience that the poems describe, food follows trajectories of exile and displacement, migration and diaspora. In these contexts, *nafas* is both embodied and mobile, exists beyond language, and produces something anew in spite of what was left behind. In this sense the cook becomes a poet, bringing new worlds into being (per Seremetakis) rather than repeating something already past. As the poem tells us, *nafas* is at once a celebration of what we have and a remembrance of what has been lost: a spirit, but also a sigh.

If food is so elusive, why write about it at all? What has this collection of essays, the outcome of writing, talking, eating, and cooking together, accomplished, if textual accounts of food are always troubled, challenged, or incomplete?

I think that sense of incompleteness stems in part from the series of tensions between seemingly opposing entities that food somehow seeks to bridge: sensory experience and discursive expression, locality and mobility, reproductive labor and commodification, the human and the nonhuman. Wherever we start when writing about food, be it a field planted with pistachio trees or a late-night falafel shop, we are inevitably drawn elsewhere. That often entails moving across the divides that typically organize scholarly work, starting with our definitions of national and regional categories. The new paths that food invites us to tread outline the possibilities that food scholarship offers to the study of the Middle East and that Levantine food offers to food studies.

To begin, food offers a way to write ourselves out of the national borders that frame much (if not most) popular and scholarly writing on modern Arab cultures. To write food cultures is to further the work of scholars of gender, migration, and diasporas who have pushed for transnational reconsiderations of a region whose political borders were recently drawn and yet are constantly crossed by people, objects, and ideas. As Azzam's poem attests, foods like za'atar travel across borders, sketching out alternative geographies for understanding Palestinian foodways even as they are rooted, literally, in historical Palestine. Writing about Levantine food in particular offers a means to recalibrate the balance of global food histories that still lean toward Europe as a habitual center. As Kyla Wazana Tompkins points out, one of the most prolific genres of both academic and popular food writing is the narrative "concerned with tracing the history of a single commodity as it is introduced to a Western consumer demographic, marketed, and disseminated through various commercial venues."[5] The simultaneous regional and global frames of the Levantine, defined both by place and by migration from it, offer a counterpoint to this model, decentering Europe without losing sight of European-driven transformations. Sara Pekow's essay in this volume, for instance, situates the transformation of sugar from a luxury item to a commodity in the context of a region with a long history of local sugar production (chapter 3).

Food's past and present also provide an account of how exclusivist national categories came into being, along with alternative narrative frames to write beyond those categories. The story of how dominant national cultures have absorbed and reclaimed minoritized and migrant foodways is just under the surface of an Istanbul kebab shop or pistachio fields in southeastern Turkey, as Samuel Dolbee and Chris Gratien explain (chapter 2). As critique, food history shows how the codification of national cuisine, like any process of canon-making, often entails erasure—whether of Armenian history in Turkey or of Palestinian heritage in Israel.

At the same time, processes of national tradition-making, like the enshrinement of kibbe as Lebanese or particular confections as Syrian, have obscured the fact that a unified food culture emerged in the modern era in the Levant that transcended political borders. The persistence of this food culture appears throughout the chapters of this book, from domestic spaces in working-class Amman where women of different national origins discuss *dawālī* (in Susan MacDougall's ethnographic account in chapter 8) to the renewed embrace of mezze in the restaurant culture of Egypt's urban elites (chapter 11).

Nudging us in these directions, food also extends beyond Zionist national narratives that start only upon Jewish migrants' arrival in Israel and downplay the complex roles that Mizrahi Jewish cooks have played in Israel's culinary history. Noam Sienna's history of *shakshūka*'s origins as a part of Tunisia's multiconfessional food heritage (chapter 9) and Dafna Hirsch's account of early encounters between Jewish settlers of Ashkenazi origin and Palestinian foods (chapter 5) counter these tendencies, broadening our understandings of Jewish food cultures in the Mediterranean world.

Finally, writing Levantine food opens up new ways to explain the material construction of political and social inequalities. Tracing the intricacies of food culture and history reveals gender dynamics and minoritized cultures not as stand-alone topics but as woven indelibly into the fabric of society and politics—even when they are rendered invisible. Adding to extensive critiques of "authenticity" in food studies, the chapters of this book show that claims to culinary authenticity are often staked in sites of privilege, from Lebanese cookbooks that reify and celebrate peasant foodways (chapter 1) to European and American restaurants that market their dishes under the banner of "Mediterranean" cuisine while eliding the history and context of those dishes' roots (chapter 10).

Meanwhile, the personal and ethnographic accounts of food presented here remind us that those roots feed living, dynamic cultures nourished by the laborious practices of women whose kitchens run according to the "embodied temporalities" of mothers and housewives pouring time and *nafas* into their cookpots, as Susan MacDougall writes, or in pomegranate orchards and olive groves that face human threats ranging from state violence to climate change. Finally, food invites us to push back against the hierarchy that divides the human from the nonhuman in the first place: Anne Meneley explains, for example, how "in Palestinian imaginaries, the olive tree is understood as an actor" and even as "nonhuman kin, expanding the terrain of kinship into the arboreal sphere" (chapter 6). This relationship between the human and nonhuman is neither folk curiosity nor recondite debate: Meneley underscores the political urgency of the relationship in the context of a protracted struggle over territory and resources. The "co-nurturing" relationship between Palestinians and their olive trees is perceived as a threat by Israeli occupiers and upheld as a form of resistance by Palestinians, for whom it is a source of nourishment as well as a crucial means to maintain a presence on their land.

Another Palestinian poet, Fadwa Tuqan (1917–2003), also evoked a human-nonhuman relationship in a poem about a beloved olive tree "on the Western slopes of Mount Gerizim" near Nablus. In describing that relationship, she invokes a sense of spirit or soul with the word *nafs*, a term closely related to *nafas*:

> Here, here, beneath the shelter of my olive tree
> The soul shatters the bonds of the earth
> And the spirit [*al-nafs*] abides forever in a solitude
> Whose silence throttles the babble of mortals.[6]

Tuqan describes a "co-nurturing" relationship with the olive tree, to borrow again from Meneley. In this instance, however, the product of that relationship is not olive oil but creative inspiration. The poem's narrator muses that her body might return to nourish the tree's roots in return—describing a cosmic cycle of mutual care, of give and take.

This image, the gesture of a person giving back to a source of material and spiritual nourishment, poses a final response to the question of what might be achieved by writing about food. In writing about food, perhaps we are drawn to return something to what has nourished us, as a means of remaking the world—or at the very least the terms with which we describe it. To do so is not to disregard political realities, from militarized borders to the unequal distribution of capital, but to reimagine them: to acknowledge and center women's unpaid labor and minoritized cultures on their terms rather than adopting the narratives of the powerful, to refuse romanticized notions of foodways that ease the silencing of violence and inequality, and to take the sensory nuances of culinary difference seriously in our understandings of human community and dignity. The aim, then, is not simply to set down in words what was grown or cooked or eaten at a given time and place but to take up food as the starting place for another form of *poesis*: to create the conditions for different conversations to take place and for something to be made anew.

## Notes

1. C. Nadia Seremetakis, ed., *The Senses Still: Perception and Memory as Material Culture in Modernity* (Chicago: University of Chicago Press, 1994), 6–7.

2. Seremetakis, *The Senses Still*, 7.

3. See Kassis's subsequent essay on *nafas* published in the *New York Times*: Reem Kassis, "Do You Have Nafas, the Elusive Gift That Makes Food Taste Better?" *New*

*York Times*, 1 April 2021, nytimes.com/2021/04/01/dining/nafas-makes-food-taste
-better.html. For another discussion of *nafas*, see Susan MacDougall's contribution to
this volume (chapter 8).

4. Zeina Azzam, "Nafas in the Kitchen," *Beltway Poetry Quarterly* 21, no. 2 (Spring
2020), beltwaypoetry.com/nafas-in-the-kitchen-to-the-israeli-officer-who-x-rayed
-and-swabbed-our-mothers-ashes-zeina-azzam.

5. Kyla Wazana Tompkins, *Racial Indigestion: Eating Bodies in the 19th Century*
(New York: New York University Press, 2012), 190. See the introduction to Tompkins's
book for a discussion of the mouth as a site of eating, speaking, and laughing.

6. Fadwa Tuqan, "Awham fi al-Zaytun," in *al-A'mal al-Shi'riyya al-Kamila: Fadwa
Tuqan* (Beirut: al-Mu'assasa al-'Arabiyya li-l-Dirasa wa-l-Nashr, 1993), 18 (translation
by author).

# Further Reading and Cooking

*A selected bibliography of cookbooks, secondary sources, and key references for the food and foodways of the modern Levant*

## Cookbooks

Baboian, Rose. *Armenian-American Cook Book: Simplified Armenian Near East Recipes.* Boston: Haig H. Toumanyan, 1964.

Bishara, Rawia. *Levant: New Middle Eastern Cooking from Tanoreen.* London: Kyle Books, 2018.

———. *Olives, Lemons & Za'atar: The Best Middle Eastern Home Cooking.* Lanham, MD: Kyle Books, 2014.

Dağdeviren, Musa. *The Turkish Cookbook.* London: Phaidon Press, 2019.

El-Haddad, Laila M., and Maggie Schmitt. *The Gaza Kitchen: A Palestinian Culinary Journey.* Charlottesville, VA: Just World Books, 2012.

Kalla, Joudie. *Baladi: A Celebration of Food from Land and Sea.* Northampton, MA: Interlink, 2018.

———. *Palestine on a Plate: Memories from My Mother's Kitchen.* Northampton, MA: Interlink, 2016.

Kassis, Reem. *The Palestinian Table.* New York: Phaidon, 2017.

Matar, Marlene. *The Aleppo Cookbook: Celebrating the Legendary Cuisine of Syria.* Northampton, MA: Interlink, 2016.

Ottolenghi, Yotam, and Sami Tamimi, *Jerusalem: A Cookbook.* Berkeley: Ten Speed Press, 2012.

Roden, Claudia. *The Book of Jewish Food: An Odyssey from Samarkand to New York.* New York: Knopf, 1996.

———. *A Book of Middle Eastern Food.* London: Nelson, 1968.

———. *The New Book of Middle Eastern Food.* Rev. ed. New York: Knopf, 2000.

Tamimi, Sami, and Tara Wigley. *Falastin.* New York: Ten Speed Press, 2020.

Tan, Aylın Öney. *A Taste of Sun & Fire: Gaziantep Cookery.* Istanbul: Yapı Kredi Yayınları, 2015.

Uvezian, Sonia. *Recipes and Remembrances from an Eastern Mediterranean Kitchen.* Austin: University of Texas Press, 1999.

Wolfert, Paula. *The Cooking of the Eastern Mediterranean: 215 Healthy, Vibrant, and Inspired Recipes.* New York: HarperCollins Publishers, 1994.

## Other Books and Sources

Abou-Hodeib, Toufoul. *A Taste for Home: The Modern Middle Class in Ottoman Beirut.* Stanford: Stanford University Press, 2017.

Abufarha, Nasser. "Land of Symbols: Cactus, Poppies, Orange and Olive Trees in Palestine." *Identities: Global Studies in Culture and Power* 15, no. 3 (2008): 343–368.

Ariel, Ari. "The Hummus Wars." *Gastronomica* 12, no. 1 (2012): 34–42.

Avieli, Nir. *Food and Power: A Culinary Ethnography of Israel.* Berkeley: University of California Press, 2018.

Bahloul, Joëlle. "The Embodied Republic: Colonial and Postcolonial French Sephardic Taste." In *Global Jewish Foodways: A History*, ed. Simone Cinotto and Hasia Diner, 139–157. Lincoln: University of Nebraska Press, 2018.

———. "Flavors and Memories of Shared Culinary Spaces in the Maghreb." In *A History of Jewish-Muslim Relations: From the Origins to the Present Day*, ed. Abdelwahab Meddeb and Benjamin Stora, 1052–1061. Princeton: Princeton University Press, 2014.

Bascuñan-Wiley, Nicholas. "Sumud and Food: Remembering Palestine through Cuisine in Chile." *Mashriq & Mahjar* 6, no. 2 (2019): 100–131.

Berg, Nancy. "Jews among Muslims: Culinary Contexts." In *Global Jewish Foodways: A History*, ed. Simone Cinotto and Hasia Diner, 70–88. Lincoln: University of Nebraska Press, 2018.

Brand, Tylor. "Some Eat to Remember, Some to Forget." In *Insatiable Appetite: Food as a Cultural Signifier in the Middle East and Beyond*, ed. Kirill Dmitriev, Julia Hauser, and Bilal Orfali, 319–339. Leiden: Brill, 2019.

Buccini, Anthony. "Western Mediterranean Vegetable Stews and the Integration of Culinary Exotica." In *Authenticity in the Kitchen: Proceedings of the Oxford Symposium on Food and Cookery 2005*, ed. Richard Hosking, 132–145. London: Prospect Books, 2006.

Canaan, Tawfiq. "Plant-Lore in Palestinian Superstition." *Jerusalem Quarterly* 24 (2005): 57–64.

Chaddad, Rafram, and Yigal Nizri. "Culinary Collisions." *Haaretz*, 22 November 2019.

*Chef's Table.* Season 5, episode 2, "Musa Dağdeviren." Directed by Clay Jeter. Netflix, 28 September 2018.

David, Elizabeth. *Harvest of the Cold Months: The Social History of Ice and Ices.* Ann Arbor: Viking, 1995.

Dmitriev, Kirill, Julia Hauser, and Bilal Orfali, eds. *Insatiable Appetite: Food as a Cultural Signifier in the Middle East and Beyond.* Leiden: Brill, 2019.

Dueck, Jennifer. "Foreign Kitchens, Foreign Lands: Middle Eastern Foodsheds for American Consumers." *Global Food History* 5, no. 3 (2019): 144–161.

Grehan, James. *Everyday Life and Consumer Culture in Eighteenth-Century Damascus.* Seattle: University of Washington Press, 2007.

Gvion, Liora. *Beyond Hummus and Falafel: Social and Political Aspects of Palestinian Food in Israel.* Berkeley: University of California Press, 2012.

Hafez, Sabry. "Food as a Semiotic Code in Arabic Literature." In *A Taste of Thyme: Culinary Cultures of the Middle East,* ed. Sami Zubaida and Richard Tapper, 257–280. London: Tauris Parke, 2000.

Helstosky, Carol. *Food Culture in the Mediterranean.* Westport, CT: Greenwood Press, 2009.

Hirsch, Dafna. "'Hummus Is Best When It Is Fresh and Made by Arabs': The Gourmetization of Hummus in Israel and the Return of the Repressed Arab." *American Ethnologist* 38, no. 4 (2011): 617–630.

Hudson, Leila. "'They Gave Us Cheese Sandwiches': Foodways of War and Flight." *Mashriq & Mahjar* 6, no. 2 (2019): 151–168.

Issawi, Charles. *The Fertile Crescent, 1800–1914: A Documentary Economic History.* Oxford: Oxford University Press, 1988.

Jureidini, Ray. "In the Shadows of Family Life: Toward a History of Domestic Service in Lebanon." *Journal of Middle East Women's Studies* 5, no. 3 (2009): 74–101.

Kashdan, Harry Eli. "Anglophone Cookbooks and the Making of the Mediterranean." *Food and Foodways* 25, no. 1 (2017): 1–19.

———. "Jerusalem in London: Yotam Ottolenghi and Sami Tamimi's Diasporic World." *Mashriq & Mahjar* 6, no. 2 (2019): 1–35.

Kassis, Reem. "Do You Have Nafas, the Elusive Gift That Makes Food Taste Better?" *New York Times,* 1 April 2021.

———. "Here's Why Palestinians Object to the Term 'Israeli Food': It Erases Us from History." *Washington Post,* 18 February 2020.

Khan, Yasmin. "You Can't Discuss Palestinian Food without Talking about the Occupation." *Literary Hub,* 5 February 2019, https://lithub.com/you-cant-discuss -palestinian-food-without-talking-about-the-occupation.

Khater, Akram. *Inventing Home: Emigration, Gender, and the Middle Class in Lebanon, 1870–1920.* Berkeley: University of California Press, 2001.

Laudan, Rachel. *Cuisine and Empire: Cooking in World History.* Berkeley: University of California Press, 2015.

Mardam-Bey, Farouk. *Ziryab: Authentic Arab Cuisine.* Woodbury, CT: Ici La Press, 2002.

Meneley, Anne. "The Accidental Pilgrims: Olive Pickers in Palestine." *Religion and Society* 5, no. 1 (2014): 186–199.

———. "Blood, Sweat and Tears in a Bottle of Palestinian Extra-Virgin Olive Oil." *Food, Culture & Society* 14, no. 2 (2011): 275–292.

———. "Discourses of Distinction in Contemporary Palestinian Extra-Virgin Olive Oil Production." *Food and Foodways* 22, nos. 1–2 (2014): 48–64.

———. "The Qualities of Palestinian Olive Oil." In *Fat: Culture and Materiality,* ed. Christopher E. Forth and Alison Leitch, 17–31. New York: Bloomsbury, 2014.

———. "Time in a Bottle: The Uneasy Circulation of Palestinian Olive Oil." *Middle East Research and Information Project* 248 (Fall 2008): 18–23.

Mishan, Ligaya. "The Rise of Palestinian Food." *T: The New York Times Style Magazine,* 12 February 2020, https://www.nytimes.com/2020/02/12/t-magazine/palestinian -food.html.

Nabhan, Gary Paul. *Arab/American: Landscape, Culture, and Cuisine in Two Great Deserts.* Tucson: University of Arizona Press, 2008.

———. *Cumin, Camels, and Caravans: A Spice Odyssey.* Berkeley: University of California Press, 2014.

Nelson, Robert. "Pitas and Passports: Arab Foodways in the Windsor-Detroit Borderlands." *Mashriq & Mahjar* 6, no. 2 (2019): 57–74.

El Nour, Saker. "Agri-Food System Dynamics in a South Lebanon Village, 1920–2015." In *The Food Question in the Middle East*, ed. Malak Rouchdy and Iman Hamdy, 61–86. Cairo Papers in Social Science, vol. 34, no. 4. Cairo: American University in Cairo Press, 2017.

Palmer, Carol. "Milk and Cereals: Identifying Food and Food Identity among Fallahin and Bedouin in Jordan." *Levant* 34, no. 1 (2002): 173–195.

Pekow, Sara. "From Farm to Table: The Foodways Connection between Rural and Urban Women in Syria after World War I." *Mashriq & Mahjar* 6, no. 2 (2019): 75–99.

Rafeq, Abdul-Karim. "The Economic Organization of Cities in Ottoman Syria." In *The Urban Social History of the Middle East, 1750–1950*, ed. Peter Sluglett, 104–140. Syracuse: Syracuse University Press, 2008.

Raviv, Yael. "Falafel: A National Icon." *Gastronomica* 3, no. 3 (2003): 20–25.

———. *Falafel Nation: Cuisine and the Making of National Identity in Israel.* Lincoln: University of Nebraska Press, 2015.

Rodinson, Maxime. "Recherches sur les documents arabes relatifs à la cuisine." *Revue des études islamiques* 17 (1949): 95–166.

Rouchdy, Malak, and Iman Hamdy, eds. *The Food Question in the Middle East.* Cairo Papers in Social Science, vol. 34, no. 4. Cairo: American University in Cairo Press, 2017.

Samancı, Özge. "The Cuisine of Istanbul between East and West during the 19th Century." In *Earthly Delights: Economies and Cultures of Food in Ottoman and Danubian Europe, c. 1500–1900*, 77–98. Leiden: Brill, 2018.

Saßmannshausen, Christian. "Eating Up: Food Consumption and Social Status in Late Ottoman Greater Syria." In *Insatiable Appetite: Food as a Cultural Signifier in the Middle East and Beyond*, ed. Kirill Dmitriev, Julia Hauser, and Bilal Orfali, 33–40. Leiden: Brill, 2019.

Seikaly, Sherene. *Men of Capital: Scarcity and Economy in Mandate Palestine.* Stanford: Stanford University Press, 2015.

Singer, Amy. *Constructing Ottoman Beneficence: An Imperial Soup Kitchen in Jerusalem*, SUNY Series in Near Eastern Studies. Albany: State University of New York Press, 2002.

———, ed. *Starting with Food: Culinary Approaches to Ottoman History.* Princeton: Markus Wiener Publishers, 2011.

Stiffler, Matthew Jaber. "Consuming Orientalism: Public Foodways of Arab American Christians." *Mashriq & Mahjar* 2, no. 2 (2014): 111–138.

Tamari, Salim. *Mountain against the Sea: Essays on Palestinian Society and Culture.* Berkeley: University of California Press, 2008.

Zubaida, Sami. "National, Communal, and Global Dimensions in Middle Eastern Food Cultures." In *A Taste of Thyme: Culinary Cultures of the Middle East* (1994), ed. Sami Zubaida and Richard Tapper, 33–45. London: I. B. Tauris, 2000.

Zubaida, Sami, and Richard Tapper, eds. *A Taste of Thyme: Culinary Cultures of the Middle East* (1994). London: I. B. Tauris, 2000.

# Contributors

**Zeina Azzam** is a Palestinian American poet, writer, and editor. She works as publications editor at Arab Center Washington DC. Previously, she was executive director of the Jerusalem Fund and director of educational outreach at Georgetown University's Center for Contemporary Arab Studies. Azzam's chapbook *Bayna Bayna, In-Between* was published by The Poetry Box. A number of literary journals feature her poems, including *Pleiades, Passager, Cordite Poetry Review, Barzakh: A Literary Magazine, Sukoon Magazine, Mizna, Voice Male,* and *Split This Rock*. Her poetry also appears in several edited volumes, such as *Tales from Six Feet Apart, Bettering American Poetry, Making Mirrors: Writing/Righting by and for Refugees,* and *Gaza Unsilenced*. Azzam holds an MA in Arabic literature from Georgetown University, an MA in sociology from George Mason University, and a BA in psychology from Vassar College.

**Samuel Dolbee** is an environmental and social historian of the Ottoman Empire and the modern Middle East. He is currently a lecturer on history and literature at Harvard University. He holds a PhD in history and Middle Eastern and Islamic Studies from New York University and an MA in Arab Studies from Georgetown University. His research has been published in the *International Journal of Middle Eastern Studies* and *Past & Present*.

**Anny Gaul** is a cultural historian of food and gender specializing in modern North Africa. She is an assistant professor of Arabic Studies at the University of Maryland, College Park, where she teaches courses on the literature, food, and cultural history of the Arabic-speaking world. She holds an MA and PhD from Georgetown University and was a postdoctoral fellow at Tufts University. Gaul is currently working on a book about food history in twentieth-century Egypt and Morocco. She has published in the *Journal of Women's His-*

*tory*, *Middle Eastern Literatures*, *Gastronomica*, and *Mashriq & Mahjar*. Her food writing has appeared in *ArabLit Quarterly* and *Eater*. She blogs at www .cookingwithgaul.com and also works as a translator from Arabic.

**Chris Gratien** is an assistant professor of history at the University of Virginia, where he teaches courses on global environmental history and the modern Middle East. He holds a PhD from the Department of History and an MA from the Center for Contemporary Arab Studies at Georgetown University. He is a former postdoctoral fellow at the Harvard Academy for International and Area Studies and Yale University's Program in Agrarian Studies. He is also producer of the Ottoman History Podcast (ottomanhistorypodcast.com), which since 2011 has featured the voices of hundreds of scholars working on the Ottoman Empire, the modern Middle East, and the Islamic world.

**Dafna Hirsch** is a senior lecturer in the Department of Sociology, Political Science, and Communication at the Open University of Israel and teaches in the master's program in Cultural Studies. She holds a PhD in history from Tel Aviv University and was a postdoctoral fellow at the Department of Sociology and Anthropology at the Hebrew University of Jerusalem. She is currently working on a book on the history of hummus consumption among Jews in Mandate Palestine and Israel. Her work has been published in various journals, including *Comparative Studies in Society and History*, *International Journal of Middle East Studies*, *American Ethnologist*, *Ethnic and Racial Studies*, *Food, Culture, and Society*, and others.

**Michel Kabalan** is a philologist and translator based at Instituto de Filosofia Universidade do Porto in Portugal, where he lectures on medieval and contemporary Arabic philosophy. Originally from Zahle, Lebanon, he earned his bachelor's. and master's from the American University of Beirut. His master's thesis analyzed the work of Taha Hussein and Mohammad Abed Al-Jabiri.

**Harry Eli Kashdan** is a scholar of food culture and migration in the contemporary Mediterranean. He holds a PhD in comparative literature from the University of Michigan and was Lauro de Bosis Postdoctoral Fellow in Italian at Harvard University before joining the Department of French and Italian at the Ohio State University as Postdoctoral Scholar in the Global Mediterranean. His work on the literary qualities of cookbooks has been published in *Food and Foodways*, *Mashriq & Mahjar*, *Quest*, and *Italian Culture*. His current projects include a monograph exploring neighborly relationships between host countries and migrants in the Mediterranean and a coedited volume (with Philip

Gleissner) of essays by American immigrant food writers on the COVID-19 pandemic.

**Reem Kassis** is a Palestinian writer whose work focuses on the intersection of food with culture, history, and politics. Her writings have been published in the *Wall Street Journal, Washington Post, Los Angeles Times,* and various academic journals. Her debut cookbook, *The Palestinian Table,* won the Guild of Food Writers Award, was nominated for a James Beard Award, and was selected by National Public Radio (NPR) as one of the best books of 2017. Her new cookbook, *The Arabesque Table,* is a one-of-a-kind collection of contemporary recipes tracing the rich history of Arab cuisine.

**Susan MacDougall** is currently a British Academy Postdoctoral Fellow in Social Anthropology at the University of Cambridge. She holds a DPhil and MSc in social anthropology from the University of Oxford and an MA in Near Eastern Studies from the University of Arizona. Her research has been published in the *Cambridge Journal of Anthropology, Ethnos,* and *Refuge: Canada's Journal on Refugees.*

**Anne Meneley** graduated with a PhD in anthropology from New York University. She is a professor of anthropology at Trent University in Canada. Her book on women's competitive hospitality in Yemen, *Tournaments of Value: Sociability and Hierarchy in a Yemeni Town,* was released in its 20th anniversary edition in 2016. Her recent work deals with the production, circulation, and consumption of olive oil in Italy and Palestine. Her work on food has appeared in *American Anthropologist, Environment and Planning E: Nature and Space, Ethnos, Food, Culture & Society, Food and Foodways, Gastronomica, History and Anthropology,* and *Jerusalem Quarterly.*

**Sara Pekow** is a PhD candidate in history at the Graduate Center, City University of New York (CUNY), with a dissertation defense planned for September 2021. Her field of study is the social history of food in modern Syria. She holds an MA from the Department of Middle Eastern, South Asian, and African Studies at Columbia University and an AB from Bowdoin College. Prior to beginning her graduate studies, Pekow was a network radio and television news writer and producer at CBS News in New York. Her work has appeared in *Mashriq & Mahjar.*

**Graham Auman Pitts** is a historian of the modern Arab world. He is a visiting professor in the Elliott School of International Affairs at George Washington

University. His current book manuscript considers food and famine in the Levant during World War I. After receiving a PhD from Georgetown's history department, he taught history and international studies at North Carolina State University. *Arab Studies Journal, Journal of the Ottoman and Turkish Studies Association,* and *Cahiers d'Orient* have published his work. Pitts held the American Druze Foundation fellowship at Georgetown's Center for Contemporary Arab Studies for two years.

**Noam Sienna** is a historian of Jewish culture in the medieval and early modern periods, with a focus on Jewish life in North Africa and the Islamic world. He holds a PhD in Jewish history and museum studies from the University of Minnesota as well as degrees in religion and anthropology from Brandeis University and the University of Toronto. His recent work examines Jewish book history, manuscript culture, and Judeo-Arabic publishing in North Africa in the early modern and modern periods.

**Antonio Tahhan** is a Syrian American food writer. Born in Venezuela to a family from Aleppo and raised in Miami, he draws inspiration from a variety of cultures. Tahhan pursued degrees in math, economics, and Spanish literature from Cornell University. As an elective course, he explored food anthropology and became fascinated by its stories, traditions, and taboos. He was awarded a Fulbright Research grant to Syria in 2010, where he studied the midday meal in three contexts: at homes, in restaurants, and in the streets. From cooking to eating, food was a natural vehicle for cultural exchange, which he continues to explore. During the COVID-19 pandemic, Antonio launched a web series called "Teta Thursdays," a virtual conversation on food, culture, and identity.

**Vicki Valosik** is the editorial director at Georgetown University's Center for Contemporary Arab Studies. Her writing has appeared in *American Scholar, Atlantic, Smithsonian Magazine, International Educator Magazine,* and other publications. She specializes in helping scholars, technical experts, practitioners, and students at Georgetown bring their ideas to a wider public through accessible storytelling and engaging writing. Valosik holds an MA in nonfiction writing from Johns Hopkins University and an MA in sociology from the University of South Alabama. For her sociology MA thesis, she conducted survey and interview research in Damascus, Syria.

**Suzanne Zeidy** is an American Egyptian restaurateur and food entrepreneur. She grew up in Cairo. After graduating from the American University in Cairo in 1992, she worked for a family-run food service. She earned her master's in business from the Stern School of Business at New York University and attended the Culinary School in New York City. Upon returning to Egypt, Zeidy set up Harvest Foods, while also starting her own restaurant, La Bodega. She co-founded Cairo Kitchen in 2011, a contemporary Egyptian food restaurant, and wrote a cookbook, *The Cairo Kitchen*, to document Egyptian family recipes.

# Index

Adana kebab: as a Levantine dish, 47–49, 51, 56–57, 59–62; working class origin of, 5–6

Aleppo: Armenian influence in, 65, 87, 90; and culinary traditions, 40, 65, 86–87; and *hayṭaliyya*, 69–70, 90; and kebabs, 54, 58; and kibbe, 30; and *köfte*, 64–65; pistachios, 49, 52–53, 54, 60, 65; and red pepper, 6, 10, 61–62

Antep, 47–49, 51–63, 68

appropriation, xii, 1, 9, 12, 94

Armenian genocide, 48, 53

Beirut, 26–31, 35; and birth of modern Levantine food culture, 2, 4–5, 11, 24–25, 40–41; and chocolate production, 77; restaurant culture in, 33–34

Bourdain, Anthony, 1, 15

bulgur wheat: and kibbe, 23, 29–30, 34–35, 37, 41, 135, 137–138; and *makhlūṭa*, 31; and Palestinian *mujaddara*, 123; and *şalgam suyu* (fermented beverage), 51

Cairo, 5, 199-202

capitalism: and cookbooks, 24; and creative destruction of tradition under, 26; history, 4, 42–43; and the Lebanese Civil War, 45; terms of exploitation under, 2

chickpeas: in *bqayla*, 175; in candy, 97; in falafel, 1, 15, 112–113; in hummus,

102, 192–193; in kibbe, 29, 34, 37; in *kusharī*, 200; in *makhlūṭa*, 31; in *qidreh*, 140–141

Choueiri, Ramzi, 25, 36–37, 41, 43, 45

colonialism, 1, 5–6, 94, 119

Columbian Exchange, 4

cookbooks, 6–10, 24–41, 170–178, 196

culinary knowledge, xiii, 173, 212

Dağdeviren, Musa, 58; *The Turkish Cookbook*, 60–61

Damascus: and ambiguity of the toponym *al-Shām*, 3, 47, 52; Armenian influence in, 65; and ice cream, 69–70; and kibbe *al-fākhtiyya*, 44; and migration to Beirut, 27; and olive oil trade with Palestine, 126; and pistachios, 11, 47, 52–53, 66; and sugar, 69, 73, 82; and sweets, 74–79

diaspora, 5, 79, 122, 178, 196, 214

dibs. *See* molasses

eggplant, 165–166, 174, 200, 211–212; introduction to the Levant of, 4; in kibbe 29–30, 34, 39, 43

Egypt, 5, 44, 50, 135, 199–204

El-Haddad, Laila, 6, 9, 125

Euphrates River, 3, 52

falafel, 1, 15, 102–105, 184–187

famine, 5

global food culture, 185, 194
Greek cuisine, 192–193

*harīsa* (stew), 31, 136
hummus, 34–35, 96–99, 101–102, 106,
   191–195

industrialization, 15, 56
Israel: and appropriation of Palestinian
   cuisine, 1–2, 12, 94, 107; and colonialism, 1, 94; and falafel, 112, 187; and
   hummus, 106, 183, 198; and immigration, 2, 182, 216; and occupation of
   Palestine, 12, 106, 117, 121, 128–129; and
   *shakshūka*, 177, 183; study of foodways
   in, 9

Jaffa: and diet of coastal towns, 99, 135–
   136; and nineteenth-century growth,
   4–5; as Palestinian "mixed city," 93,
   96–97; 99–101, 103, 105–106
Jerusalem: Israeli occupation of, 128; and
   *lahmeh bi–l–waraq*, 144; as Palestinian "mixed city," 93, 96, 100–101;
   and restaurant culture, 98–99; and
   *zibdiyyeh*, 135
Jordan: and class, 159; and colonialism,
   5; and gendered social norms, 160,
   162–163; as part of the Levant, 3, 14,
   156; Palestinian cuisine in, 159, 166;
   and Syrian refugees, 79

kebab: döner paired with pizza, 188–192;
   with Egyptian mezze 200; in Italian
   fast-food, 185; in Mandate Palestine,
   98, 102, 105–106; and Ottoman history, 49–50
kibbe: Egyptian *kubayba*, 203, 205–206,
   208; as Levantine staple dish, 23–24,
   31, 40; made in a food processor, 35;
   origin of, 41; raw (*nī'a*), 34–35, 135, 137;
   seasonal aspect of, 30
kitchens: in bourgeois Beirut 28; in
   Egypt and Palestine 43; gendered
   labor in, 29, 36, 159–160, 163, 216; and
   Lebanese tradition, 32–33
*knāfeh*. See *kunāfa*

kubba. *See* kibbe
*kunāfa*, 74, 146

Lebanon: construction of national cuisine in, 25, 32–42, 196; and creation
   of modern borders, 23–24; and the
   Ottoman period, 31; as importer of
   staple foodstuffs, 4; and migration, 5,
   26; and similarity with the cuisine of
   the Galilee, 135; and sugar, 71–73

Mediterranean cuisine: healthy aspect
   of, 116; and hummus, 192; and olive
   trees, 117–118, 122; as vague label, 3,
   6, 185, 188, 192–196; vegetable stews
   in, 175
mezze, 34, 97–98, 199–208
molasses, 26, 39, 69, 90, 135

*nafas*, 162, 213–214, 216–217
Nakba, 95, 118, 120

olives, 4, 16, 115–129
Orientalism, 10, 176

Palestine: British Mandate, 95–96; and
   café culture, 97–100; and cookbooks,
   10; food venues as contact zone in,
   93–95; Mizrahi Jews in, 101–103;
   olive harvest in, 122–124; olive oil in,
   115–118, 124–127; and production of
   sweets, 78; Zionist colonialism in, 1,
   100–101, 118–122; Zionist perceptions
   of local food, 103–107
pistachios, 52–53; and Armenians, 48,
   51; in baklava, 47, in *kunāfa*, 74,
   146–147
pizza, 185–198

recipes: beetroot tahini, 207; carrot tahini, 208; *harīseh*, 136; *hawseh*, 139;
   kibbe, 28, 30, 35–37, 42; *knāfeh*, 146;
   *kubayba*, 205–206; *kubbeh niyeh*,
   137–38; and *lahmeh bi–l–waraq*, 144;
   *qidreh*, 140; rice pudding, 89; *shakshūka*, 170, 175–78; *zibdiyyeh*, 142
Roden, Claudia, 6–8, 17, 23, 40, 46

Said, Edward, 8, 18, 210

Sarkis, Khalil, 24–31, 33–34, 36–37, 43–45, 173

*shakshūka*, 12, 170, 175–176, 183

stuffed grape leaves: or *dawālī* (Amman), 153–156, 159, 164–165; or *laḥmeh bi-l-waraq* (Jerusalem), 144–145; in Ottoman Lebanon, 31

Syria: as coterminous with the Levant, 3, 27, 52–53, 156; and grain production, 29; and *karam* (generosity), 87; and sweets, 69–70; 74–79; and Turkish cuisine, 47–49, 53–56, 60, 63


tahini: in Egypt, 200, 202, 203, 207–208; and fish, 135; hummus without, 102; and kebab, 98, 106; and kibbe, 29, 34, 38, 44; as traditional peasant food, 26

tomatoes: in Aleppan kibbe, 30; as broth,165; in Gazan cuisine, 135, 142; introduction to the Levant, 4; in Israel, 177; in Jewish Tunisian cuisine, 174; in Lebanese kibbe, 38; in salad, 190, 200; and sauce for vegetable stews, 98, 175; in *shakshūka*, 170, 175; stuffed, 157

Turkey: and appropriation of Arab and Armenian food culture, 2, 12, 48, 215; and boundary of the Levant, 3, 48–49; and xenophobia, 47


wine, 4, 18, 30, 117, 203

women: and Arabic in Tunisia, 172; and labor, 16, 25, 36, 156–157, 160, 173, 217; in Palestinian cafes, 97, 105


Zubaida, Sami, 6–7, 51, 101